How Congressmen Decide

How Congressmen Decide:
A Policy Focus

E 70

AAGE R. CLAUSEN
Ohio State University

ST. MARTIN'S PRESS   *New York*

To: Claus and Minnie; steerage circa 1905

Preface

This preface is being written during a time when the news media are giving headline attention to a confrontation between the Presidency and Congress. That confrontation is dramatically referred to as a "constitutional crisis" because it concerns the powers and prerogatives of these two branches of government, each one intent upon pressing its interpretation of its authority under the Constitution. To the casual observer of American politics who relies upon the popular media for information, this so-called constitutional crisis may appear to be a dramatic new event. However, the specialist in American government—journalist, political scientist, or historian—will recognize the confrontation as being unusual in degree rather than in substance, for the battle over congressional and executive prerogatives is as old as the Constitution itself. In the *long-term perspective*, the current episode emerges as little more than an unusually interesting page in the annals of, congressional-executive conflict rather than as an exciting new political phenomenon.

It is with such a long-term perspective that I have investigated the ways in which congressmen decide on policy questions. It is my conviction that individual members of Congress look at and vote upon policy questions in terms of enduring personal policy views, their perceptions of constituency interests and views, their relations with interest groups, and their party loyalties. I view these factors as relatively stable and unchanging, so that if one understands the policy stance of Congress today one can predict with a fair degree of accuracy its general policy stance tomorrow and, in many instances, even ten years from today. Congress is not, of course, immune to change; indeed, it is my argument that Congress changes more than do individual members, most obviously by the transfusion of new blood and a letting of the old.

In addition to the long-term perspective, I have also sought a *broad-gauge perspective* on decision-making in Congress. Thus, my focus is upon *general* policy concerns, such as this nation's level of international involvement and the extent to which the federal government should exercise responsibility for the welfare of the individual and the society. After identifying the congressmen's policy orientations with regard to these larger policy questions, I focus attention on the factors that determine policy positions on such general questions. One of the products of this analysis is an understanding of the policy divisions within the Congress, which, in turn, reflect the political life of the nation.

Throughout the book an ever present, although sometimes subliminal, theme is that the individual members of Congress, when seen behind the trappings of office, are persons of few extraordinary endowments. The congressman is not a political virtuoso constantly performing political maneuvers of great complexity with an unerringly delicate sense of political balance. Members of Congress are best understood as typical participants in the politically activist segment of our citizenry, with no special calling to the ministry of policy-making. Their decisions result from a blend of prejudice, reason, and practicality. Those decisions are sometimes based upon much information and at other times upon little; they are sometimes the product of political necessity and at other times the result of unencumbered judgment. Whatever the blend of these decision elements, an understanding of congressional decision-making does not depend upon a complex theory of decision behavior.

The research that has contributed to the writing of this book, both directly and indirectly, has been in progress for a number of years. Essential to this extended research effort have been the support provided by the Survey Research Center of The University of Michigan and the Research Committee of the Graduate School of the University of Wisconsin; a grant from the Committee on Governmental and Legal Processes, Social Science Research Council; and a grant from the National Science Foundation. Most recently assistance has been provided by the Polimetrics Laboratory and the Department of Political Science of Ohio State University. The importance of the service provided by the Inter-university Consortium for Political Research, University of Michigan, in making the roll-call data records available in analyzable form, cannot be overstated.

I am indebted to a number of individuals who have contributed to this research and writing enterprise. Most directly associated with me in this work, and most instrumental in carrying it out, have been Richard Cheney, Juanita Hamilton, Kay Klipstine, Ann Rappoport, Brian Silver, and Steven Shull. Others whose time, effort, criticism, and encouragement have been most helpful are John Kessel, Warren Miller, Samuel Patterson, and Randall Ripley.

I have refrained from expressing my appreciation to my family until last. My most supportive wife, Geri, and tolerant son, Jon, have borne the burdens of little time, no vacations, and my grumpy disposition with remarkable grace. More than that, my wife's wit, charm, and critical eye have been constant sources of refreshment during the long trek.

A. R. C.

Contents

1
Introduction

The member of Congress has been the object of scrutiny by observers who come away with widely differing impressions of the merits and functions of this national political actor. To some, the congressman appears to be the passive register of political pressure; to others, he is the zealous guardian of local interests and congressional folkways. Some look upon him as the political manipulator extraordinary, while still others regard him as the ombudsman of citizens' interests in the face of a powerful and inattentive federal bureaucracy.

Differing impressions of the member of Congress, the senator and the representative, are a function not only of the peculiar perspectives of different observers but also of the multifaceted character of the congressman's role in relation to other parts of the political system. The congressman is involved in a complex web of relationships due to his part in the ongoing drama of policy-making. He is involved in each of the three acts of this play: policy formulation, policy enactment, and policy implementation.

There is a growing consensus among critics that congressmen seem to be more effective in enacting policy than in formulating policy, which is being dominated more and more by persons in the executive and bureaucratic realm of government. Nevertheless, it would be unwise to ignore the policy initiatives that *do* come from Congress. Even though policies may bear the executive label, consultation with congressmen has usually taken place, in spirit if not in body, and has often influenced the policy course.

Congressmen also become involved in policy implementation through a variety of devices: consultations with administrators on an informal day-to-day basis; formal presentations to congressional com-

mittees by administrative program heads; frequent formal congressional investigations of corruption, waste, and sloth committed by
policy administrators; and the unsystematic overseeing of the bureaucracy that occurs when a constituent complains to the congressman
that the administrators of policy appear lacking in equity and em-
pathy.

In an oblique response to the critics of Congress who accuse it of
inaction, ineptness, and irrelevance, let me suggest a different perspective. Instead of viewing the function of Congress as that which is
suggested by the title "lawmaker," it might be more useful to think of
Congress as one of the major intersections of a policy communications
network that extends across most policy domains. Congress receives
formal and informal messages from the president, responding to some
and ignoring others. It also receives messages from the bureaucracy,
usually requests for money, and commonly responds with an injunc-
tion to spend less and do more. Its constituency also sends messages,
some of which are passed on to the president and the bureaucracy,
while others are allowed to accumulate and possibly gain the support
and momentum that compel a legislative response. Interest groups
have some of their views aired in committee hearings, and other views
are shared in more private surroundings.

Congress also initiates messages by raising issues and generating
support for policy positions. Not all congressmen wait to be prodded
into action—many are self-starters. Sometimes their actions result in
the initiation and formulation of legislation within the Congress; other
times the issues that are raised gain a place in the president's program.

When Congress is seen as a center for the exchange of policy communications, as well as a transmitter of policy commands in the form
of legislation, it takes on a relatively positive appearance. However,
it is easy to chastise Congress for its ineptness when it is viewed only
in its role of lawmaker, because it is then subject to an unflattering
comparison with the executive branch's centralized mechanism for
initiating legislation.

Whatever one's evaluation of congressional performance and influence relative to the performance and influence of other branches
of government, there seems to be at least a grudging recognition that
the U.S. Congress ranks high among legislatures of the world as a
wielder of influence. Even more relevant to the present study is the
fact that individual members of Congress have a level of independence

and political influence beyond that of members of all other legislative bodies. Thus, it is important to understand the factors that enter into the policy decisions of individual senators and representatives.

The policy decisions of members of Congress have an important effect on the lives of all U.S. citizens. Think of any aspect of life in the United States—education, welfare, transportation, taxes, religious freedom, quality of products (from food to fly poison)—and chances are that your congressman has made some decision bearing on it during the last ten years or less. Indeed, the policy decisions of congressmen are of substantial importance to citizens of other nations as well, because of the impact that American economic, political, and military activities have on the world community. The variety of congressional concerns would be exhausting to review; suffice it to say that the number of decisions to be made is counted in the hundreds for the two-year life of each Congress.

Today there are 435 representatives and 100 senators to make the necessary decisions. Although the task is shared by all of them, with a large number of important preliminary decisions on legislation being made in the specialized policy committees, each member must still face the moment of decision time and time again. If it is personal responsibility he shirks, he wishes for the "voice" vote, becomes somewhat uneasy when a standing "division" is called for, and experiences more anxiety when the "teller" vote compels him to declare his position by rising and filing by the tellers of the yeas and nays. Yet in these instances the word of his decision is not likely to travel far beyond the legislative chamber. However, when a roll call is taken his vote is recorded and published. There it stands for all to see, to be coupled with praise or condemnation.

The question for us here is: *How do congressmen arrive at their decisions on policy,* given the substantive variety, the large number, and the importance of these decisions? The individual member cannot study each legislative proposal at length, even if he is so inclined. Some responsible compromise method, short of the laborious study of each item of legislation, must be worked out by the legislator if he is to survive the decision ordeal. Furthermore, the process of individual decision-making in Congress must be one that is compatible with the fact that the members of Congress do not possess extraordinary intellectual capabilities and suffer from the usual limitations of time and energy. Congressmen are citizens who, for a variety of understandable but unpredictable reasons, have been elected to legislative office. They tend to be a cut above the average in their social and economic status, and in their educational accomplishments. And there are those for whom the quest for political power is an overwhelming characteristic. Still, the most distinctive feature of a member of Congress is his presence in that body. Greatness among congressmen, as among others, is rare.

When we make congressmen larger than life they are miscast; when we denigrate them because of their immersion in politics they are abused. Their qualities do not entitle them to the stature of storybook heroes, nor do their political pursuits provide us with the basis for casting them as villains. We can best understand the behavior of members of Congress and how it reflects the nation's political situation if we recognize that *their qualities of character and range of talents are those possessed by the much larger body of politically alert citizens from which they are drawn.*

In the study that follows two themes are stressed in viewing congressmen and their decision-making behavior. First, the methods for decision that are used by congressmen are methods commonly employed by most persons faced with choices of products, people, and programs of action. This theme is discussed in a section of the present chapter, "Premise." Second, the policy positions of members of Congress are reasonably representative of the positions of those citizens who participate in the political life of this nation. Consequently, a study that looks into the origins of the policy positions of members of Congress is also a study of the political life of the nation and the major forces working within it. The expansion of this theme, preceded by a brief description of the time setting of the study, constitutes the following section on "Political Representation."

Political Representation

The main part of this study of the policy decisions of members of Congress encompasses twelve years, a brief span in the life of a Congress which will celebrate its 200th birthday in 1989. During the dozen years, 1953–1964, Americans enjoyed the best kind of peace likely to be observed in the twentieth century: a condition in which there was a minimum commitment of American combat troops to the battlefield. The first year of this period marks the ceasefire in the Korean War, and the last year precedes the sharp increase in American commitments and casualties in Vietnam. It was a period when national resources and attention could be directed to domestic problems, despite the chill caused by the continuation of the Cold War. In this climate social cleavages, economic antagonisms, and political divisions could experience full growth, unstunted by the draining demands of war and unsuppressed by the call for national unity.

In deference to those who doubt the validity of projecting behavior patterns observed in the past onto the present, I have conducted an analysis of the Congress of 1969–1970. If its members are seen to behave in a manner consistent with the pre-1965 group, perhaps it will be easier to accept the currency of the findings from the twelve-year core of the study.

A study of the actions of senators and representatives provides an extraordinary vantage point from which to observe the larger political scene. In common with other democratically elected assemblies, the U.S. Congress provides a somewhat distorted, but clearly recognizable reflection of the political values, attitudes, and beliefs of the voters to whom it is responsible. The amount of distortion, of course, can become quite severe, and as such should be a matter of serious public concern.

There is no question that Congress is *not* a representative assemblage in terms of the nonpolitical characteristics of its membership. We know that this group is wealthier, whiter, older and "male-r" than a cross section of American voters. And lawyers are as overrepresented as manual workers are underrepresented. However, most Americans accept the possibility that political representation may be achieved without economic, religious, racial, and sexual balance. More important than these characteristics is the candidate's long-term residence in the area he is to represent, presumably as a form of assurance that he understands and has a "feeling for" the values of the people. In short, the focus is upon the *political* representation the candidate will provide his electors.

On the other hand, the very fact that some categories of citizens— the black, the female, the young—are underrepresented in Congress attests to the fact that Congress represents the *effective* forces in the political life of the nation. For it is incontrovertibly the case that some groups of citizens are not effective forces because they have been heartily discouraged from joining in. Undoubtedly, political representation is highest for those who are most involved in political affairs and lowest for those who either will not or cannot take part.

This situation is not necessarily fair, and neither is it likely to be different in the future. It does, however, point up one of my main arguments: the study of Congress can be much more than the study of a political institution and its functions; it can also be a study of the political life of the entire society. Congress mirrors the fact that the effective forces get representation, while those which are not active (by choice or otherwise) do not.

Premise

Observations on American politics are abundantly blessed with ideological clichés running the gamut from "thunder on the Right" to "radical chorus on the Left." The politics of the nation can be seen as following a liberal course in one decade and taking a conservative direction in the next. Eras are designated as isolationist and internationalist. Candidates, parties, movements, administrations, and courts are labeled as conservative, moderate, liberal, reactionary, and radical. The common characteristic of these labels is that they represent attempts to group larger numbers of individuals, organizations, and actions into a much smaller number of categories. Such attempts at classification pervade all areas of life, and so we may designate this phenomenon as the *law of categorization*.

Used in the context of behavioral predictability, categorization involves the attempt to characterize tendencies in past behavior in order to anticipate tendencies in future behavior. For example, one who has taken moderate positions in the past will be expected to take moderate positions in the future.

People must classify their observations in order to communicate understanding, but the tool of classification is used in another way, as well. We classify the complexity of the world through which we move on our daily rounds in order to be able to act. Therefore, one of the tasks of the scholar, journalist, or general observer is to create ever more useful categories. Being cognizant of the complexity of human behavior, we demand simplification. We need better categories that minimize distortion and misclassification.

The categorical mode of cognition (the process of attaching meaning) makes it possible to seek out the similarities of otherwise unique phenomena and to classify them in terms of their similarities and differences (e.g., the categories "deer" and "deer hunters"). When this classification is coupled with similar responses to "apparently similar" phenomena, the individual gains a measure of security and freedom subject to the constraints established by the predictability of behavior (deer hunters nearly always shoot deer, not hunters). The observer's success in analyzing human behavior is dependent upon his ability to abstract the ordering principles, including the cognitive categories used by the actors.

Congress: A Premise Fulfilled

The law of categorization is highly visible in the efforts of observers to comprehend the complexity of the policy-making process in the United States Congress. Senators and representatives are continually categorized, labeled, and stereotyped. One reason for writing this book is my dissatisfaction with the categories commonly used, e.g., liberal, moderate, conservative. It is my view that these do not give congressmen their due. Such classifications are too crude; they do not cut cleanly into the tissue of national politics, but tear, rip, and disfigure. Popular political writers and journalists are perhaps the worst offenders in using this kind of labeling. Most are aware and many despair of the distortions and inaccuracies conveyed along with the labels, but few are favored with the opportunity to articulate satisfactorily the complexity of legislative politics. The exigencies of headlines and deadlines are often not amenable to more elaboration than "conservative opposition to the liberal elements of the president's program is growing as election day approaches."

The journalist who takes the time to gather his impressions and knowledge of Congress into a book, the historian, and the political scientist can proceed at a more leisurely pace, but they also need the descriptive convenience provided by the classification of events, people, and programs into a manageable set of categories. No one can write in great detail about 435 congressmen or 100 senators. Reference must be made to voting blocs, coalitions, ideological groupings, interest-groups, and categories of legislation (e.g., civil rights, foreign aid, labor). Thus, no study of Congress, whether it focuses upon the styles and accomplishments of individual leaders, particular pieces of legislation, or Congress as a whole, can proceed without the formation and labeling of categories.

Just as it necessary for the observer of Congress to rely on general classificatory schemes, *the manifold tasks of the congressman would be impossible to perform without the aid of principles of classification and habitual modes of response.* The member of Congress would be overwhelmed and frustrated into either immobility or erratic behavior if he had to respond to every constituent, every lobbyist, and every policy proposal as a wholly unique phenomenon.

The congressman's need for the tool of classification is no more evident than in the area of his activity with which this book is concerned: the making of individual decisions on a wide variety and a large number of legislative topics. If judgments on each legislative motion were totally independent, as though no item of legislation and no amendment thereto shared anything in common with any other legislative motion, the task of decision-making would be beyond human capability. It is imperative, then, that the congressman develop categories which subsume specific legislative motions, so that a common response can be made to all items of legislation included within a more general category.

This study of legislative decision behavior is based on the premise that the categories used by congressmen are highly similar to those employed by the press, the schools, the full array of political and government actors, and the ordinary citizen to sort out the multifarious policy concerns. These categories include civil rights, civil liberties, social welfare, economic policy, farm policy, defense and foreign policy. I am suggesting that congressmen make their decisions, in part, by using a limited set of policy content categories to which legislative proposals are assigned.

Another important part of the congressman's response to the decision task is the use of a limited set of decision premises which are matched up with the limited set of content categories. Thus, the *basis* for a congressman's decision on a particular item of legislation included within a general content category is the same as for other items of legislation classified within that category. Furthermore, the decision premises are not drawn from "esoterica" but take such common forms as the "party line" handed down by party leaders, ideological positions, conceptions of the appropriate domain of government responsibility, economy in government, and other considerations abounding in the political culture *that are shared by legislators and lay people.*

Indeed, why should the categories of policy and the premises for decision employed by congressmen differ greatly from those used by their fellow citizens, many of whom might well have taken their seats in Congress? The unspoken assumption may be that one aspect of the professionalization of congressmen is the development of highly complex and politically sophisticated orientations to policy questions that set congressmen apart from their fellow citizens. Surely, the argument continues, with extended exposure to the intricacies involved in the government of a society, the congressman must refine his evaluations of policy alternatives and elaborate his categories of policy content. By the same token, the congressman's immersion in a presumably complex process of decision-making, replete with coalition building, bargaining, political and parliamentary maneuvering, and old-fashioned logrolling, would seem to require a complex theory of decision-making in order to understand congressional behavior.

The thrust of this book is that a great deal can be learned about congressional decision-making without heavy reliance upon conceptions of the decision process that emphasize complexity—a reliance that all too often adds up to the single unedifying conclusion that the process is simply too complex to comprehend. I would agree that the politics surrounding certain pieces of legislation may involve every instrument of the politician's trade. But even in such cases, plus the greater majority of instances where the level of political intrigue makes a pretty dull tale, the outcome of the *decision process is heavily influenced by the general policy positions of the participants*. Furthermore, these policy positions are likely to be quite stable over time, affecting congressional decisions in a predictable manner through many terms of congressional service. The points offered in this section will be fully elaborated in subsequent chapters.

In Broad Outline:
A Study of Policy Positions

A single study of the policy-making process in the United States Congress must, of necessity, take a particular slant on this process. This, in turn, predicates a focus on particular aspects of legislative decision-making, both in terms of the types of legislative behavior to be explained and the sources of behavior to be used in the explanation.

In this study, analysis is made of the policy *positions* assumed by congressmen rather than of the *process* of policy-making. It is my contention, however, that policy positions established for individual congressmen on the basis of roll-call votes are representative of policy positions taken in the various other aspects of their legislative activity. I suggest, further, that one who wishes to understand the politics of this nation would do well to examine the record of congressional voting decisions. A strong evidential base for insights into the operation of the American political system is provided by a voting pattern analysis which is sensitive to the policy content of the motions voted upon, the factors related to the voting decisions, and the stability and change in voting behavior over time.

This study involves a search for a comprehensive pattern in congressional voting that stands in marked contrast to the buzzing, blooming confusion so often ascribed to legislatures by political observers, as well as by the participants themselves. As the title of the concluding chapter indicates, a major goal of this research is to specify the "Patterns of Influence" that bear upon congressional decisions. These patterns are observed with respect to different general policy areas and are spelled out in terms of three general sources of influence on policy decisions: party, constituency, and the executive.

The research here is strongly oriented to policy content. I expect the mix of party, constituency, and executive influence to change as the policy focus shifts. This may appear to be relatively obvious but it is not a point to which political scientists have devoted much attention in their research. Instead, concentration has been on the process of policy-making without sufficient regard for the variations in process that accompany variations in policy content.[1]

Policy Dimensions

The content of the policy positions of congressmen is specified in this study in terms of policy dimensions. Given the way in which policy dimensions are conceptualized and measured, congressmen are ordered according to their policy positions. This placement is analogous to the ordering of people along the two dimensions of height and weight. A different ordering on each dimension is implicit in the variations of body structures; similarly, different orderings of congressmen can be expected in relation to different dimensions of policy.

A full description of the policy dimension concept is given in Chapter 2. However, an understanding of the general character of a policy dimension may be facilitated at this stage of the presentation by referring to the propensity of political observers and participants to order voters and office-holders in the United States on an ideological dimension of liberalism-conservatism. The use of this dimension construct normally suggests confidence in the possibility of predicting people's positions on various policy questions according to their positions on the liberal-conservative dimension. Thus, it is anticipated that there is a very strong likelihood that the ultraconservatives, on one pole of the dimension, will take positions diametrically opposed to those of the extreme liberals, on the other pole, on a wide range of policy matters.

More than enough is known about the organization of the policy positions of voters and congressmen to reject the validity of relying simply upon a liberal-conservative dimension to provide an accurate picture. Consequently, an adequate description and explanation of policy orientations requires a study of more precisely defined dimensions. One such dimension that has emerged from this study is civil liberties. Congressmen are ordered according to the degree to which they support federal policies designed to further the civil liberties of United States citizens.

The ordering of representatives and senators on the civil liberties dimension, as well as the idea that there is a civil liberties dimension, is inferred from the results of the application of objective procedures for measuring policy dimensions in roll-call voting. This objective determination of policy dimensions and policy positions is applied to all roll-call votes, procedural motions excepted, which exhibit a split with at least ten percent in the minority position.

Although it is inappropriate at this time to go into any of the details of this "dimensional analysis" it may be helpful to report on the products. The result of the dimensional analysis of both Senate and House voting over a twelve-year period, 1953–1964, is the measurement of five major policy dimensions, one for each of five policy domains: foreign and defense, farm, social welfare, economic, and civil rights and liberties. Evidence of minor dimensions is found, but attention will be confined almost entirely to the five major ones.

References

1. Austin Ranney, "Study of Policy Content: Framework For Choice," in Ranney (ed.), *Political Science and Public Policy* (Chicago: Markham, 1968); see especially Lewis A. Froman, Jr., "The Categorization of Policy Contents," pp. 41–54.

2

The Policy Dimension
Theory of
Congressional Decision-Making

The idea of a policy dimension and the associated theory of decision-making are used throughout this study to give meaning to
thousands of voting decisions made by senators and representatives.
Some readers will object that not enough of the complexity of the
individual congressman's decision-making process is brought out and
that I go too far too fast in my simplification of this complexity.

Granted it is simplification to assign a single index or scale score to
represent each congressman's position on each of the five policy
dimensions for each two-year congressional term covered in the
study. The result is that the votes of congressmen on approximately
three-quarters of all the roll calls taken during each Congress are
summarized by five scores. Such parsimony is likely to chill the
spectator of politics who warms to the drama of political conflict
and delights in tales of intrigue.

On the other hand, five scores for each congressman, reflecting
his policy positions on *five different policy dimensions,* provide rich
variety compared with the *single* index used by a variety of interest
groups and publishers to represent the "rightness" or "wrongness"
of the congressman's voting record. Furthermore, the parsimony that
emerges in the description of *individual* decision-making is not something foisted upon the congressman without regard for his process
of decision-making; it is, rather, an indication of *his need to reduce
the decision-making chores by simplifying the decision process.*
Congressmen, like other people, when given a choice between a complex time-consuming procedure and a simpler time-saving method,
will usually opt for the simpler approach. Even were the consci-

entious legislators disposed toward a more thorough process for making individual decisions, there is little doubt that this option would be exercised rarely, given the large number of decisions and other demands upon their time.[1]

However, agreement on the proposition that congressmen make policy decisions by some relatively expeditious means, far short of close examination of each legislative motion, does not resolve the debate over the particular form of the decision-making process at the individual level. Actually, that process encompasses two separate, but related decisions: (1) The congressman must determine the policy content on which the decision is to be made; and (2) he must determine the rule for making the decision—whether according to the President's wishes, for example, or in line with the party majority.

It is the assumption of the policy dimension theory of decision-making to be stated here that, with rare exception, the decision rule is chosen *after* the policy content has been determined. This excludes the possibility that decisions are made without consulting the policy content—a situation cynically (and tragically) illustrated by the image of the legislator huffing onto the floor, buttonholing the first colleague he encounters, ascertaining his voting position, and doing likewise. The lore of legislative politics suggests that this occurrence is not so rare as one might wish. Yet I am disposed to object that the perceptive observer might not notice such behavior if it were not exceptional, in contrast with the pervasive form of more responsible behavior. I object further that such a frantic latecomer, even in his haste, will find a colleague whose views are in accord with his. Therefore, the vote he casts with the compatible colleague is likely to be equivalent to a vote cast after careful consideration.

This theory of decision-making also rules out the casting of votes according to the example or dictates of a subsample of colleagues to whom the decision role has been abdicated. Such abdication may appear to be the rule in legislative bodies in other parts of the world where party discipline in roll-call voting is strict. However, I do not regard a roll-call vote in such parliamentary bodies to be the manifestation of the policy position of the individual nor the outcome of an individual decision process, except in the most trivial sense. Rather, it is the policy position of the party, which is the outcome of a collective decision process. Only during this collective process does the individual legislator have an opportunity to express the policy position formed in accordance with his legislative role.

In less disciplined party legislatures where party is nevertheless the most pervasive basis of cleavage, such as the United States Congress, I can accept the view that party is an important element in the individual decision.[2] However, the present theory holds that the choice to follow the party leadership, or to vote with the majority of the party, is dependent upon the policy content of the roll calls. It is clear that party cues are not accepted on many roll calls. Thus, I come back to the assumption that the congressman chooses the decision rule after he has determined the policy content. Let us proceed from this assumption to a statement of the policy dimension theory of congressional decision-making, always to be understood as a *partial* theory.

In skeletal form, the policy dimension theory states that legislators reduce the time and energy requirements of policy decision-making by (1) sorting specific policy proposals into a limited number of general policy content categories and by (2) establishing a policy position for each general category of policy content, one that can be used to make decisions on each of the specific proposals assigned to that category. These two statements of the theory parallel the *policy content–decision rule* sequence presented as an assumption of the theory.

The theory holds further that the policy position taken by the individual, when acting as a congressman, consists of more than his personal attitudes. It is based also on his view of his *policy-making responsibilities* vis-à-vis his constituency, his party, the president, and cherished interests. The mix of these components is different for different congressmen and changes with policy content. Whereas one congressman's policy position may be contrary to his personal attitudes with respect to a particular policy, another's personal attitudes may be indistinguishable from his policy positions. Most congressmen, however, will work out some accommodation of personal attitudes and political responsibilities involving neither extreme condition.

In the following sections, I shall spell out the meaning of the policy dimension theory of decision-making with reference, first, to the policy content categories and, second, to the properties of the congressman's policy position. The civil liberties dimension will then be used to illustrate theory and method. Finally, the policy dimension theory will be compared with other views on the manner in which congressmen make their decisions.

Policy Content:
A Few Widely Used Concepts

A basic proposition of the theory, one that is subject to test in the present analysis, is that legislators will concur in the classification of specific policy questions according to a relatively small number of *policy concepts.*

Let me illustrate a policy concept by way of analogy. The use of the term "chair" will produce a mental image of a *chair* in most users of the English language. Different persons will "see" different images, but if the different images could be superimposed on each other by means of independent tracings on the same piece of paper, they would reveal a common chair form in the higher concentration of trace lines, representing the concept, chair. Similarly, if a number of Americans were asked to give their meaning of *civil liberties,* one would expect a superimposition of their definitions to show a high density of common terms and a scattering of less common ones.

To continue the analogy, the concept of a chair is enormously useful in classifying and giving meaning to (cognizing) a large variety of materials arranged in an immense number of specific shapes. The policy concept of civil liberty is equally useful in classifying and cognizing policies constructed in a wide variety of specific forms. Other examples of policy concepts are social welfare, international involvement, and economic regulation.

The relation of the specific policy proposal to the policy concept is the relation of the specific case to the general class. The process of giving meaning to a specific proposal involves the "trying on" of concepts until one is found whose general form can be fitted to the specific form of the proposal. (Although more than one concept may fit, that possibility is excluded in the interest of theoretical simplicity; its exclusion is considered but a slight loss in the explanation of legislative decision-making.)

The trying-on process is too complex to describe in detail; it involves more than a simple matching of the objective outlines of a proposal with the form of the policy concept. Rather, it entails the accommodation of the perception of the attributes, or characteristics, of the policy proposal with the necessarily limited cognitive capacity of the individual to give meaning to the proposal. The attributes of a proposal—*who* gets *how much* from *whom* through *what agency*

—are like messages from a source in space. These messages must be interpreted by the Earthman (congressman) in order to arrive at some understanding of the source (policy proposal). The interpretations most likely to arise are those that provide an understanding of the messages in terms that are familiar to Earthmen, that is, the messages are coded according to available concepts.

Somewhat more formally, the policy concept specifies a category of policy into which specific policies may be put. It is an element of the cognitive apparatus of the human mind, not a property of the policy proposal. It guides the perceptual mechanism in searching out *recognizable* attributes of the policy proposal as a means toward interpretation. Thus, the policy concept is something that is ascribed to a specific proposal by each individual. It is not an objectively identifiable property of the proposal, as is its title. For example, several pieces of legislation may "appear" to involve civil liberties, but some of the legislative items may be cognized in terms of a policy concept other than that of civil liberties.

A major implication of the proposition that legislators will concur in the classification of specific policy questions *according to a relatively small number of policy concepts* is that there is a limited set of policy concepts that are widely shared. (This does not preclude the existence of a large number of policy concepts that are *not* widely shared.) It is my contention, furthermore, that the widely shared policy concepts employed by legislators are commonly used by other citizens, especially those most interested and active in politics.

The proposition that a small number of policy concepts is widely shared in a political system is not nearly so unreal as it may at first appear. It is through the use of policy concepts of high generality that political discourse is possible. A policy concept provides a summary of the detailed statement of a policy proposal in shorthand terms understood by others. Furthermore, the generality of policy concepts is functional to political communications which are heavily dependent on the mass media. Even legislators depend, at times, on the media to inform them of the activities of their colleagues! But severe limitations of time and space in the media necessitate the most simplified presentations of political alternatives and policy views. Nor are there many consumers of the media who desire more detail. Therefore, a characterization of different policy proposals in terms of a limited stock of widely shared concepts is predictable.

This proposition also becomes more tenable to the extent that we rid ourselves of the illusion that people, like ourselves, do more than assign policies into broad categories, for evaluative purposes, except for the particular policy question with which we become concerned for a period of time. Nor is there strong reason to suppose that congressmen are all that different from the active citizen in this respect. Indeed, Congress has recognized the limitations on human capabilities by establishing committees with subject matter specializations.

We shall return to further consideration of these points as the analysis unfolds within the framework established by this theoretical statement. Let us proceed to the next step of the decision process, having taken the first step of labeling the policy proposal with a policy concept.

Policy Positions: Their Properties

In the second step of the decision process the congressman compares (1) the level of support for a particular policy concept, such as civil liberties, that exists in a piece of legislation, with (2) his own supportiveness of civil liberties. In other words, the congressman compares his *position* on the policy dimension of civil liberties with the legislation's *position* on the civil liberties dimension—highly supportive, moderately supportive, minimally supportive. Hence, the first property of a legislator's policy position on a policy dimension is equivalent to the level of support that he is willing to provide for the policy concept, e.g., civil liberties that are the substance of the policy dimension bearing the same name.

The congressman's response to a legislative proposal in terms of a policy decision depends on the relation between the congressman's position and the position stated in the proposal. If the legislator's level of support for the policy concept is exceeded by the legislation, he will *reject* it, by either working against it or voting it down. The congressman will *accept* the legislation if the level of support granted by the legislation is equal to, or less than, his ideal level, *providing* that the only perceived alternative is weaker, or no legislation at all; in other words, half a loaf is better than none. This is consistent with the observation of two "organization" theorists, "Most human decision-making, whether individual or organizational, is concerned with the discovery and selection of satisfactory alternatives; only in exceptional cases is it concerned with the discovery and selection of optimal alternatives." [3]

This theoretical statement is in need of one modification. It does not imply that the legislator can discriminate sharply between a piece of legislation that matches his ideal and one that implies a level of support for the policy concept that exceeds his ideal by a very small increment. I do maintain, however, that the likelihood of a congressman's accepting legislation exceeding his ideal support level diminishes rapidly as the discrepancy increases. Thus, a moderate on social welfare will be very likely to reject very liberal legislation; I am less certain about his reaction to legislation that is slightly more liberal than his position.

Assume, as illustration, that civil liberties is the policy concept ascribed to a piece of legislation by most legislators. According to the theory, congressmen are ordered on a continuum from low to high support for civil liberties. Persons taking a *high support* position will accept most, if not all, legislation furthering civil liberties. They place a high value on the civil liberties of the individual and may be less concerned with national security, the maintenance of orderly conditions, and the curtailment of unAmericanisms. This is not to say they may not value the latter just as highly, but they find them quite compatible with a first priority on civil liberties.

Toward the middle of the continuum we find *moderates* who favor civil liberty but may be less sanguine about an easy resolution of the contradiction between freedom and security which has plagued political philosophers for so long. Furthermore, they may have some real doubts about the efficacy of legislation in guaranteeing civil liberties. For whatever reason, the moderates respond less enthusiastically to legislative promotion of civil liberties.

At the other end of the continuum from the high-supporters are legislators whose positions are sometimes referred to as *anti*–civil libertarian, a designation that I avoid because it is inappropriate to suggest, without strong evidence, that someone is opposed to civil liberties; that is a harsh judgment, to be reserved for the "villains" of history. Instead, I refer to *low-supporters* for civil liberties, including those who place higher values on the benefits perceived to accrue to the enactment of legislation that ensures a measure of control or security.

The *second property* of the policy position concerns its determinants. As indicated earlier, the policy position is an adaptation of the individual to his role as a congressman. It need not express his personal attitude toward a policy concept; indeed, it is more likely to be a position taken after an assessment of his policy-making responsibilities as a representative of a particular constituency, as a member of one of the political parties, as an exponent of an ideological point of view, as an advocate of specific group interests, and as a member of Congress in loyal opposition to, or in support of, the administration. Mixed in with all these components of his policy position are the member's own points of view—not to mention those of the member's spouse.

A *third property* of the congressman's policy position is its transferability to various stages of the decision-making process. This implies, and quite importantly, that the policy position manifested in roll-call voting is effective also in nonrecorded votes on the floor, in decisions in committees, and in articulations of policy positions to colleagues and other persons involved in the legislative work.

It should be recognized that this property of the policy position is simply assumed by the theory and is not subject to test within the confines of the present study. Nor is it necessary to an explanation of roll-call voting in terms of the policy dimension theory of decision-making. It is important, however, as a statement that policy positions measured on roll-call voting are representative of the policy positions taken by members of Congress in their several legislative activities. Hence, *if a constituent is informed of the policy position of his representative through the means utilized in the current study, he has a good measure of the policy representation afforded him by his man on the Potomac.*

This assertion of a good match between roll-call voting and other legislative behavior will go down hard for many people who have been persuaded that the roll-call vote affords the congressman a chance to project a favored image, part fact and part fiction, while revealing his true identity only in the really "important" decisions made offstage in cloakrooms and committee meetings—in other words, that the congressman throws his weight in one direction off the floor and in another on the floor.

I am disposed to reject this as a facile deduction from an unsubstantiated theory of conspiratorial politics, which explains much but understands little. In its crudest expression, it holds that politicians never mean what they say. Abetting this conspiracy theory is the fact that congressional reputations are fair game for congressmen's enemies; attacks, founded and unfounded, take their toll on the congressional image over time. However, I find it impossible to imagine the legislative system functioning at all if more than a handful of congressmen consistently contradicted private with public decisions. Above all, the functioning of Congress, like any other sizeable social organization, is dependent upon its members taking consistent positions and holding to their commitments, thus being fairly predictable in their behavior. This is an important compensation for the inevitably inadequate communication between individuals.

Although I derive the most delight from debunking the conspiracy theory of politics, which should have been laid to rest by several decades of open congressional support for oil depletion allowances, the more telling defense of the openness of congressional policy positions rests on the force of numbers. The proportion of bills in which a legislator is likely to have an interest strong enough to compel the public masking of a private evil is small indeed. There may be a scoundrel here and there, but one cannot easily dismiss the view that the public record is a reasonably accurate representation of the total legislative record compiled by individual congressmen.

Finally, there is a *fourth property* of the congressman's policy position, one to be tested in the present analysis. This is the property of stability. The expectation is that the individual congressman will hold the same policy position across numerous terms of office, because there is little change in the determinants of the policy position.

During the term of service of the average congressman, changes in the constituency, for example, are gradual and limited. In the first condition, the changes are little noticed; in the second, they have little impact. Contributing to the stability of the policy position is the congressman's enduring identification with the same party, an identification formed, more than likely, at a very early age.[4] The resultant encrustation of values, attitudes, and beliefs is relatively impermeable and highly protective of policy views formed before entering Congress. Also, group affiliations and attitudes have been taken in and nourished over the years. The one source of the congressman's policy position that can change, and does so swiftly and with some impact, is the president.

Up to now the discussion has been conducted at a general, or formal, level with only passing reference to policy substance. A better understanding of the policy dimension theory can be achieved by examining its application. Such an examination serves the additional function of indicating, in a general way, the methods used in obtaining the measures of the congressmen's positions on policy dimensions. We shall therefore look closely at the procedure on a single policy dimension: civil liberties.

Illustration of a Policy Dimension: Civil Liberties

Let us first examine briefly the political context and the steps taken to make the initial definition of the civil rights and liberties domain, from which the *civil liberties dimension* is drawn.

The study encompasses the Eighty-third through the Eighty-eighth Congresses. This twelve-year period, 1953–1964, spans a Republican administration (Eisenhower, 1953–1960) and a Democratic administration (Kennedy-Johnson, 1961–1964). During this period, a Republican majority in both houses of Congress gave way to a Democratic majority in both. The Congress and the nation wrestled with a variety of policy matters of major importance: foreign aid, civil liberties, national security (external and internal), farm subsidies, educational policy (pre- and post-Sputnik), business-government relations (the Eisenhower slogan was to get government out of business and put businessmen in government), the utilization and control of atomic energy, McCarthyism, economic stagnation at both the local level (for example, in Appalachia) and the national level (the recession of 1958), among other questions of national concern.

POLICY DOMAINS AND POLICY DIMENSIONS

Strategic research considerations led me to sort virtually all substantive questions voted upon by senators and representatives into general policy domains. Five such domains were defined on the basis of the following criteria: (1) The domains should be similar to the policy categories used extensively in the political system as organizational rubrics and policy concepts. (2) They should be distinct enough that most people could agree on the particular policy domain to which a legislative motion should be assigned. (3) The similarity of content within each domain should be high enough that there would be no insurmountable problems in the way of an interpretation of the policy dimensions extracted from each. An additional criterion for defining the policy domains is based on the findings of previous research respecting the policy dimensional structure of congressional voting. The result is the five policy domains given in Chapter 1: *foreign and defense, civil rights and liberties, social welfare, farm,* and *economic.*

It pains me not at all to grant that other investigators would settle upon different policy content categories; rules of categorization are inevitably subjective. This means also that the categories I have used may not necessarily be the ones that congressmen used in assigning roll calls to policy concepts. Therefore, it is imperative that an attempt be made to discover the categories *employed by congress-men* in their search for order and meaning in the jumbled bag of policy questions submitted for their consideration. Nor does the method used here prevent the discovery of categories that include policy questions from different domains, a point discussed elsewhere. In other words, the subjectivity in my designation of policy domains and assignment of roll calls to them does not preclude objectivity in the search for categories of policy content used *by congressmen* when they make their decisions.

CONSENSUS ON POLICY CONTENT:
REQUISITE FOR A POLICY DIMENSION

The policy dimension is based on a consensus among legislators that a subset of roll calls is concerned with a common policy concept. The existence of this consensus is induced from an objective measurement procedure, which compares the vote of every legislator with every other legislator on each roll call; it also compares the alignment of legislators on each roll call with their alignment on every other roll call.[5] The technical aspects of this measurement procedure are well known, and the measures are widely used for a variety of human behaviors.[6] Here and elsewhere I shall eschew the discussion of methodological topics of the more technical or complex variety. However, it is relevant to the present level of discourse to point out that the policy dimension that is inferred from voting behavior is based on the legislators' *own* sorting and labeling of roll calls according to *their* categories of policy content, or policy concepts. Thus, it is the policy questions that most of the legislators agree belong to a single policy concept that become associated with a policy dimension in this study.

An investigation of the voting of senators and representatives on roll calls originally sorted into the civil rights and liberties domain indicates the existence of a civil liberties policy dimension. (The discrepancy in the titles of the domain and the dimension will be duly explained.) This judgment is based on the objective measurement procedures; it is not a judgment that necessarily follows from the initial sorting of roll calls performed by me. According to this judgment, legislators in both the House and the Senate are in substantial agreement that the policy content of a subset of the roll calls in the civil rights and liberties domain is that of civil liberties.

Let me post a very important reminder at this point. This concerns the meaning of a policy concept as it is used in the present study. As I stated earlier in drawing an analogy between a policy concept and the concept of a chair, not all versions of the policy concept are identical. Therefore, my name for and definition of a policy concept constitute, at best, only an approximation to the policy concept (including both name and definition) that is employed by any congressman. Assigning a single policy concept to the category of specific policies associated with a policy dimension is an effort to indicate, in very brief terms, the points of commonality characterizing the different policy proposals. The commonality is something for which empirical evidence is available in the methods used in this study; the naming of the policy concept that denotes the commonality is a matter of judgment.

Two points must be made with respect to the relation between the policy dimension and the policy domain in this particular case. First, some of the roll calls that *I* assigned to the general domain are *not* included on the civil liberties dimension. This suggests the intrusion of other policy considerations, partisanship, and nonsubstantive parliamentary maneuvering.

The second point is that the policy dimension is referred to as the civil liberties dimension whereas the domain was designated as the civil rights and liberties domain. The domain tag denotes a measure of ambivalence, for I thought it quite possible that the question of civil rights for blacks would be judged to be a different issue from that raised by the long-term concerns for individual liberties, privileges, freedoms, and justice. However, this distinction was not observed and a single civil liberties dimension emerges which subsumes civil rights for blacks.

Dominating the specific policy questions included in the domain of civil rights and liberties is black civil rights. The same holds true for the civil liberties dimension. The question of black civil rights is posed in the most pointed fashion by the various civil rights acts proposed during the twelve years under study. It is also implicit in legislation governing the District of Columbia, given its large black population. The dominance of the black civil rights question on the civil liberties dimension is so great that one is tempted to refer to a civil *rights* dimension with an implicit reference to blacks. Nevertheless, the civil liberties label is more appropriate as a more inclusive concept subsuming civil rights, because additional roll calls associated with this dimension touch on employee rights under national security regulations, crime legislation, legislative apportionment, control of subversives, sex discrimination, and restrictions on campaign financing.

It is no great surprise to find that congressmen of both houses agree on the substance of roll calls taken on legislation dealing with the rights of blacks. To this extent the concept of a policy dimension, based on a consensus among congressmen as to the policy substance of a set of roll calls, is certainly neither abstract nor esoteric. Not so obvious, nor so easily acceptable, is the consensus that black civil rights issues fit into a category of policy with a variety of civil liberty questions.

I share the skepticism of those who become uncomfortable when too great a variety of policy concerns are crowded under a single policy concept. The worry is that the phenomenon is happenstance, temporary, or an unwarranted imposition of a high degree of order on the part of the observer. This unease is allayed in the present case by the observations that the same categorization occurs, not in just one house, but in both houses of Congress, and not in the two-year life of a single Congress, but in six two-year terms. Thus, we are not observing a phenomenon peculiar to one of the houses nor to the membership of either at a single point in time. There is the passage of time, an implicit test of any observation on human behavior—as, for example, of marital fidelity. Furthermore, there is the recruitment of new members into both houses, who apparently bring with them the concept of civil liberty as an attribute that can be generalized to a variety of policy questions. This suggests that the civil liberties dimension measured in Congress is relevant to at least that segment of the electorate from which congressmen are recruited. Thus the tenacity of a policy dimension is enhanced by its roots in the citizenry.

EXCEPTIONS TO THE CIVIL LIBERTIES DIMENSION

An understanding of the meaning of a policy dimension, as the term is used here, can be furthered by a brief consideration of the roll calls in the civil rights and liberties domain that were *excluded* from the civil liberties dimension. It is important to note that these include roll calls that appear to involve civil liberty questions similar to those that were included.

A prime example is the set of amendments seeking to write nondiscrimination clauses into legislation not primarily concerned with civil rights, such as public housing. The circumstances surrounding these amendments suggest that each is proposed by an opponent of the policy that is the heart of the legislation. An indication that a political maneuver is underway, which is not based on a concern with civil rights of blacks, is the Democratic joining of hands to counter the Republican strategists. If black civil rights were truly at issue, such fellowship would be unlikely between southern and northern Democrats.

In addition to the nondiscrimination clauses referred to above, votes on the censure of Senator Joseph McCarthy of Wisconsin show partisan cleavage. On the surface, the censure debate was considered a likely candidate for the civil liberty and rights domain in view of the criticisms of the senator's behavior as destructive of such liberties. Nor is this possibility totally denied by the exclusion of the censure votes from the civil liberties dimension. However, the partisan element is sufficiently strong to destroy the consensus needed to identify the censure votes with the dimension.

Roll calls in the Senate on the legal status of the Communist party also failed to pass muster as civil liberty questions, although no one would have objected strenuously if they had. Here again partisanship inserts its waspish stinger into the soft decorum of Senate debate. And revenge is the motive. The stinger is an effort on the part of the Democrats to harass the Republican administration by passing legislation that deals severely with the Communists but appears to be unworkable. This is in return for Republican criticisms of previous Democratic administrations for being soft on Communists.[7]

The point of the discussion of the characteristics of the roll calls in the civil liberty domain that are excluded from the civil liberties dimension is that it is not valid to identify such roll calls with the civil liberties dimension. For example, on the roll calls concerning the censure of McCarthy, many Democrats may have supported the censure because they perceived the senator as a threat to civil liberties, but many others may have done so out of a stronger partisan motivation to repay McCarthy for his political attacks on them. Similarly, many Republicans may have opposed the McCarthy censure, not because they were any less sensitive to threats to civil liberty, but out of a sense of partisan loyalty. Therefore, the votes on the McCarthy censure are excluded from the civil liberties dimension.

SCORING ON A POLICY DIMENSION

Given a set of roll calls meeting the criterion of policy homogeneity, we can score the positions of all congressmen on a policy dimension. This scoring is based on the legislators' votes. The more often the legislator takes a support position, the higher his score on the relevant dimension. This scoring procedure is highly similar to that performed by various publishers and political organizations,[8] which publish indexes scoring congressmen on their liberalness, conservativeness, and various other "-nesses" and commonly implying an ordering of "rightness" as determined by the agencies' voting standards. The scoring is often based on a simple count of the number of "right" votes.

The critical difference between the procedure that I follow and the one followed by politically motivated organizations with an axe to grind is clearly not in the scoring but in the selection of the roll calls. The only axe I have to grind is the one that sharpens our delineation of the policy dimensions effective in congressional voting and marks the policy positions of congressmen on these dimensions. Thus, with respect to the dimension of civil liberties, the difference in my procedure and that of a political organization might arise, for example, in the treatment of the McCarthy censure votes. I exclude them from a measure of civil libertarianism, whereas the political agency might include them. The consequence is that the more inclusive measure will be based not only on civil liberty attitudes but on partisan loyalty as well and a Democrat may get credit for a civil libertarian response when he is only expressing partisan loyalty, while a civil libertarian Republican may be docked for being a partisan loyalist.

When "wrongness" and "rightness" are the criteria, the vacuum sweeper approach to measurement may be acceptable. It is not appropriate when the purpose of the analysis is to represent the congressman's position on policy, taking into account his own understanding of the policy at issue rather than that of the observer. Looking at it from another perspective, I am interested, not in the ultimate implication of the congressman's vote, but in the meaning he attaches to it at the time of the vote. The censure of McCarthy may well have blunted the attack on civil liberties, but a congressman's vote for censure may not have been cast with that in mind.

Each of the scales representing the civil liberties dimension gives an ordering of congressmen on this dimension. At one pole are legislators who exhibit a high level of support for legislation protective of civil liberties. At the opposite pole are those who provide the least support for such legislation. Between the two poles are arrayed the rest of the members of the legislative bodies.

It is hoped that this illustration will allay the concerns of those who feel that something called a dimension must be highly mathematical and terribly complex. It is neither. A policy dimension, viewed in very general terms, consists of a broad statement of the direction of policy in a domain of potential government activity—in this case, government support of civil liberties—and an ordering of individuals (legislators or citizens) according to their support for government activity in a particular sphere of human activities. Given a knowledge of the individual's position on the dimension, and assuming he does not change his position, we can predict that he will oppose most government activity in support of a policy concept, or support most, or take a middle road, supporting some and rejecting some. Actually, the ordering of congressmen that we are able to achieve is more precise than a three-point scale, but the general idea is the same.

Before moving on to a discussion of complementary theories of decision-making, let me acknowledge my debt to those in whose footsteps I follow.

Anyone familiar with research on legislative decision-making, particularly roll-call voting, will be aware of the origins of the policy dimension theory.[9] Some may sniff and observe disdainfully that it is nothing but an old wine in a new bottle. I don't mind the metaphor, since I regard the wine to be of an excellent vintage and also value a good bottling job.

Essentially, what I have done is to use the bare bones of behavior theory contained in the most commonly used forms of dimensional analysis and fleshed out a theory of decision-making applicable to the decision processes of individual legislators.[10] The justification for doing so is found in the general applicability of the methods of dimensional analysis to legislative voting behavior, as certified by previous studies, and possibly even understated by them because of the severe criteria sometimes used in establishing evidence of unipolicy dimensions.[11] I feel justified in offering a theory of decision-making based upon policy dimensional analysis, not only because this form of analysis has been successful, but also because those of us conducting such analyses have an obligation to articulate as fully and as explicitly as possible the theory of behavior that is implicit in the method of analysis.

I have gone beyond the duty imposed by the obligation specified above to suggest that the dimensional structure of congressional decision-making is, in its main and enduring properties, of a low order of complexity. Therein, as I see it, lies my main bid for controversy, not in the exposition of the policy dimension theory, which resides on a firm foundation of past practice and success.

Complementary Theories

A comparison of the policy dimension theory of decision-making with other views of the manner in which congressmen decide, or normatively speaking, how congressmen should make their policy decisions, may help to avert the needless controversy that stems from misconstructions of intent. Such controversy is especially likely to develop if the policy dimension theory is presented as an alternative to other theories. Such is not my intent. I believe that the policy dimension theory is not at variance with other conceptions of the ways in which individual legislators arrive at their policy decisions.

Let me modestly declare, at this time, that I share with others the concern that any set of statements used to provide understanding of a set of behaviors is entitled to be called a theory. Several devices are commonly used to circumvent this problem. One is simply to go ahead making the statements without calling them anything. The other is to use terms such as "pretheory," "theoretical framework," "preface to a theory," "conceptual framework," or "model." One may get into less trouble using such terms because they appear less pretentious; yet I am not certain that the error of faulty labeling is avoided, since such terms are seldom well-defined either.

Given the lack of a consensus on the meaning of any of these terms, including the meaning of "theory" when one deviates from a strictly deductive system, I shall use the term "theory" even though its application is to statements that purport to provide no more than a partial explanation of behavior or a way of looking at behavioral phenomena that provides some potential for explanation.

The discussion of theories of legislator decision-making is indebted to a critique by Donald R. Matthews and James A. Stimson, who have referred to them as models. An outline of the models discussed by Matthews and Stimson, including a model of their own (all henceforth referred to as theories within the limited meaning attributed to this term), plus my own brief review of two other theories, is presented in conjunction with my assessment of their complementarity with the policy dimension theory.[12]

In their critique, Matthews and Stimson describe the *public interest–statesman theory,* the *instructed delegate theory,* and the *ideologist theory* of decision-making.

According to the *public interest–statesman* theory, the member of Congress assesses the content and consequences of a piece of legislation using standards consistent with the public interest. The member of Congress, in this view, is responsible, not merely to his electoral constituency, but to the nation. Matthews and Stimson criticize this view, as would many others, because it is totally unrealistic to expect anyone to define a public interest that encompasses the needs and aspirations of millions of human beings.

The criticism is irrefutable if the theory refers to some objective statement of the public interest. However, it is much less devastating if the theory is taken to refer to the congressman's judgment of the public interest. In this event it is *his* conception of the public interest that becomes his decision rule. Only the member of Congress casts the vote, so it is only his subjective definition of the public interest that matters. Even so, the level of omniscience to which the member must lay claim in order to justify his being a judge of the public interest leads many of us to doubt that more than a few congressmen take this route in arriving at their decisions.

The intersection of the public interest–statesman theory with the policy dimension theory is easily identifiable. The commonality of the two theories is most clearly evident when we consider the determinants of the policy position taken by the legislator. In the policy dimension theory, the congressman arrives at a policy position after consulting his policy responsibilities vis-à-vis various groups and individuals. In the public interest–statesman theory the congressman consults his policy responsibility *to the nation.*

Furthermore, the public interest theory does not exclude the possibility that "public interest" congressmen share the use of general policy concepts with other congressmen operating on a less lofty plane. In addition, the consultation of the public interest may determine the policy position identified with each policy concept which, in turn, determines positions on specific policy proposals.

In short, there is nothing in the statement of the public interest–statesman theory that puts it at odds with the policy dimension theory. It simply does not articulate the several aspects of the individual decision-making process that are presented in the policy dimension theory.

The *instructed delegate* theory is a dinosaur of democratic theory that perishes when the body politic becomes too large for electors and elected to consult on a person-to-person level or when no meeting place can accommodate the full citizenry. In brief, the representative cannot act as a delegate carrying out the wishes of his constituents because he cannot possibly ascertain their instructions.

Representation can, however, be accomplished, without explicit instructions from constituents, through the medium of the congressman's perceptions of the policy requirements of his constituents. The accuracy of these perceptions is enhanced by a variety of information sources, though none is so broadly based as the "instructions" implicit in the instructed delegate theory.

The instructed delegate theory fits easily within the framework of the policy dimension theory. Like the public interest–statesman theory, it is silent with respect to the manner in which congressmen perceive and give meaning to legislation and is concerned only with the decision rule. The rule is simply to abide by constituency instructions, for the policy responsibility of the congressman is only to the constituency. Thus, the policy position of the congressman is the policy position of his constituents.

The instructed delegate theory, in its purest form, may conflict with the policy dimension theory in that the latter's emphasis upon general policy concepts and general policy positions is of little meaning where the member is instructed on every single vote. This, of course, is the aspect of the instructed delegate theory that makes it irrelevant to the functioning of legislative institutions. However, if the theory is loosened up a bit to permit instructions of a more general sort (the major point being that the representative is the servant of his constituency in every way) then the policy concepts and general policy positions of the policy dimension theory may be quite appropriate.

Moving on to the *ideologist* theory, as described by Matthews and Stimson, "when a specific policy proposal comes to the floor, all the member need do is compare its probable consequences with a structure of beliefs he carries around in his head. If the policy and his ideology agree he supports the measure; if not, he votes against its acceptance." [13] Their first argument against this theory is the lack of evidence. This argument raises methodological issues that I discuss elsewhere.[14] The import of my counterargument is that the lack of evidence is partly a function of the methods cited by Matthews and Stimson as appropriate for gathering evidence on ideological voting; other methods might provide support for the ideologist theory. The more convincing arguments put forth by Matthews and Stimson are (1) that ideology is *in*frequently at issue on a specific item of legislation and (2) that instead of an all-embracing ideology, congressmen use more specific policy concepts in evaluating legislation.[15]

I am in full accord with the critique of the ideologist theory. In fact, the policy dimension theory is offered as a means of differentiating between different policy concerns currently bundled together in the liberal-conservative dimension. Thus, a policy is labeled as being conservative or as being liberal, and the assumption is made that liberals and conservatives in Congress will take opposite sides. However, all people labeled as conservatives do not always agree, nor is there some undifferentiated bloc of liberals always taking the same position. Different alignments form as the policy content changes.

If we can agree that liberal and conservative ideologies do not provide the bases for many, many policy decisions—and there appear to be no other viable candidates for the role of ideology—the ideologist theory appears to have serious shortcomings as an explanation of congressional decision-making. It is too gross a simplification of the decision-making apparatus of the typical congressman, so proud of his pragmatism and so scornful of ideological straitjackets.

The ideologist theory, like the two aforementioned ones, complements the policy dimension theory through its specification of a decision rule. According to the ideologist theory, the policy position of the congressman is determined by his ideological stance. Also like the instructed delegate and public interest–statesman theories, it says nothing about the manner in which congressmen cognize policy proposals. Actually, it does not exclude the possibility that the ideology incorporates the several policy dimensions in the present study and defines a policy position on each.

Two other theories of decision-making, not included in the Matthews-Stimson critique, are the *bloc* and *coalition* theories. The terms "bloc" and "coalition" are sometimes used interchangeably, at other times they are differentiated. I adhere to what I consider to be a stricter definition of each than is commonly implied. In my view, these theories imply a continuing pattern of interpersonal communications concerning legislative strategies that will maximize the bloc or coalition members' control over the legislative machinery. The primary difference between the two legislative combinations is that members of a bloc share similar origins and usually a single interest, whereas members of coalitions coalesce to maximize each other's somewhat disparate interests.

An example of a coalition (at least, it is often called one) is the conservative alliance of Republicans and southern Democrats; the disparateness of the two wings of the coalition lies in their different party affiliations. The most recent example of what may be considered a bloc has been the farm bloc, a set of representatives with a single interest and an influence reputed to be in excess of its numerical strength, thereby implying an advantage gained from a conscious unity.

However, some question remains as to the validity of the bloc and coalition designations in these two instances. Clearly, there are policy questions on which a majority of the southern Democrats align with a majority of the Republicans; and there are policy questions on which farm representatives concur. But this does not permit us to infer that either the farm representatives or the renegade Democrats and conservative Republicans vote in concert because of prior and continuing consultations over legislative goals and strategies.

The problem is that without evidence on interpersonal communications within a legislative body it is difficult to distinguish between voting behavior that results from similar, but individual, conceptons of policy responsibilities and that resulting from coalition or bloc arrangements. Representatives of farm constituencies can appear to be a bloc even though each member votes his constituency interest; similarly, Republicans and southern Democrats may appear to coalesce although they are doing no more than registering individual conservative biases.

Whatever the facts of legislative behavior, my view of the individual's decision process is not in conflict with theories of coalition and bloc behavior, as they apply to *blocs and coalitions of some permanency*. The loyalty to a long-standing coalition that is activated by certain policy concerns is consistent with the idea of general policy concepts, one of which may be the object of the coalition behavior. Moreover, the stable policy position associated with a policy concept can be based on a long-term coalition or bloc position. For example, in the case of the farm bloc the relevant policy concept may be that of agricultural assistance. This concept subsumes a variety of specific farm programs. The associated policy position is the equivalent of the bloc posture of strong support for agricultural assistance programs.

The review of decision theories concludes with the cue-taking theory, supported by Matthews and Stimson, as being more realistic than those they have reviewed. This theory states that

> *when a member is confronted with the necessity of casting a roll-call vote on a complex issue about which he knows very little, he searches for cues provided by trusted colleagues who—because of their formal position in the legislature or policy specialization—have more information . . . to make an independent decision. Cue-givers need not be individuals. When overwhelming majorities of groups which the member respects and trusts—the whole House, the members of his party or state delegation, for example—vote the same way the member is likely to accept their collective judgement as his own.*[16]

Through the use of the cue-taking device

> *it is possible for the ordinary Congressman both to vote in a reasonably rational fashion and to do so on the basis of exceedingly little information.* Outside the area of his own policy specialization, the member need only decide which cue-giver or cue-givers to follow on what sorts of issues.[17]

Given the above quotation, I want to draw attention to the sequence in the decision process which is posited by the cue-taking theory. First, the *sort* of issue is determined, then the *cue-giver for the decision* is selected. This formulation of the decision process squares perfectly with the assumptions undergirding the policy-dimension theory: That the decision rule is selected *after* the policy content is determined by the congressman.

The decision rule in the policy dimension theory is the policy position that the congressman holds relative to a general policy concept; in the cue-taking theory the decision rule is provided by the trusted colleague, where the "trust" is transferred from one colleague, or set of colleagues, to another according to the content of the legislation. Succinctly, the cue-taking theory substitutes the policy person for the policy position of the dimension theory.

Within the terms of the policy dimension theory, the cue-taking theory complements the former by specifying one of the ways in which the congressman may compare his policy position on a dimension with the position of the legislation on which a vote is about to be cast. For example, when the congressman knows that the substance of the legislation is civil liberties, but is not well enough informed on the particulars of the legislation to determine the level of support it provides for civil liberties, he can turn to a colleague whose position on the dimension is known to be similar to his own and follow his voting lead.

The complementarity of the two theories is also found in the equivalence between the "sort of issue" of the cue-taking theory and the "policy concept" of the policy dimension theory. The policy concept provides a further definition of what is meant by the sort of issue. In addition, the policy dimension theory is explicit in its statement that the policy concept is a relatively permanent component of the legislator's cognitive structure, which is used in successive sessions to sort the same kinds of specific policies into given categories. I presume that the "sort of issue" to which Matthews and Stimson refer is also a relatively stable designation of issues for the individual congressman. For if the classification of individual proposals according to the sort of issue kept changing, the member of Congress would continually have to be finding the appropriate cue-senders to fit the different "sortings." This would not be in accord with the time-saver principle on which the cue-taking theory rests, in part.

Although the compatibility and complementarity of the policy dimension and the cue-taking theory is substantial, there does remain a clear difference in emphasis. Whereas the policy dimension theory focuses on the congressman's definition of policy content, as well as upon the decision rule, the cue-taking theory bores in on the decision rule. In doing so, it leaves little room for the possibility that congressmen may develop policy positions that are activated with no more information on the substance of the question on the floor than is needed to activate the search for the appropriate cue-giver.

The cue-taking theory clearly places the individual legislator in a state of high dependence upon the cue-giver. However, it does not explain how the cue-giver arrives at his vote decision. This may be of little importance if the cue-givers are a very small, select number of members in the legislative body. One can, for example, accept the idea that the president, a few party leaders, and high-ranking members of the committee responsible for the legislation being voted upon are the cue-givers, without requiring an explanation for their behavior in a theory of legislator decision making. This explanation would certainly be useful, but it is not essential to a theory that *does* explain the behaviors of hundreds of legislators. However, the cue-taking theory permits the cue-givers to be group majorities, including the majority of the whole house. Furthermore, in known tests to date it is the group cue-givers that are far and away the most important. Thus, the failure of the theory to explain the decisions of the cue-givers is no small matter.

In conclusion, let me stress two major points. The policy dimension theory of individual decision-making enjoys complementarity with other theories because it refers to an aspect of the decision process not attended to by them. These other theories are mainly concerned with the rule for making the decision—public interest, constituency instructions, personal attitudes—a concern shared by the policy dimension theory. The difference is that the policy dimension theory is concerned also with the process whereby the legislator identifies the meaning of a specific policy proposal—by referring it to his stock of policy concepts. The decision rule follows.

The policy dimension theory reflects the view that politics is centrally concerned with policy. At times, personalities, the drama rather than the substance of political conflict, and strategic maneuvering may obscure this core concern of politics with policy. The nature of the mass media coverage helps to bury policy under a cover of other political facts and fictions. However, succeeding chapters in this study will demonstrate the importance of the policy content of politics, leaving no doubt that as the content of policy varies, so do the terms of the political equation.

References

1. Donald R. Matthews and James A. Stimson, "Decision-Making by U. S. Representatives: A Preliminary Model," in Sidney Ulmer, ed., *Political Decision-Making* (New York: Van Nostrand Reinhold, 1970), pp. 15–17.

2. Documentation of the level of party cleavage, along with an extensive discussion, is found in Chapter 5.

3. James G. March and Herbert A. Simon, *Organizations* (New York: Wiley, 1958), pp. 140–141.

4. Angus Campbell, *et al.*, *The American Voter* (New York: Wiley, 1960), pp. 146–147; Robert Hess and Judith Torney, *Development of Political Attitudes in Children* (Garden City, N.Y.: Doubleday, 1967), pp. 110–111, 247.

5. I have used the same technique as MacRae, with minor modifications. See Duncan MacRae, Jr., "Method for Identifying Issues and Factions from Legislative Votes," *American Political Science Review* 59 (December 1965), pp. 909–926. For a detailed discussion of the techniques used in this study see Aage R. Clausen and Richard B. Cheney, "A Comparative Analysis of Senate-House Voting on Economic and Welfare Policy; 1953–1964," *American Political Science Review* 64 (March 1970), pp. 139–140.

6. See Duncan MacRae, Jr., *Issues and Parties in Legislative Voting* (New York: Harper & Row, 1970), especially chap. 1.

7. *Congress and the Nation: 1945–1964* (Congressional Quarterly, 1965), p. 1646.

8. The scoring of congressmen on a policy dimension in each of the Congresses was accomplished as follows: First, the roll calls belonging to a particular policy dimension were identified. Second, the member received a score of 1.00 on each roll call on which he took the position that was more supportive of the relevant policy concept, of 3.00 on each roll call on which he took the less supportive position, and 2.00 on each roll call on which he failed to indicate a position either by a pair or a response to a *Congressional Quarterly* poll. Third, a mean score was calculated for each congressman on each policy dimension, based upon the scores received on the individual roll calls in the policy dimension set. The result was an ordering of congressmen on the policy dimension, from those whose mean score reflected the highest support position, 1.00, to those whose mean score of 3.00 reflected the lowest level of support for the policy concept. Congressmen who failed to register a position on over 50 percent of the roll calls identified with a particular policy dimension in a particular Congress were not scored. The rationale for this scoring procedure is advanced in Aage R. Clausen and Richard B. Cheney, "A Comparative Analysis of Senate-House Voting on Economic and Welfare Policy: 1953–1964," *American Political Science Review* 64 (March 1970), p. 140.

9. Duncan MacRae, Jr., *Dimensions of Congressional Voting* (Berkeley: University of California Press, 1958); George M. Belknap, "A Method for Analyzing Legislative Behavior," *Midwest Journal of Political Science* 2 (November 1958), pp. 377–402; Warren Miller and Donald Stokes, "Constituency Influence in Congress," *American Political Science Review* 57 (March 1963), pp. 45–56.

10. A very general statement which links a theory of response behavior (the responses of individuals to test items) to the problems of measurement is provided by Paul F. Lazarsfeld, "A Conceptual Introduction to Latent Structure

Analysis," in Paul F. Lazarsfeld, ed., *Mathematical Thinking in the Social Sciences* (New York: Free Press, 1954).

11. Lee F. Anderson, *et al.*, *Legislative Roll-Call Analysis* (Evanston: Northwestern University Press, 1966).

12. Matthews and Stimson, *op. cit.*, pp. 18–23.

13. *Ibid.*, p. 20.

14. Aage R. Clausen, "State Party Influence on Congressional Policy Decisions," *Midwest Journal of Political Science* 16 (February 1972), pp. 86–87.

15. Matthews and Stimson, *op. cit.*, pp. 20–21.

16. *Ibid.*, pp. 22–23.

17. *Ibid.*, p. 23.

3

Five Major
Policy Dimensions

The Premise of this work referred to the liberal-conservative dimension that permeates much of what one reads and hears of American politics. At one time it was believed that most Americans could be ordered, in at least some crude fashion, along the liberal-conservative continuum. This belief persists in many circles. Furthermore, it was believed that the individual's position on this dimension would determine his views on a wide variety of nonpolitical questions as well as political ones. A liberal on social welfare was expected to be a liberal on civil liberties and farm and economic policy, a liberal with respect to morals, religion, and child-rearing practices, and a liberal on anything else one might imagine. The liberal, conservative, or moderate outlook of an individual was no less than a basic orientation to his total environment, determining his responses to its political, economic, and social aspects.

Social scientists who finally got around to examining citizen attitudes, instead of making assumptions about them, had little difficulty in recognizing the multidimensional character of public attitudes and so rejecting the concept of a single-dimension organization. One of the earlier findings was that of a distinction between an economic and a civil liberty dimension, formerly indistinguishable in liberal-conservative terms.[1]

Numerous studies have since shown the fallaciousness of the notion of a single liberal-conservative dimension on which all people can be ordered and from which one can predict attitudes on an infinite array of topics. Indeed, some evidence suggests that few people organize their attitudes on any two or more topics into a pattern shared by others.[2] In this perspective, pessimism attends the attempt to predict the attitude on one topic given the attitude on any other for a representative sample of Americans. Instead of one dimension, such as the liberal-conservative, this view implies a multitude of dimensions.

However, narrowing our focus henceforth to *political* attitudes only, we find that the disarray in public attitudes can be overstated as well as understated. This overstatement may result in part from the evidence chosen to measure political attitudes, notably, a failure to present policy questions that are most meaningful to the people surveyed. There has been some tendency to pose questions that are important to political scientists, editorial writers, and news commentators but are hardly dinner-table conversation in most of the homes in Gary, Indiana. In addition, there *is evidence of coherence in public attitudes on policy questions within limited domains,* such as welfare policy, civil liberties, or facets of foreign policy.[3] It is important to note also that success in finding sets of mutually consistent attitudes on different types of policy questions within specific domains increases among people who follow politics more closely and are more involved in the political fray.[4]

Congressmen are recruited from the ranks of the most highly involved citizens and can be expected to possess the desire and the ability to organize their attitudes on public policy within certain domains such as foreign, farm, or welfare policy. Some may even develop a set of attitudes that spring from a single dimension or a central impulse: humanitarianism, egocentrism, generosity, aggressiveness. However, the evidence of this and other studies indicates that coherence in public attitudes is restricted to more limited policy domains.

A sneak preview of the manner in which congressmen order their policy positions was provided in the Introduction. There I referred to five policy domains, each of which yielded a single major policy dimension. This early glimpse left some detail untold, however. The present chapter will give more detail, including brief descriptions of the *content* of each of the five policy dimensions and the *history* of each dimension in American politics. These historical excursions will consume very little time because little information on these dimensions was gathered before World War II. The political scientists' "benign neglect" of historical analysis and the historians' distaste for systematic quantitative analysis, shared by most political scientists prior to the present generation, contribute to the deficiencies in the scholarly record.

Civil Liberties

Content

The concept of civil liberties includes specific aspects of civil liberty, such as freedom from unsanctioned violence on the part of enforcement officers and the sanctity of private life, and the right to fair trial. The ideal of justice before the law is widely recognized, perhaps because of childhood exposure to clear moral condemnation of exceptions to this ideal in the ubiquitous low-budget film features: "westerns" and "cops and robbers." And the concept of equal treatment of equal citizens finds ready acceptance and understanding, although in practice there is much deviance from the ideal.

These and other general norms making up the democratic ideal way of life, with immediate effect on process rather than policy, and initially concerned with nonmaterial rather than material values, are the components of the general *concept of civil liberty*. Civil liberty may be defined more abstractly as "the sum of the rights and immunities of all the citizens of an organized civil community concurrent with the guaranteed protection against interference with such rights and privileges." [5] In this view equality and civil rights are subsumed under the concept of civil liberty. Certainly "civil liberty" is the more general term today when civil rights are almost exclusively identified with the blacks' struggle for full membership in American society.

A further point of clarification is important to our understanding of the civil liberties dimension in congressional decisions. The concept immediately involved is that of *federal government support* for civil liberties. It is conceivable that a person may oppose a civil libertarian policy at the federal level, not out of opposition to the principle involved, but because of doubts about the propriety of *federal* activity He may prefer state action, or action at a lower level of government, or he may feel that the same guarantees must be worked out by nongovernmental agencies. However, let us not overlook the further possibility that avowed preference for nonfederal action may be used as a blind for the support of the status quo.

This point of clarification holds for all of the policy dimensions, for the concept each time involves only the governmental role at the federal level. Incidentally, this is another good reason for not inferring that the congressman's policy position is his personal attitude; it may only represent a position that is suitable to the performance of his congressional responsibilities.

History

The civil liberties dimension first appears in the present study in the Eighty-fourth Congress (1955–1956). The relative scarcity of civil liberty roll calls in the prior Congress, the Eighty-third, on which the study originated, precluded measurement of a dimension. Similarly, in the Eighty-second Congress there was little civil liberty action. Although, a study of voting in the House of Representatives yields good evidence of the civil liberties dimension in the Eighty-first Congress (1949–1950),[6] insufficient analyses of congressional decision-making in the civil liberties domain make it impossible to project the civil liberties dimension back into time beyond 1949.

International Involvement

Content

The *international involvement dimension* emerges in the analysis of roll calls assigned to the foreign and defense policy domain. This domain includes all nondomestic policy questions: foreign aid, trade, participation in international organizations and conferences, presidential "doctrines" such as the Eisenhower Mideast Doctrine, and lesser questions of international content. Defense policy was included within this domain because the number of votes on this matter was too small to warrant separate treatment, but the principal reason was the strong likelihood that it is closely linked to foreign policy.

It is clear from the analysis that senators and representatives do not derive all their positions on foreign and defense matters from their position on a single dimension. From the evidence, it is apparent that foreign trade and foreign aid involve different policy concepts. Defense policy is independent of both. Immigration decisions involve yet a different concept. Let me emphasize, here, that these are not findings based only on this study; they appear in other studies in some historical depth.

What this means is that knowing that a congressman supports foreign aid does not allow one to assume that he also favors a relatively open immigration policy and is a free-trader. Certainly, there are some congressmen who take all three positions, but this can not be established without a full examination of each person's record in all three areas.

Although there exist several policy dimensions within the foreign and defense policy domain, one is clearly the most general, accounting for nearly all voting decisions on the foreign aid program, both economic and military. It is not just a foreign aid dimension. In the House it includes votes on a variety of international activities, but not trade, immigration, and defense. The generality of this dimension is less marked in the Senate (generality referring to the proportion of roll calls in the domain that can be assigned to this dimension), although the diversity of policy concerns is similar to that embraced by the dimension in the House.

That a number of roll calls in the Senate "escape" the dominant dimension is attributed to the opportunities that senators have for considering the more detailed aspects of international policy on the floor. These relatively extensive deliberations facilitate the expression of specialized concerns (minor dimensions if you will), that are confined to committees and informal discussions in the House. There are many fewer House votes on amendments; conversely, there are proportionally more roll calls on the full piece of legislation under consideration. This means that House members are usually voting on the main outlines of policy where a general dimension of international affairs is most appropriate. Senators, in contrast, are often voting on policy refinements, where a general policy position is less useful as a premise for decision.

The policy concept that defines the substance of the dominant dimension in this domain is international involvement. Congressmen are considered to be ordered on this dimension from those who favor restraint to those who favor an activist policy. This description deliberately avoids the connotations of the old internationalism-isolationism dimension, which seems inappropriate to post–World War II Americans with the rank of congressman.

On the international involvement dimension suggested here, the *activist* is one who supports the use of national resources to influence the course of international affairs; he does not necessarily envision a world government (which the term "internationalist" can imply). The proponent of international *restraint* counsels the husbanding of national resources and takes a skeptical view of the gains achieved by committing those resources to affect international relations, but he does not hold the view that international affairs can be ignored (which the term "isolationist" suggests).

History

More research on congressional activity in the area of foreign and defense policy has been done on earlier periods of American history than is true of any of the other policy domains. Evidence is readily available for any period immediately after World War I, which is as far back as I care to go; it marks the beginning of a time in world history when United States foreign policy decisions carried weight, even though the decisions reflected a severe level of international restraint. That is to say, we possessed enough power potential that our failure to use it could be as important as our willingness.

Prior to World War I the primary interest of Congress in international relations centered on what was referred to as the tariff question. Since then, trade policy has continued to be distinguished from other questions in foreign policy, but congressional involvement was greatly reduced in the 1930s with the enactment of the Trade Agreements Act of 1934, which turned decisions on individual tariff items over to the executive branch, relieving congressmen of the responsibility for setting the duty on everything from steel ingots to sewing needles.

The distinction between foreign trade, as a policy dimension on which congressmen are ordered from protectionist to free-traders, and international involvement (dominated by foreign aid) appears to be a viable one since just before World War II. Support for this is found in a study by Leroy Rieselbach, who looked at congressional voting in 1939–1940, 1947–1948, 1953–1954, and 1957–1958.[7] And in a study of House voting 1949–1950, Duncan MacRae observes the same trade-aid distinction to be a very sharp one.[8] In sum, since foreign aid has become a major instrument of American foreign policy, it, along with other items of international involvement, has been identified with a policy dimension distinct from that of foreign trade.

The historical depth of the international involvement dimension is well enough supported to claim that its presence in the 1953–1964 period is not a time-bound observation. Some might question its identity with the isolationist-internationalist dimension of pre-World War II, a doubt that can be resolved only by returning to a study of congressional voting in the 1920s and 1930s.

Certainly, popular historical perspectives give the impression that people in this country are ordered along the same dimension in both periods but that the center of gravity of public opinion has shifted toward the activist position. It would also appear that the bipolarization on this dimension has lessened since World War II and as a function of a general awareness that we are involved in international affairs, like it or not. Thus, isolationists have become advocates of restraint rather than celibacy in international relations, while the internationalist position at the other extreme has failed to attract additional adherents and perhaps has even suffered some losses in the face of the dis-United Nations.

Agricultural Assistance

Content

One of the least secure industries of this country has been peacetime farming. During wartime the demand for agricultural goods increases, farmers are encouraged to expand their operations, and overinvestment often ensues. Following the cessation of physical hostilities, the demand and the prices for farm products decline, but interest payments, maintenance costs, and prices for farm supplies do not.

In the twentieth century the government has been asked to extend a helping hand in the periods following both major wars. The concept of *agricultural assistance* became firmly entrenched in national politics during the thirties, when the postwar farmer blues became an angry lament caused by a general economic depression combined with a windblown drought. The farmer demanded his share of the Roosevelt New Deal of the 1930s. He received credit, mortgage moratoriums, payments for planting less and adopting more anti-erosion procedures, assistance in obtaining cheap fertilizer, and many other forms of aid. Included was the farm commodity subsidy.

The farm subsidies provide a minimum floor for farm prices on designated commodities. If the market falls below this floor, the farmer sells to the government. Unfortunately, the surplus production, partially encouraged by the price floor, becomes a storage problem for the government. Nor does the government seem to have the same facility in making corn, wheat, and oats disappear that it has with the money it collects. The less-than-pleasing paradox is the continuing high cost of food on the market, accompanied by unused food in the government granaries and higher taxes to defray the expenses of storage and subsidy. Such was the problem faced by the administration and the congress during the period under study.

Nearly all of the roll calls included on the agricultural assistance dimension are concerned with farm subsidies. The opponents took the classical, free-market, social Darwinian survival-of-the-fittest approach: The withdrawal of government support for farm prices would compel the more inefficient farmers to close down operations, and the long-range benefit would be a healthier farming industry. Concomitantly, there would be lower consumer prices and lower taxes. What could be more reasonable?

Proponents of agricultural assistance feared that the conditions of a free market might cause a farm recession which would spread to other industries. They also questioned the wisdom of forcing the farmers into the city and possibly onto the unemployment and welfare rolls. Finally, there was the romantic symbol of the family farm, the ideal environment for the growing child and mature adult but an institution that would be hard pressed to survive in a laissez-faire economy.

Congressmen and other citizens were scattered along the full continuum from those who favored what amounted to a guaranteed farm income, through those who favored a floor but not a prop under farm prices, to those who wanted the removal of even the floor.[9]

When the agricultural assistance dimension is viewed in this fashion, not original with me, it is difficult to ignore the loud sounds of an ideological battle waged on a familiar political-economic terrain. Old arguments over the government management of the economy versus unfettered free enterprise provided much of the firepower.

History

Evidence of the agricultural assistance dimension is clear in 1949–1950, but none is available for the 1951–1952 Congress, the one prior to the first included in this study.[10] By no evidence, I mean that there is literally no systematic evidence either affirming or denying its content or generality in these years. This is more generally true of the studies of the activities of Congress on farm policy prior to 1949. We shall have to be content with the evidence of an agricultural assistance dimension dating from 1949 through 1964, without in any way ruling out its greater historical duration.

Social Welfare

Content

The concept of *social welfare,* and federal government responsibility for it, is so widely employed as to need no introduction. I offer a definition used previously: "Legislation on the welfare dimension involves a relatively direct intercession of the government on behalf of the individual, cushioning him against the jolts administered by the economy, assisting him in coping with more powerful economic elements, and aiding him in getting the equal chance that the ideal of equal opportunity demands." [11] Included in this legislation are proposals dealing with public housing, urban renewal, labor regulation, education, urban affairs, and employment opportunities and rewards.

History

There is no clear evidence of a social welfare dimension in previous studies because it has been interwoven with the government management dimension drawn from the economic policy domain, to be described next. Roll calls on what I have referred to as economic and welfare policy have often been included in single measures of domestic liberalism-conservatism. Or they have been lumped together as indicators of government economic interventionism or as measures of attitudes towards the federal role.

The mixing of policies from the economic and welfare policy domains is quite understandable in view of their content similarity. Furthermore, it is often the case that superficial or routine statistical analyses of voting decisions are insufficiently sensitive to distinguish one dimension from another simply in terms of the voting patterns. The interweaving of the two policy dimensions—social welfare and government management—occurred in the present study, also, but a distinction between the two was possible, largely because of the longitudinal character of the study; an historical perspective can often be of great value, even to a quantitatively oriented political scientist.

This problem of the undesired fusing of conceptually distinct policy dimensions, and its resolution, has been dealt with in previous publications; disbelievers are invited to consult these earlier works.[12] For the rest of us, time is served better by moving on to the related dimension in the economic policy domain and by observing its substantive differences from the social welfare dimension.

Government Management

Content

The economic policy domain includes legislation concerned with the government ownership and regulation of economic enterprises, government spending on public works as opposed to incentives to private business to maintain and restore the economy, private versus public development of natural resources (for example, water power and atomic energy for electricity), regulation of business activities, distribution of the tax burden, conservation, setting of interest rates, and balancing the budget. The policy concept of the policy dimension that preempts this domain is that of *government management* of the economy and the resources of the nation.

The concept of government management implies a rather direct intervention of the government in economic affairs and in the disposition of natural resources. As used here, it is biased toward *immediate* benefits to the *mass* of the citizenry, as in public works expenditures during periods of unemployment, rather than a system of incentives to private business to encourage expansion and employment. There is also a bias toward broader distribution of the wealth, less concern for the sanctity of private enterprise, and willingness to expand the role of government as manager without undue concern for the growth of the power of government. The concept of government management leans toward a preference for the demands of the poor over the rich, the consumer over the producer, the public over the private interest, and the borrower over the lender.

Illustrative of legislation associated with the government management dimension is that dealing with air and water pollution (yes, even then), antitrust policy, the sale of government-owned rubber plants, wage and price controls (once thought to be a thing of the past), public power utilities, housing mortgage and interest policy, and public works (including antirecession measures). Also included is legislation concerning land reclamation projects, mineral and timber rights on public lands, and conservation.

A major difference between the welfare and the government management dimensions is the difference between providing assistance directly to the individual, according to his current condition, and creating an economic and physical environment favorable to the great mass of the citizenry. Under the welfare policy concept the individual is assisted with respect to education, housing, wages, working conditions, retirement benefits, and "relief." The effects on the individual of the policies subsumed under the government management concept are less direct and not always easy to predict. Certainly, this applies to the choice between business incentives and government "pump priming"—the jobs may be made available, but the individual must seek them out; this is quite different from assistance in the form of a check through the mail or handed out at the unemployment office. Similarly, the effect, upon individuals, of government regulation and ownership of industry, conservation policies, and setting of housing mortgage policy, is indirect.

History

As stated in the discussion of the social welfare dimension, no distinction between it and the government management dimension has been made in studies of earlier periods. My expectation is that with the appropriate methods of analysis, such as the ones used here, such a distinction could be made even in the pre–World War II period. Regardless of what might have been, it is impossible to piece together a clear picture of historical continuity, or discontinuity, beyond the pale of the present study.

As a postscript to this review of the five policy dimensions, let me comment briefly and as nontechnically as possible on the evidence regarding other dimensions. Two properties of the evidence supportive of the existence of additional dimensions were instrumental in my decision to confine the study to the five major dimensions. In the first instance, the evidence in support of additional dimensions was weak because the measures of these dimensions usually consisted of a small number of roll calls. This is damaging to the inference of a policy dimension because the validity of the measurement of a dimension increases as the number of roll calls increases.

In the second instance, the evidence in support of additional dimensions was weakened because it was usually based on the voting in a single Congress. Thus one has good reason to wonder whether such a measurement might be no more than a transient constellation of voting decisions on a number of roll calls that "happens" to fit the model used to detect the existence of a policy dimension. Indeed, one of the advantages of a longitudinal study based on several Congresses is that the criterion of recurrence can be used to separate the gold from all else that glitters.

Conclusions

In the conclusion to this review of the five policy dimensions to which the remainder of the study is devoted let me red-flag two results of the analysis producing the five dimensions. First, it is important to remember that the analysis of the structure of congressional voting, *performed independently* on the Senate and on the House, has revealed *parallel forms of the five policy dimensions* in the two houses. Of course, it is not wise to be dogmatic about the judgment that the dimensions are the same in both houses; that is virtually impossible to establish. However, I am encouraged to make this judgment because not only is the content the same, but, as later analyses will show, the party and regional divisions of the two bodies are highly similar on each of the five dimensions.

Second, it is equally important to recall that the *same five policy dimensions persist over a period of twelve years* during which there is a continuing influx of new members and the sad exodus of old ones. During this period, in which the Senate reached the present size of 100 members, nearly twice that many individuals, 186, held seats in that upper chamber. Compared with the usual House membership of 435, there were 786 individuals who held membership. Yet despite the turnover of members, bringing new men and women into the decision process, the same dimensions persist.

The *continuity* of the policy dimensions over three presidential administrations and their *parallel forms* in two quite different legislative bodies suggest that these dimensions have strong footholds in the politically alert public. In the absence of rapid socialization of new congressmen into the congressional ways of viewing policy, it is certainly reasonable to think that these dimensions penetrate into that portion of the citizenry from which members of Congress are drawn. Otherwise one would expect to see the breakup of old dimensions of voting and the intrusion of new ones as new members of Congress are recruited.

In this chapter I have sought to provide a perspective on congressional decision-making that is both general and substantively meaningful. The policy dimensions whose content and history have been described are the very heart of the analysis and understanding of policy cleavages in the Congress and in the United States. Consequently, it seemed necessary and useful to bring them to a front and center position on our stage of consciousness by describing them in their most familiar terms: their policy content.

I have also stressed the high level of continuity in the patterns of decision-making in Congress, over time. The full meaning of this picture of congressional activity is conveyed in the expectation that a member of Congress who left after having served in the first Congress in this study (the Eighty-third) and returned eight years later to serve in the last Congress of the series (the Eighty-eighth) would have felt quite at home again.

In the next chapter, two questions are raised with respect to the continuity of policy dimensions over time. (1) Do the dimensions of the 1953–1964 period extend into the present? (2) What is the nature of the evidence that I have used to come to the conclusion that there are these five dimensions—government management, social welfare, agricultural assistance, civil liberties, international involvement—which span the six Congresses under study?

The first question leads to an extension of the dimensional analysis to the Ninety-first Congress to see whether the same five dimensions are still operative in 1969–1970. The second question, concerning the evidence of dimensional continuity, requires a closer look at the data than offered heretofore.

Indeed, many readers may find that the following chapter focuses too narrowly on methodology (how do we know what we claim to know?) to be of sufficient interest to warrant a thorough reading. The reader who is willing to accept my judgment on the meaning, and meaningfulness, of my measures of the five policy dimensions, is encouraged to skim the next chapter, touching down on only the high spots. For although the next chapter is important to the close student of congressional behavior, it is not essential for an understanding of the discussion in the chapters that follow it.

References

1. For a review of this literature see Seymour M. Lipset, *Political Man* (Garden City, N.Y.: Doubleday, 1960), pp. 87–126. For a case in point see V. O. Key, Jr., *Public Opinion and American Democracy* (New York: Knopf, 1965), p. 171.

2. Philip E. Converse, "The Nature of Belief Systems in Mass Publics," in David Apter, ed., *Ideology and Discontent* (New York: Free Press, 1964), pp. 206–231.

3. Warren E. Miller and Donald E. Stokes, "Constituency Influence in Congress," *American Political Science Review* 57 (March 1963), pp. 45–56.

4. Converse, *op. cit.*

5. *Webster's New Collegiate Dictionary* (Springfield, Mass.: Merriam, 1956), p. 484.

6. Duncan MacRae, Jr., *Dimensions of Congressional Voting* (Berkeley: University of California Press, 1958).

7. Leroy N. Rieselbach, *Roots of Isolationism* (Indianapolis, Ind.: Bobbs-Merrill, 1966).

8. MacRae, *op. cit.*

9. *Congress and the Nation: 1945–1964* (Congressional Quarterly, 1965), p. 664.

10. MacRae, *op. cit.*

11. Aage R. Clausen and Richard B. Chaney, "Comparative Analysis of Senate-House Voting on Economic and Welfare Policy," *American Political Science Review* 64 (March 1970), p. 141.

12. *Ibid.*, pp. 140–152; Aage R. Clausen, "Measurement Identity in the Longitudinal Analysis of Legislative Voting," *American Political Science Review* 61 (December 1967), pp. 1020–1035.

4

Continuity and Stability: 1953-1970

The understanding of the decision-making behavior of members of Congress is facilitated to the extent that this behavior exhibits a fairly stable pattern, with behavioral components that exhibit constancy over time. If the processes leading to the policy decisions of members of Congress were constantly changing, in both substance and form, it would be difficult to arrive at a general understanding of congressional behavior.

In the search for the elements of constancy in congressional behavior, and in an effort to describe the regularity observed in the behavior of individual congressmen, the spotlight is brought to bear on two related phenomena. One of these is the *continuity of policy dimensions* through different terms of Congress; the second is the *stability of the policy positions* held by individual congressmen over some period of time.

The time period, and the Congresses, most thoroughly studied with respect to these two phenomena of *dimensional continuity* and *positional stability* extends from 1953 through 1964, from the Eighty-third through the Eighty-eighth Congresses. For reasons to be given later, an additional time period (1969–1970), and Congress (the Ninety-first), is also included in this analysis.

It may be helpful if the examination of these two properties of congressional voting is set within a framework consisting of three propositions included in the policy dimension theory put forward earlier: (1) The large number of specific policy questions associated with individual roll calls are referred to a limited number of general policy concepts by the individual legislators as they strive to reduce the complexity of their decision-making chores; each specific question is given meaning in terms of the policy concept that it activates in the mind of the individual. (2) The general policy concepts used by an individual member of Congress are stable components of his cognitive map, highly resistant to change even over fairly long periods of time. (3) The positions that congressmen hold with respect to the general policy concepts, from low to high support, are relatively stable over time.

The finding of five dominant policy dimensions that account for approximately three-quarters of all roll calls is consistent with the first proposition: that congressmen refer a large number of specific policy questions to a very limited set of general policy concepts. For there is but one general policy concept, shared by most legislators, associated with each dimension. This policy concept (social welfare, for example) is the content of that particular dimension.

The continuity of the five policy dimensions over the six Congresses, from 1953 through 1964, is consonant with the second proposition of the policy dimension theory: that policy concepts are enduring components of the congressman's cognitive mapping, or categorization, of the great variety of specific policy questions. I have not yet supported this assertion of dimensional continuity; that task is undertaken in the present chapter.

Nor has evidence yet been produced with respect to the third proposition drawn from the policy dimension theory, regarding the stability of policy positions held by congressmen. This, too, is a matter to be dealt with shortly, in conjunction with the treatment of continuity.

The importance of these two properties of individual decision-making, stability and continuity, extends beyond their centrality to the policy dimension theory. Similarly, the theory's importance extends beyond its usefulness as a reconstruction of the individual decision process. So before getting into the descriptive detail, let us consider the implications of the presence, and absence, of dimensional continuity and the implications of variations in positional stability.

Continuity of Dimensions: Implications

One of the implications of a finding that a policy dimension spans several Congresses is that its policy concept is either so important in (if not to) the functioning of Congress that newly recruited members are rapidly introduced to its use. Alternatively, it is a policy concept that is widely employed beyond the halls of Congress and thereby accessible to the new members of Congress even before they take their seats. I have presented the argument that the latter is the case.

If my argument is correct, at least to some significant degree, the finding of dimensional continuity is much more than a convenience in the study of Congress. It is also an indication of a mesh in the policy orientations of congressmen and their constituents, providing evidence of a sharing of policy concepts between congressmen and at least those constituents who form the pool of potential candidates and their active supporters.

The sharing of policy concepts between legislators and their constituents is highly important to the representational process. The policy concepts can serve as mediums through which policy position statements are communicated. Impulses flow either way through the medium. Legislators send messages that communicate their stands on the general policy concepts, but they also receive positional communications from their constitutents. Thus, a limited set of policy concepts, associated with dimensions displaying a high degree of continuity, express a condition with a strong potential for policy representation at the general level considered in this research.

If, instead, legislators were to change their stock of high-use policy concepts frequently, the sharing of those concepts with their constituents would be much less likely. On the other hand, gradual change in the dimensional structure (and the underlying policy concepts) from Congress to Congress could be the result of changes in policy concerns, or ways of viewing policy alternatives, that might be shared by both congressmen and the more active and involved citizens. In any event, indications are that congressmen favor the familiar over the new and thus stay in touch with a greater share of their constituents, at least in terms of the categories used to classify policy matters.

Facing in the other direction, what, might one ask, would be made out of contrasting evidence that the dimensional policy content, along with the dimensional structure, changes markedly from one Congress to the next? By looking in this direction for a bit we may gain a better appreciation of the implications of dimensional continuity.

One possible interpretation of congressional voting that exhibited a constantly changing dimensional structure might be that the houses of Congress are legislative bodies in which changing strategies of coalitional advantage become confounded with policy content. What is cognized by the individual congressman, and responded to on a roll-call vote, is not simply policy, but policy-plus-strategy. In such a situation, a general policy concept would be useless as a coding device; nor do I know what a general policy-plus-strategy concept might look like. I suspect that it would be much less stable than a simple straightforward general policy concept, for the mix of policy and strategy considerations would be highly subject to change. Actually, this view of the congressional forum is probably closer to popular conceptions than the one espoused in this book.

Another interpretation of a changing dimensional structure, also compatible with popular speculations about the behavior of Congress, is that the changes are due to the forces generated by and expressed in the election of a new Congress. If the elections were truly effective formative processes, in relation to policy matters, and if each new Congress were a unique assemblage of perspectives wrought from the blazing forge of electoral debate and conflict, one might expect new dimensions in congressional politics. But the forge of electoral debate and conflict, while ringing loud, usually does not achieve the proper mixture of air and fire to reshape old tools of discourse into new.

It should be clear to anyone who has followed me this far that I find both truth and charm in the French expression, "the more things change the more they remain the same." The finding of continuity in the dimensions of policy that order congressional re-actions to policy questions while the membership changes, presidential administrations come and go, and manifestations of change abound in the society and receive abundant notice, is compatible with this French observation. However, I do not wish to over-emphasize the impermeability of Congress to change and will move away from that emphasis in discussing the level of stability in the policy positions held by individual members.

Stability of Policy Positions

In relation to the continuity of policy dimensions, it is important to note that policy positions may exhibit the widest possible range of variation, from concretized immobility to frenetic movement, while the dimensional framework of decision remains constant. For example, the civil liberties dimension may span several Congresses, thereby suggesting a lack of change, but individual congressmen may change their positions along this dimension, moving from low to high support or in the opposite direction. In addition, freshmen congressmen may take quite different policy positions than their predecessors while viewing the legislative options in terms of the same general policy concept of civil liberties.

The major implication of a finding that the policy positions of individual legislators are quite stable is readily apparent. If legislators tended to anchor their policy positions in granite, the only way of altering the policy output of Congress would be to blast some congressmen out of office.

Certainly positional stability is a very strong likelihood, since human beings are not noted for their readiness to change their points of view. This is likely to be particularly true for the general and basic points of view associated with the five policy concepts explicated in this study. Actually, the expectation that congressmen will appear stable in their policy positions is based on previous studies of roll-call voting behavior, in addition to a more general knowledge of human behavior. This expectation is consistent also with the recently prevailing understanding among political scientists that lobbying efforts directed at legislators whose positions are known to be contrary to the lobby position are an expensive and relatively ineffective use of resources.[1]

Another implication of the finding of positional stability is that, given a knowledge of the factors underlying policy positions on different dimensions—knowledge that may be related to the properties of incoming congressmen—one may be in a position to make predictions about the collective policy position of the new Congress relative to the preceding one. For if the policy positions of the members who are held over from one Congress to the next remain substantially the same, an evaluation of the policy position of the new Congress is dependent only upon an assessment of the change introduced by the freshmen congressmen. In other words, one does not have to begin from point zero in the assessment of the new Congress.

The promise of predictability in the behavior of newly elected Congresses, based on our knowledge of previous Congresses and a pattern of behavioral constancy over time, brings us squarely up against the question: Of what current utility is the study of congressional decisions made a decade ago? In the specific case here, what does the analysis of voting in the Congress during a prior period, 1953–1964, tell us about policy decision-making at the individual level during the current Congress?

Current Relevance

The current relevance of a study of congressional behavior during previous Congresses is a point that can be addressed on two levels. On the most general level, one may make the argument that the mechanism of decision-making employed by individual congressmen is unlikely to change, for example, the use of general policy concepts to give meaning to specific policy proposals. This will be current practice although the *particular* policy concepts may not be the same ones as in previous periods. This argument draws upon the proposition that the processes underlying human behavior are much less likely to change than is the substance entered into the process. Consequently, general properties of behavior may be extrapolated beyond the time-specific context of a particular study.

In deference to those for whom every day's events are a novel experience to be treated as unique phenomena, and for the benefit of the casual observers of human behavior not yet persuaded of the powerful and persistent forces of habit, inertia, and routine that govern the lives of individuals and their institutions, I have repeated the dimensional analysis for the last full Congress available for analysis at this writing. This is the Ninety-first Congress of 1969–1970.

With respect to the Ninety-first Congress, the point of relevance is addressed by asking the following question. Are the voting decisions of the members of the Ninety-first Congress comprehensible in terms of the same five policy dimensions that describe the voting of the Eighty-third through the Eighty-eighth Congresses? If so, the case for the complaint that the 1953–1964 period is historically unique, (1) with respect to the assertion of the policy dimension theory that decisions are made with reference to a limited number of policy concepts, and (2) as regards the content of the five dimensions, is greatly diminished. By the same token, we will have greater confidence that the same five dimensions are *still* ordering congressional policy perceptions and policy positions.

On the other hand, we may find that some of the five dimensions are currently viable whereas others have disappeared by 1969–1970. In the latter instance, it is anticipated that new dimensions will have emerged in place of the old. But this is no cause for anxiety; rather, it is a reason for excitement, as the dynamics of change have a potential for exposing the conditions that produce new policy dimensions and cause the demise of the old. Of course, if there is a massive reshuffling of policy dimensions, the problem of historical uniqueness confronts us—*relative to the particular substance of policy dimensions.*

The Case for Continuity

I have asserted, without presenting systematic evidence, that there are five policy dimensions that dominate voting in both the House and the Senate for a twelve-year period. This assertion is based on confidence in the validity of the procedures by which the dimensions are measured and their continuity over time is established. Discussion and illustration of the procedures with respect to two of the policy dimensions, government management (previously referred to as economic policy) and social welfare, have been published previously where they may be read by those who are unsatisfied with the general character of the description offered here.[2]

The procedure of analysis is as follows: On the basis of content classifications used in other studies and content categories more generally employed by publicists, teachers, and practicing politicians and statesmen, five domains of policy were delineated: social welfare, economic, foreign and defense, civil rights and liberties, and farm. Within each of the Congresses, and within each of the houses, roll calls were assigned to one of these five domains. A few roll calls were omitted because motions were procedural or the substance was *both* trivial and incompatible with the policy domain specifications.

Do keep one fact in mind: The roll calls were assigned to policy domains *independently* for each house and congressional term *prior* to doing the dimensional analysis on any house or Congress. The assignment of roll calls to policy domains was not assisted by looking at the results of a dimensional analysis.

Following the domain assignment, the voting patterns within each policy domain, for each house and Congress, were examined in search of evidence of policy dimensions. This involved finding subsets of roll calls that fit together; that is to say, the voting divisions on the individual roll calls were similar to each other in a way that is expected when two or more roll calls are voted upon in terms of a single policy dimension. The "fit" was determined by using statistical techniques widely accepted by social scientists as appropriate instruments for measuring a variety of dimensions of human behavior, attitudes, and traits, given the responses of individuals to a battery of questions or statements. In the present study, it is legislators who are responding to a battery of roll-call motions presented over the term of a Congress.

Let me illustrate and explain the procedure. In doing so, I shall adopt a convention that will be followed throughout the remainder of the book. When discussing methods, methodology, and in some cases the results of an analysis, I shall on occasion go into a level of technical detail that will be of little interest to readers primarily concerned with substance and willing to accept my conclusions. On these occasions the technical discussion will be set off from the more general presentation by solid horizontal lines demarking the boundaries of the technical discussion. Without loss, the reader can simply keep on the highroad, so to speak, treating the technical presentations as detours or optional side routes leading back to the main road.

Consider, as illustration, the analysis of the roll calls sorted into the social welfare domain for the House of Representatives in the first Congress of the study, the Eighty-third. A subset of roll calls is found that fit together, according to the statistical evidence that they are voted on in terms of a common policy dimension.

The statistical evidence consists of the finding that the average correlation between the pairs of roll calls in the subset, for all possible pairings, is 0.7 or greater, using the gamma coefficient. In addition, the correlation is never lower than 0.6 for any single pairing within the subset. Finally, the subset must contain three or more roll calls. Even that number is usually too small to warrant the inference of a policy dimension, as opposed to some fortuitous combination of factors producing similar alignments on different roll calls.

Looking at the content of the specific policy questions posed in the roll calls in the subset in this illustration, I made the judgment that the general policy concept to which each of these roll calls had been referred by most of the House members was social welfare. Examples of specific policy questions commonly identified with the social welfare dimension are federal aid to education, a minimum wage increase, an extension of the coverage of unemployment compensation benefits, public housing, and increased aid to dependent children.

The finding is that there is one subset of roll calls in each policy domain, in each house and Congress, that almost always includes at least twice the number of roll calls in the next largest subset. Furthermore, the largest subset is nearly always the one that appears to measure the policy dimension that extends across the six Congresses of the core study. This serves as confirmation of the validity of the domain definitions and indicates that policy domain designations that are very familiar on the American political scene are inclusive of, and highly similar to, the policy concepts employed by congressmen.

The next step was to score the members of the House in a way that would reflect their ordering on the policy dimension—in this particular case, from low to high support for the policy concept of federal government responsibility for social welfare. Essentially, these scores are the equivalent of a simple calculation of the proportion of times the individual member has voted for social welfare legislation, given only the subset of roll calls that have been identified with the social welfare dimension.

After this procedure was completed for every policy domain, defining as many subsets of roll calls as fit together within each domain, within each house, and Congress, the next and most difficult phase of the analysis was undertaken. This is the analysis with which this chapter is concerned: assessing the continuity, or the persistence, of the policy dimensions throughout the succeeding Congresses. The question being asked is, How do we know that a subset of roll calls in the Eighty-third Congress, which I have defined as measuring the policy dimension, social welfare, really is measuring the same policy dimension as a subset of roll calls similarly designated in the Eighty-fourth Congress, and in the Eighty-fifth Congress, and so on?

The first, easiest, and most naturally appealing answer is that the content of the legislation associated with the social welfare dimension is the same in each Congress. This is a good criterion to use in assessing the continuity of a single policy dimension and plays a major part in this assessment, but it is insufficient *by itself*. The insufficiency stems from the fact that what looks to *us* like social welfare legislation, that is, what fits our concept of social welfare, may not have appeared as social welfare legislation in the congressman's mind. (This point was made in the discussion of the civil liberties dimension in Chapter 2.) To the congressman the policy question may have been one of government intervention, or economy—or race, for that matter. And it is the perceptions and cognitions of the congressmen that matter. In truth, it will never be possible to establish with a high degree of certainty that the content of a policy dimension in Congress A is the same as the content of a dimension measured in Congress B. We can, however, try to bring as much evidence to bear upon the question as possible, given limitations on available resources.

In addition to looking at the content of the roll calls associated with a policy dimension over time it is possible to employ another criterion of continuity. The expectation is that *the ordering of congressmen* on a policy dimension measured in Congress A will be highly similar to the ordering of congressmen on the same dimension in Congress B. This raises the question, How similar is highly similar? A partial answer is that highly similar orderings on the *same* dimension are orderings that are more similar than those observed on *different* dimensions. For example, it is expected that the ordering of congressmen on the social welfare dimension in the Eighty-third Congress will be more similar to the ordering of congressmen on the social welfare dimension in the Eighty-fourth Congress than to the ordering of Eighty-fourth Congress members on international involvement. This is no more than common sense. All that is being said is that the policy positions taken by congressmen are likely to be more similar with respect to the same topic, even though the occasions for taking the positions are some time apart, than policy positions taken on different topics, also some time apart.

An important assumption is being made, however, in applying the second criterion. This is the assumption, built into the policy dimension theory and subject to test, that the policy positions of individual congressmen will be stable over some period of time. This can be a very dubious assumption, as, for example, when the White House is the home for two presidents from different parties during the span of years under study. Nevertheless, the assumption of positional stability appears to be valid enough often enough that it is a very useful piece of evidence to consider, along with the continuity of the content of the roll calls, in determining whether or not the same dimension is reappearing in successive Congresses.

A third criterion is used for establishing dimensional continuity, one concerned with the characteristics of the ordering of individual congressmen on the different dimensions. Thus, one would expect that the ordering of congressmen on a dimension will exhibit some characteristic that is particularly meaningful to that dimension and that this characteristic will appear in the ordering of congressmen on the same dimension in different Congresses. A clear example of what I mean is the North-South division that is expected on the civil liberties dimension, given its civil rights component. This division is expected on the civil liberties dimension in every Congress during the period under study. Similarly, it is anticipated that an urban-rural, as well as a party, division will characterize the ordering of congressmen on the social welfare dimension. As this expectation is confirmed in one or two Congresses, it is then anticipated that these characteristics will continue to adhere to the orderings on the different measures of this dimension. When they do not, it gives us pause, because one piece of evidence has failed us. The case for continuity is not destroyed by the lack of one piece of evidence, but it is weakened, and this must be taken into account in the final judgment.

In the next section, some of the evidence used to support the conclusion that particular policy dimensions persist through the terms of two or more Congresses is advanced. This will be done in relation to the five policy dimensions described in the preceding chapter. Of the three criteria of dimensional continuity just proposed, evidence will be shown pertaining to two of them. The criterion not reviewed is the one that requires the content of the roll calls associated with a policy dimension in different Congresses to be the same. The findings in this respect have been discussed in the preceding chapter, at least in general terms. Anyone wishing more detailed analysis of roll-call content may consult prior publications.[3] The less skeptical reader may choose to skim quickly through the next few pages, which are much more oriented to method than to substance.

Continuity: 1953–1964

The case for continuity will be made first for the Congresses in the core study, those serving from 1953 through 1964. Whether or not the same dimensions appear in the Ninety-first Congress, 1969–1970, is a matter to be taken up later.

Our first look at the evidence bearing upon the case for continuity focuses upon the question, *Do the measures of a given policy dimension, constructed in different Congresses, produce orderings of congressmen that are more similar to each other than they are to orderings of congressmen on measures of different dimensions?* For example, is the ordering of House members on the measure of the government management dimension in the Eighty-third Congress more similar to the ordering on the same dimension in the Eighty-fourth Congress than to the ordering of members on any of the measures of the other four dimensions? If the answer to this question is no, there are at least two ways to go with the analysis. One way involves the rejection of the case for continuity on the grounds that the measures are hopelessly intertwined and we are unable to separate one policy dimension from another. The other way is less negative and involves the consideration of additional evidence, in the knowledge that none of the criteria of evidence is either sufficient or necessary by itself.

The results of the analysis of the similarity of the orderings of members on different measures of what is apparently the same dimension, given the content of the roll calls included in the measures, are presented graphically in Figure 1 (A for the House, B for the Senate).

For each house, the similarity of the member orderings on measures of the same dimension is compared with the level of similarity characterizing the member orderings on different dimensions. Three summary scores are given relative to each of the five dimensions. The first score is the mean level of similarity between measures of "itself." The second score is the similarity

Figure 1(A)

Average Similarity of House *Member Orderings on Measures of Same Dimension Compared with Measures of Different Dimensions*

☐ Least similar   ▤ Most similar   ▓ Similarity on
   other dimension   other dimension   self measures

GOVERNMENT AGRICULTURAL SOCIAL   CIVIL   INTERNATIONAL
MANAGEMENT ASSISTANCE   WELFARE   LIBERTIES INVOLVEMENT

Eisenhower Congresses: 83rd-86th

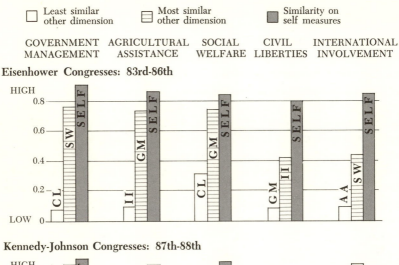

Kennedy-Johnson Congresses: 87th-88th

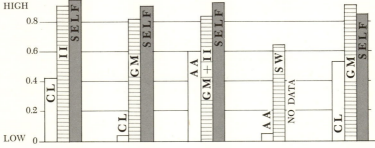

Eisenhower → Kennedy-Johnson

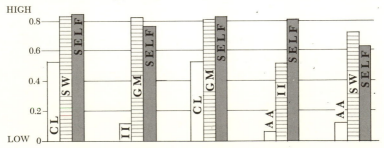

Figure 1(B)

Average Similarity of Senate *Member Orderings on Measures of Same Dimension Compared with Measures of Different Dimensions*

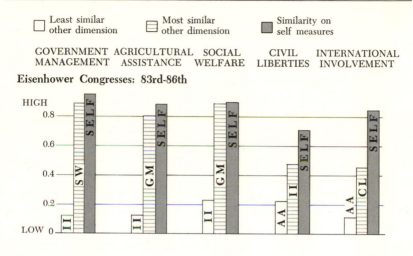

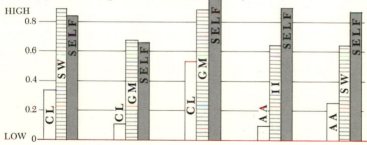

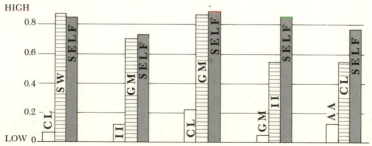

between the orderings on its measures and the measures of the one other dimension whose orderings are *most* similar to the dimension in question (the most similar dimension is designated in the bar graph). A third score gives the same information for the dimension whose ordering is *least* similar to the policy dimension in the spotlight. To meet the criterion of continuity, the score for the similarity of the "self" measures should be the highest of the three.

The analyses were conducted separately for the Eisenhower Congresses, the Kennedy-Johnson Congresses, and for the pairings of measures involving one each from the two administrations. The statistical coefficient used to measure the similarity of orderings was the Pearson *r*.

In general, there is substantial satisfaction of the *ordering similarity* criterion of dimensional continuity. In the Senate, some problems do arise with respect to the two dimensions of government management and social welfare. The similarity between legislator orderings on social welfare and government management measures is *sometimes* greater than the similarity among some measures of the government management dimension. Said another way, the orderings of senators on the two dimensions tend to be highly similar. Consequently, one has to ask, Do we have measures of two distinct dimensions that display parallel continuity across the five Congresses, or is there really only one welfare-economic dimension? It is a fair question, particularly in view of a tendency among many political observers and participants to think in terms of a single dimension including the specific policies found on both of our dimensions. My answer is that I find substantial evidence, drawn from other quarters, to support the distinctiveness of these two dimensions. Some evidence will be presented very soon; additional evidence will emerge in other contexts in which the behavior of the congressmen on the five policy dimensions is analyzed.

The criterion of ordering similarity is challenged also by the behavior of the international involvement dimension measures in the House. There is a convergence of the legislator orderings on the international involvement scales and the social welfare and government management scales in the Kennedy-Johnson Congresses. In the Eisenhower Congresses, on the other hand, there was no problem.

This behavior of the measures of the international involvement dimension will be fully explained later in the book in terms that do not call into question either the continuity or the distinctiveness of the international involvement dimension. For now, the explanation is that the effect of a Democratic president, relative to a Republican president, is to cause a party bipolarization to take place on the international involvement dimension. Consequently, the legislator orderings on this dimension under the Kennedy-Johnson administration were brought into line with the party divisions generally characteristic of the social welfare and government management dimensions (to be shown later in this chapter).

Finally, there is the hardly noticeable problem with the ordering similarity criterion in the case of the agricultural assistance dimension in the House. Orderings on this dimension in the Eisenhower Congresses are less similar to orderings on measures of the same dimension in the Kennedy-Johnson Congresses than they are to orderings on the government management dimension. Again we have an instance of two highly related dimensions on which some movement takes place *between* administrations. However, it is important to note that the criterion of continuity is satisfied when we consider just those measures of the dimensions that are constructed within each administration. If the latter were not the case, and if other evidence on the distinctiveness of the agricultural assistance dimension were not available (such as the policy content of the agricultural assistance roll calls), I would be tempted to conclude that agricultural assistance legislation evoked a legislative response in terms of the government management dimension. But this would actually obscure a policy content differentiation that finds support and utility in later analyses.

In brief conclusion, the requirement that measures of the same dimension produce orderings of congressmen that are highly similar over time is well met. As shown in Figures 1(A) and 1(B), the level of similarity is high in absolute terms (see bars designated "self"). And in relative terms, measures of the same dimension are usually more similar than measures of different dimensions—in terms of their ordering of legislators. Where the latter is not true, compensating evidence in support of the case for continuity is available. Some of this evidence will appear as the full analysis unfolds, although its relevance to the question of continuity may not be explained as such. An illustration of the type of evidence to which I refer follows.

Unique Properties
of Legislator Orderings
on Individual Policy Dimensions

One criterion of continuity previously advanced is that the orderings of legislators on a particular dimension should be characterized by some property or properties meaningful to that dimension and characteristic of each of the measures of the dimension. Also, one may expect to find that measures of different dimensions are related to a given property in different ways, and consistently so over time. The display in Figure 2 exemplifies what I mean.

In Figure 2 the partisanship of the orderings on five dimensions is shown for both House and Senate in terms of a summary measure of partisanship calculated for each of the two administrations, Eisenhower and Kennedy-Johnson. Approximately the same level of partisanship characterizes each dimension across the two administrations. The major exception is the international involvement dimension, which tends to display a partisan bipolarization under a Democratic president which is muted or absent under a Republican president. Thus, we have a general pattern of partisanship in relation to the policy dimensions that remains the same over time, with the measures of the various dimensions falling into the niches assigned to their policy dimension.

In this pattern, the government management dimension is consistently most highly partisan; that is to say, the partisanship on the measures of this dimension is highest under both administrations and in both houses. The lowest level of partisanship is observed most consistently on measures of the civil liberties dimension. With the exception of international involvement, the measures of the remainder of the dimensions exhibit a moderately high level of partisanship under all four conditions in which the measurements were taken.

If, in contrast, the partisanship on different measures of what appears to be the same policy dimension had changed, from one measure of this dimension to the next, in an irregular fashion that defied explanation, it would have been necessary to consider the possibility that the different measures were not of the same dimension, despite an apparent similarity in policy content. For we do expect that the policy positions of members of Congress on a particular dimension

Figure 2
*The Level of Partisanship as a Consistent Property of the
Five Policy Dimensions Under Two Administrations:
Eisenhower and Kennedy-Johnson*

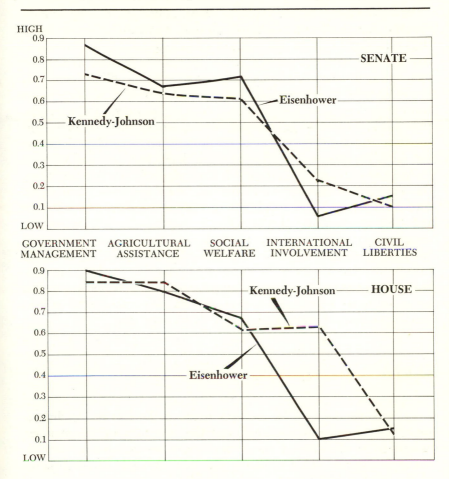

are determined, in large part, by the same set of factors over some
period of time and that the effect of any one factor on a given policy
dimension will remain relatively stable over time.

It is also anticipated that a particular factor, such as party, will
have different effects on different dimensions, being strong on one,

weak on another, and noneffective on yet others. Thus, partisanship will be high on some dimensions, moderate on others, and weak or nonexistent on the remainder, as was found to be true for the five policy dimensions in this study.

In sum, the case for continuity is based, in part, on the expectation that the factors affecting decisions on policy will differ across policy dimensions, but that the effect of any one factor on a given dimension will remain relatively constant across several Congresses. This is the common-sense view that congressmen, like other people, refer to different sources of information, advice, and expertise as they move from one general category of decisions to another (for example, from social welfare to government management) and that they tend to return to the same sources in different Congresses when decisions are made on questions similar to those dealt with previously,

As stated above, the case that I have made for the continuity of the five policy dimensions across the six Congresses from 1953 through 1964 does not rest on the evidence presented thus far. It will be buttressed by the continuing analysis of the behavior of the congressmen with respect to these dimensions, as we observe behavioral differences across the five dimensions. Very shortly, we shall turn to the last Congress in the analysis, the Ninety-first, and ask the same question about continuity. For the moment, however, the focus shifts to a consideration of the stability manifested in the policy positions of individual congressmen over time.

Stability of Members' Policy Positions

In building the case for the continuity of the five policy dimensions, one criterion of evidence was the similarity of the member orderings on measures of the same dimensions constructed in different Congresses. That evidence provided also the first indication of the level of stability of members' policy positions in that a high level of similarity in the orderings is dependent on the stability of the members' positions over time.

In this section, I propose to go behind this general observation for a closer look at the characteristics of the stability phenomenon. This is warranted in view of the centrality of this phenomenon to the policy dimension theory, a centrality not fully demonstrated by its contribution to the case for continuity.

An important component of the policy dimension theory is the proposition that the policy positions of individual members will be highly stable. This does not deny either the fact or the possibility of change, but considers substantial change to be the exception. The finding of stability enhances the policy dimension theory in that it fits with the general view that congressmen seek to simplify and otherwise reduce their decision-making tasks. Certainly one of the better ways of reducing the burdens of policy-making is to avoid the process of reevaluating policy positions that have served in the past.

The stability of individual policy positions is assessed by examining the similarity of the scale scores assigned to congressmen on the same dimension in different Congresses. Of course, the scale scores are not totally accurate representations of the legislators' "true" positions on the dimensions. However, inaccuracy is reduced in the larger scales, those based on the larger number of roll calls. Just as the general ability of a student to handle the subject matter of a course is more accurately measured with a larger number of test items, so the congressman's general position on a policy dimension can be measured more precisely when we have his decisions on a larger number of roll calls. Accordingly, I have selected the two largest scales on each dimension as the best indicators of the stability on that dimension.

A graphic presentation of the stability of the policy positions of individual congressmen on the five dimensions in each house appears in Figure 3.

The scatterplots in Figure 3 display the distributions of legislators in terms of the individual legislators' positions on the two scales chosen for each dimension. The greater the departure of the data points, representing the individual legislators' simultaneous positions on the two scales, from the diagonal line joining the lower left and upper right corners of the enclosing square, the greater the change in policy position. Actually, all points in the diagonal corridor represent congressmen whose policy positions probably have not changed because the scores are subject to measurement error. Since some amount of error

Figure 3

*Stability of Members' Policy Positions Shown for Two Largest Scales
Constructed on Each Dimension During Eisenhower Congresses*

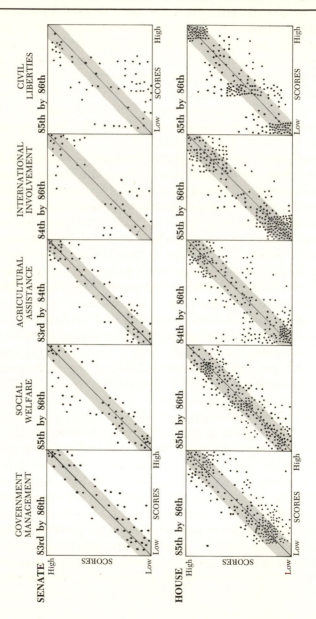

is to be expected the scores assigned to congressmen at two points in time may be different even though there has been no change in the policy position.

The evidence is convincing that congressional policy positions are remarkably stable. The most notable departure from this general pattern is on the civil liberties dimension in the Senate. Yet even in this case, most of the movement takes place either *within* the lower half of the scale or *within* the upper half, with few Senators crossing the Great Divide between low and high support positions.

Not only are members' positions stable from one Congress to the next, this stability characterizes representatives and senators located all along the policy dimension, moderates as well as high- and low-scorers. It is not surprising to find that persons holding more extreme positions hold them quite dearly; [4] such legislators are expected to resist the vagaries of transient policy winds, being much less prone to change than those forever testing the political atmosphere with a moist finger. However, I did expect to find that congressmen located in moderate positions on one scale would reappear on another scale in one of the more extreme positions. In other words, it would not have been surprising if the moderate position represented little more than a temporary deviation from a stable end position taken in another Congress. Thus, in one particular Congress an individual member might have a moderate score because of an unusual aggregation of idiosyncratic factors pushing him away from a more normal end position. But this is apparently not the case; congressmen holding moderate positions tend to remain within a range of moderate positions. Granted, there is slightly greater stability among high- and low-scorers, but it is not markedly so.

Nor are the moderate positions as sparsely populated as one might expect, given a decision format that discourages fence straddling by always forcing a member to vote either yea or nay, when he would often prefer a modified form of the legislation being voted upon. While there is a tendency toward bipolarization of congressmen on the several dimensions, there is also a pretty fair distribution all along each of the dimensions.

This graphic demonstration of stability will not be accepted by everyone as the full story, since but a subset of the dimensional measures, consisting of the two largest scales from each dimension, was involved. It is possible that these scale pairs are unrepresentative in other respects than size. This possibility is enhanced by the fact that the two largest scales were often from adjacent Congresses, hence there is the possibility that the limited time periods involved are unique with respect to the high level of stability in policy positions. Two scales chosen from another time period might exhibit much less stability in policy positions. It is also the case that the largest scales were drawn from the Eisenhower congresses and there may have been something unique about congressional service during this period, since presidents do differ in their relations with congress.

The base for the analysis of the stability of the policy positions of individual Congressmen was broadened by including all of the scales constructed on the five dimensions in the six Congresses under study. A summary measure of stability was calculated for the set of scale pairings in the Eisenhower administration and for the pairings in the Kennedy-Johnson administration. This measure of stability reaches a maximum of 1.0 when there is no change in positions from one Congress to the next, and drops to 0.0 when a congressman's score in one Congress gives no indication how he will score in a later Congress.

The summary measures of stability are computed *within* each administration and compared with the same measure computed on the two largest scales. The reason for confining the analysis of stability within administrations is derived from the policy dimension theory of congressional decision-making. In this theory it is recognized that a change in an important policy client of the congressman, so to speak, can alter the congressman's position. Having moved to a new position, stability sets in again until some other major change occurs in the congressman's clientele. These major changes are thought to be quite rare; however, the facts argue that one such major change is that of a turnover of the presidency from one party to another. Results of the analysis are given in Figure 4.

In relation to the scatterplots presented previously, the summary measure of stability used here is a statement of the amount of dispersion of the data points relative to the diagonal. The greater the dispersion, the lower its value and the higher the level of instability.

The coefficient used as the summary measure of stability is the Pearson *r*. Although the maximum value of 1.0 is consistent with the absence of a change in scores, it is also true that the

Pearson *r* can reach 1.0 with any amount of change in scores if every congressman moves exactly the same distance in the same direction as every other congressman. It is in the latter respect that the Pearson *r* is used elsewhere as a measure of the similarity of orderings on different measures of policy dimensions.

Using the Pearson *r* as a measure of the stability of a congressman's policy positions, something additional to the similarity of the ordering of congressmen on measures of the same dimension, does make sense if one is willing to assume that the set of roll calls offered in one Congress is equivalent to the set in another Congress, as regards their properties as tests of a congressman's support for a particular policy concept. From my experience in working with these data, this assumption seems fairly reasonable.

The stability of policy positions is shown using three sources of data. These are (1) all six Congress pairings that are possible within the term of the Eisenhower administration, on which an average stability measure was computed after weighting the contribution of each Congress pairing by the number of members serving in both Congresses of the pair; (2) the single pairing of the two Congresses of the Kennedy-Johnson administration; and (3) the two largest scales used in the previous demonstration of stability.

It is quite apparent that most congressmen adopt a position on a policy dimension and stick with it. With but two exceptions, the level of stability exceeds 0.8 on a scale ranging from 0 to 1.0. Neither of the exceptions is marked by a level low enough to contradict the generality of the pattern of stability.

The comprehensive summary measures of stability make it clear that the earlier demonstration of the stability of members' policy positions was typical. While the two largest scales drawn from the Congresses of the Eisenhower administration show a higher level of inter-Congress stability than the average computed on the pairings of all Congresses in this administration, the difference is not great. This difference is also commensurate with the expectations of greater measurement error for the smaller scales.

The general point to which this discussion leads is that there must be powerful ordering mechanisms at work which induce a pattern of behavior so regular that our measuring instruments, so crude

Figure 4
Stability of Policy Positions Held by Senators and Representatives

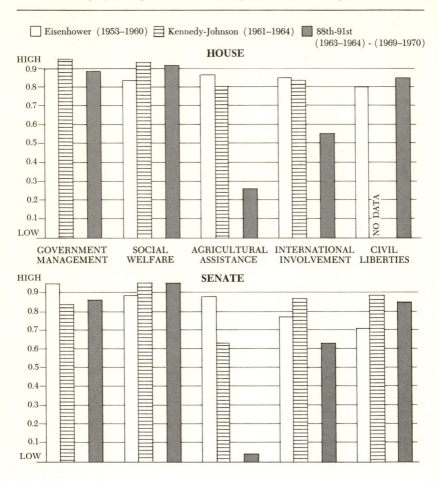

compared with the instruments in the laboratory of the physical scientist, can produce an ordering of congressmen that holds from one Congress to the next, to the next, to the next, . . . The marvel is clearly not the measuring instrument, although its ingeniousness is not to be discounted, but the behavior of congressmen, both senators and representatives.

Let us return now to the specific question posed concerning the continuity of the five policy dimensions from the dim historical past of 1953–1964 to more clearly seen yesteryears of 1969–1970 when the members of the Ninety-first Congress cast their yeas and nays. Are the same five policy dimensions still operative? And are the policy positions of the members still the same as they were in 1963–1964?

The Ninety-first Congress: Continuity and Stability

The voting behavior in the Ninety-first Congress will be described in a much less mechanical, step-by-step fashion. Both the rules of evidence and the forms of evidence used to establish the case for continuity should be clear by now and will often be implicit in the statements about the Ninety-first Congress. Similarly, the measurement of stability will be of the same form.

There is clear evidence that four of the five policy dimensions operative in the core Congresses of the study continue to be effective in the Ninety-first. The one dimension that seems to disappear is the agricultural assistance dimension. Yet even in this case it is not clear that the original dimension has died. Granted, a different dimension dominates the farm policy domain in the Ninety-first Congress, so a substitution appears to have taken place. But as we look at the data more closely, we shall see that there remains some question as to the demise of the old dimension.

There is also an interesting development in the foreign and defense policy domain at the same time that there is evidence of the continuity of the international involvement dimension. For alongside the international involvement dimension there is a policy dimension that actually affects voting on more roll calls than does the continuing dimension. I will not label this companion dimension at this time, but it is clear that it springs out of concerns with foreign policy and

defense questions that arose in conjunction with the expansion of
our involvement in Vietnam.

Finally, it appears beyond a reasonable doubt that congressmen
have not changed in their orientations towards policies normally associated with the three dimensions of government management,
social welfare, and civil liberties. This is not surprising in view of
the lack of any indications, from public debate and headline news
stories, that a major reorientation in thinking about policies has
occurred in the areas with which these dimensions are concerned.
Certainly, there have been harbingers of change with respect to
welfare policies, where the current of dissatisfaction has been swell-
ing. However, this current has apparently not achieved enough force
and volume to cut new channels of policy conceptualization.

The one piece of evidence that contributes most to our overall
view of the pattern of voting in the Ninety-first Congress, relative
to the prior Congresses, is the measure of the similarity of the orderings on the five dimensions. This measure is taken on the members
of the Ninety-first Congress who served also in the last Congress
of the core study, the Eighty-eighth. (Curiously, this continuous
membership is 66 percent of the total membership in each house:
66 members of the Senate and 278 members of the House.) The
measure of the similarity of the orderings of members between the
two Congresses is compared with the same measurement taken on
the Congresses of the Eisenhower years and on the Congresses of
the Kennedy-Johnson administration (Figure 5).

With respect to the three dimensions, government management,
social welfare and civil liberties, the degree of similarity of the
orderings of congressmen across the Eighty-eighth and Ninety-first
Congresses is very high. In other words, the similarity is just as high
as the general level observed among the Congresses of the core
study.

At the other extreme is the case of the agricultural assistance
dimension. The ordering on the measure of this dimension in the
Eighty-eighth Congress bears little or no similarity to the ordering
in the Ninety-first, depending on which house you are viewing. The
"no similarity" description applies to the house of Representatives,
the "little similarity" observation, to the Senate. In short, there is
strong evidence that the agricultural assistance dimension has not
carried over from the earlier Congresses to the Ninety-first. Nor is

Figure 5

*Similarity Between Legislator Orderings in Ninety-first Congress
(1969–1970) and Eighty-eighth Congress (1963–1964)
Relative to Stability Among Earlier Congresses*

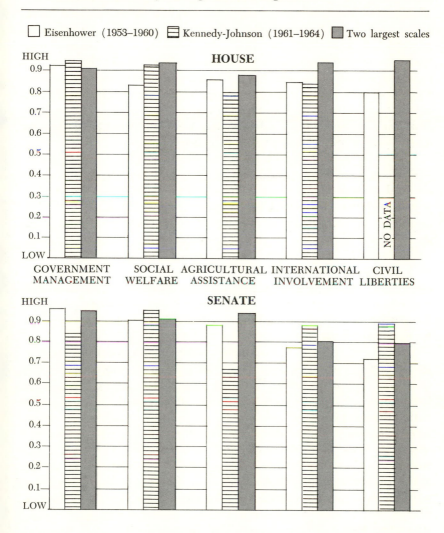

there any reason to anticipate that countervailing evidence can be adduced from other sources to support the claim of continuity.

The in-between case, as regards the similarity of legislator orderings, is the international involvement dimension. Paradoxically, I would have had more questions about the continuity of the international involvement dimension if the similarity of the orderings in the two Congresses had been high. For this would have been a break with the normal pattern for this dimension. In this pattern, a reordering of many of the congressmen's positions takes place when the presidency shifts from one party to the other.[5] The shift that took place between the Eighty-eighth and Ninety-first Congresses was the change from the *Democratic* Kennedy-Johnson presidency to the *Republican* presidency of Richard Nixon.

Thus, it is evident from these data that there are four dimensions continuing into the Ninety-first Congress and one dimension, agricultural assistance, that has come on hard times. Let me briefly report on other evidence confirming this interpretation.

It will be recalled that the partisanship on the government management dimension was consistently higher than on any other dimension in the core Congresses; this holds true in the Ninety-first, in both the Senate and the House. Similarly, the party division on the social welfare dimension remains at a moderate level, a couple steps below the government management dimension. In addition, the partisanship on the civil liberties dimension remains at the lower levels observed on the earlier Congresses.

On the international involvement dimension the level of apparent partisanship is lower in the Ninety-first Congress. However, this is consistent with expectations drawn from earlier analyses to the effect that the party division on international involvement declines under a Republican president.[6]

This leaves the agricultural assistance dimension, which does not appear to have been measured in the Ninety-first Congress. Here we find that the "new" dimension is as lacking in partisanship as the agricultural dimension is endowed. This new dimension is no more partisan than the civil liberties dimension, which has ranked low on this property. Consequently, I am disposed to be even more firmly convinced that it is truly a new dimension.

This completes the review of the statistical evidence on the continuity of the five policy dimensions, which falls short of making the case for continuity on the agricultural assistance dimension. I

May we ask your help?

We are pleased to send you this complimentary examination copy of
HOW CONGRESSMEN DECIDE by Aage R. Clausen. It would be extremely
helpful to us in estimating our stock requirements if you would use
this postpaid card to let us know of any plans you may have to use
HOW CONGRESSMEN DECIDE in your classes. Whatever your plans, we
would be grateful for your comments.

_____I plan to adopt this book.   _____I am considering adopting
                                           this book.
_____Enrollment

Comments:_____

_____

_____

_____

_____

_____

_____

Name_____

Department_____

College_____

City, State, Zip Code_____

FIRST CLASS
Permit No. 1147
New York, N.Y.

BUSINESS REPLY MAIL NO POSTAGE STAMP NECESSARY IF MAILED IN THE UNITED STATES

Postage will be paid by

ST. MARTIN'S PRESS, INC.

College Department

175 Fifth Avenue

New York, New York 10010

want to turn now to a closer look at the content of the roll calls associated with the measures of the policy dimensions in the Ninety-first Congress and at the extent to which the major policy dimensions dominate each of the policy domains.

We first look at the three policy dimensions that are behaving in the most normal and unchanged fashion in the Ninety-first Congress: government management, social welfare, and civil liberties. With respect to each, and in each house, the measure of the continuing policy dimension contains over twice as many roll calls as the next largest potential measure of a policy dimension in the same domain.

Thus, there is no evidence, in these three policy areas, of a challenge to the supremacy of the "old" dimensions that have exerted their hegemony over their respective policy domains.

There are also few surprises in the topics associated with the three dimensions; indeed, little has changed since the earlier Congresses. The fact of the matter is that innovative legislative programs are the exception rather than the rule. Consequently, it is not surprising that these three dimensions just keep rolling along.

The one difference from the earlier Congresses is the inclusion of a much greater number and variety of legislative proposals on the civil liberties dimension that are *not* concerned with the rights of blacks. This buttresses the conclusion offered on the earlier Congresses to the effect that the civil liberties dimension is broadly inclusive of a number of issues concerned with individual rights and liberties.

Moving away from the normal and almost ritualistic patterns of voting on the domestic policies discussed above, we cross over into the farm policy domain. Here we may have an instance of a disappearing dimension. The agricultural assistance dimension, operative primarily in legislation on farm subsidies, has dominated the farm policy domain in prior Congresses.

What happened in the Ninety-first Congress? Taking center stage were proposals to limit the amount any single producer could receive in subsidy payments. The administration proposed a limit of $110,000 per crop per producer; the final legislation settled on half that amount, $55,000, and suggestions were made to limit the payment ceiling to $20,000 and less. This new element in the consideration of the subsidy program was also the most controversial, dominating the debate on farm legislation in the Ninety-first Congress.[7]

In this debate the issue was not support for the subsidy program, nor the general subsidy level for different crops, as had typified earlier congressional considerations of the farm program. Rather, it revolved around the question of what is to be done in the cases of individual producers, most of them agribusinesses, who do not require the financial support so necessary for the maintenance of the small producers, the family farms. Yet, because of their large operations, these farm giants get large subsidies when paid at the same rate as the small producers.

The subsidy limitation question would appear to fall outside the boundaries of the general concept of agricultural assistance. Certainly, there is a different partisan lineup. For example, the southern Democrats are found to have been in opposition to northern Democrats whereas previously the northern urban Democratic wing had joined southern Democrats in giving strong support to the general subsidy program. Support for the farm economy is one thing, but it is another for urban Democrats to support agricultural subsidy payments to large corporation farmers with the tax money of their urban constituents.

Given this information on the events that transpired in the area of farm legislation in the Ninety-first Congress, what is to be concluded? It is my view that the policy questions raised by the injection of the ceiling limitation on individual payments were not responded to in terms of the agricultural assistance dimension. It is conceivable that the old dimension will appear again when, and if, the ceiling question is settled and attention returns to the general merits of a subsidy program for farmers. On the other hand, it is also possible that there has been a restructuring of the perceptions of the farm programs, leading to new positions not easily abandoned. However, let me post my doubts about the latter possibility on the grounds that predicting change in congressional behavior is much riskier than predicting a return to old and familiar pathways to policy-making.

The fifth policy dimension, international involvement, appeared again in the Ninety-first Congress, as it had in the Eighty-third through the Eighty-eighth. As usual, legislation on this dimension was largely concerned with foreign aid and other forms of international cooperation, excluding defense, trade, and immigration policy. So it is not the continuity of the international involvement dimension that piques my interest, although it is significant as an additional indicator of the durability of policy dimensions within the Congress.

What is of particular interest is the second dimension that appears in the foreign and defense policy domain.

The finding of a dimension separate from the old standby is especially interesting because many people have expressed an opinion that the Vietnam War debate in 1969 and 1970, and before, produced new orientations and new alignments on foreign policy questions. Instead, what appears to have occurred is that the conditions associated with the Vietnam war generated an *independent* general policy concern, which may or may not develop into a durable policy dimension.

One of the principal legislative topics associated with this dimension is that of defense and military policy. For the first time in the period under study, defense legislation was subjected to extensive congressional voting, a development that is linked to, if not caused by, the Vietnam War. What emerges then in this dimension is evidence of the fairly prevalent popular impression that a significant portion of the population, and congressmen, was moved to a state of general apprehension about the military arm of our foreign policy.[8] Within the terms of this general apprehension are a set of specific concerns. One concern is over the effectiveness and utility of U.S. military operations in Vietnam and the rest of Indochina. A second point of concern is the advisability of providing other nations with armaments, through arms sales and military aid, with which to start local wars, some with a potential for expanding into major international conflicts. Related to this are misgivings about the possibility that national economies, bolstered by our economic aid, will be weakened by the costs of weapons procurement, which tend to escalate. Finally, there is the more general dissatisfaction with the alleged degree of esoterica, superfluity, and waste in the defense program.

Equally strongly felt concerns, relevant to the same dimension, were expressed over the possibility of an imprudent undercutting of our military capability, flexibility, and credibility. Related to this was the felt need to continue the support of Indo-Chinese allies. As for the cessation of arms sales to other countries, would not this simply turn the market over to other nations, to the detriment of our relations with the recipient countries?

Within the scope and focus of the current study, the relevant point is that there exist the makings of a policy dimension that has a strong potential for survival for the duration. Yet, at the same time, the international involvement dimension continues to affect decisions

on international policies not so directly tied to military questions and
the Vietnam War. Thus, there is the possibility of two major dimensions in the domain of foreign and defense policy projecting into
future Congresses. Just as the international involvement dimension
of post–World War II found its origins and sustenance in the cold
war, a prime force behind our foreign aid program, so this new
dimension has originated in a hot war and may be sustained by the
issues raised in the conduct of this war.

Conclusions

One general conclusion drawn from the analysis described in this
chapter is that the study of the decision-making behavior of individual congressmen during the period 1953–1964 is much more than
the study of a unique historical period of congressional activity.
Not only does the same general theory of individual decision-making,
the policy dimension theory, hold into the most recent Congress,
five and six years later, but four out of the same five policy dimensions reappear in the later Congress. Furthermore, three of these
dimensions appear destined for a long life, to judge by their record
to date: government management, social welfare, and civil liberties.
The continuing existence of the international involvement dimension
through succeeding Congresses is less certain, although prediction of
an early death is clearly premature and without a solid foundation.
This leaves the agricultural assistance dimension, which dropped
from sight in the Ninety-first Congress; whether it came to rest in a
graveyard for old dimensions or was the temporary victim of an
elephant trap is not known. The elephant trap in this instance would
have been the failure of Congress to vote on legislative proposals
that activated the general policy concept of agricultural assistance.
Instead, the primary concern was with the size of payments to very
large individual producers of farm products, a specific matter not
related to the desirability of the general program of economic support for America's farmers. So the agricultural assistance dimension
may appear again—and probably will. Other conclusions follow.

The continuity of the five major policy dimensions across the six
Congresses of the core study, and the continuation of four of the
five dimensions into the Ninety-first Congress, demonstrates a high

degree of constancy in the use of a limited stock of general policy concepts. This is consistent with the policy dimension theory.

Another element of the policy dimension theory is the proposition that legislators, like other people, will remain fairly stable in their policy positions. Again the evidence is consistent with this proposition. Indeed, the level of stability is just short of the unbelievable when it is recognized that the "true" level of stability is greater than that observed on the scores assigned to represent the policy positions of individual members, due to the inevitability of some amount of measurement error.

An important aspect of the stability phenomenon is that it characterizes congressmen positioned all along the policy dimension and is not just a property of legislators anchored into opposing polar positions. Furthermore, there are sizable numbers of senators and representatives occupying moderate as well as end positions. In short, I am gratified with the capacity of the measures to discriminate reliably among congressmen at a higher level of differentiation than that provided by the designation of pro and anti groups or by the traditional trichotomy, pro, moderate, and anti. This is important to the rest of the study, which focuses upon the behavior of senators and representatives as represented by these dimensional measures or scales.

But let us now move on to use the measures of the five policy dimensions in an analysis of the six core Congresses. We may do so with a high degree of confidence that, even with respect to the substance of the policy concepts, these dimensions are continuing into the most recent Congress, with the possible exceptions already noted. Thus, results of the study of the six core Congresses can, I feel, be extrapolated to the Ninety-second Congress, and the Ninety-third, and on to some Congress in the indefinite future. Those readers *still* not sharing this view of congressional behavior will perhaps grant that the study of the earlier Congresses is useful as a description of the modes of individual decision-making and as a basis for observing the actions of today's senators and representatives in the United States Congress.

References

1. Malcolm E. Jewell and Samuel C. Patterson, *Legislative Process in the United States* (New York: Random House, 1966), pp. 297–298; Harmon Zeigler and Michael Baer, *Lobbying* (Belmont, Calif.: Wadsworth, 1969); Lester Milbrath, *Washington Lobbyists* (Skokie, Ill.: Rand MacNally, 1963); Raymond A. Bauer, *et al.*, *American Business and Public Policy: Politics of Foreign Trade* (New York: Atherton, 1963), p. 398.

2. Aage R. Clausen, "Measurement Identity in the Longitudinal Analysis of Legislative Voting," *American Political Science Review* 61 (December 1967); Aage R. Clausen and Richard B. Cheney, "A Comparative Analysis of Senate-House Voting on Economic and Welfare Policy: 1953–1964," *American Political Science Review* 64 (March 1970), pp. 140–152.

3. Aage R. Clausen, "Foreign Policy Voting in the U.S. Congress: 1953–64," paper delivered at Midwest Political Science Association Convention, April 30–May 2, 1970; Clausen and Cheney, *loc. cit.*

4. Robert Lane and David O. Sears, *Public Opinion* (Englewood Cliffs, N.J.: Prentice-Hall, 1964), p. 105.

5. Evidence of this statement is provided in full in Chapter 9.

6. Clausen, "Foreign Policy Voting in the U.S. Congress: 1953–64."

7. 1969 *Congressional Quarterly Almanac* (Congressional Quarterly, 1969), p. 329; 1970 *Congressional Quarterly Almanac*, p. 637.

8. For a discussion of the congressional role during the 1960s see Arnold Kanter, "Congress and the Defense Budget: 1960–1970," *American Political Science Review* 66 (March 1972), pp. 129–143.

5

Party and Ideology: Patterns of Policy Cleavage

The everlasting complaint about American politics is that it is so disorderly that not even the lifelong participant can talk about it very long without contradicting himself. In the eyes of most observers, the apparent absence of order in American politics stems from the lack of ideology and the unwillingness of the Democratic and Republican parties to formulate coherent policy programs to which individual members must adhere, in both word and deed. In this chapter we shall look fairly closely at the evidence in support of this complaint about chaos in American politics. More specifically, what is the evidence regarding the effectiveness of party as a source of policy cleavage, and to what extent is there evidence of a commitment to ideological points of view?

The contributions of party and ideology to order in American politics are assessed on the basis of voting patterns in Congress. However, let me reaffirm the point, made much earlier, that I regard the Congress assembled as a fair representation of the effective individuals and groups in the full political system. Consequently, the association of party and ideology with the patterns of policy cleavage in Congress is considered to be an association that characterizes the broader citizenry of effective and interested political types.

Dealing first with party as a potential source of order in American politics, our concern is with the evidence behind the common complaint that "you can't tell the parties apart" even with a scorecard. The evidence is drawn from a description of the party lineups on the five policy dimensions. In the search for ideology the policy positions of individual members on the five policy dimensions are examined for evidence of ideological coherence in the configurations of policy positions.

It is well to be prepared for something less than a definitive conclusion about the roles of party and ideology in American politics, on the basis of the investigation in this chapter. On the other hand, the method of investigation is such that it should yield a reasonably clear wide-screen view of the American political terrain, one that will serve as a point of general orientation as we probe more deeply into the fissures of national politics.

The Role of Party

The Democratic and Republican parties are often criticized for their unwillingness to commit themselves to broad policy programs and for their opportunistic approach to issues as means of election to office rather than as reasons for election. According to their detractors, both parties are so anxious to take the middle of the road that the policy tracks of the one become indistinguishable from those of the other. Politicos of the Left as well as those of the Right complain that the parties do not have coherent and distinct programs by which to tell them apart and measure their value. The barroom lawyer opines that the choice is between two sets of thieves, equally well disguised and pursuing the same parasitic purpose.

Defenders of the two major parties view the critics with ill-concealed contempt, particularly those critics who lament the dearth of ideology. The defenders are annoyed by the failure of the critics to appreciate the value of the compromises that are made *because* the parties avoid the bloody drama of ideological warfare. Pro-partisans, American style, are leery of those who would have sharp distinctions in place of blurry differences and would heap upon us the entangling nets of ideological gladiators.[1]

Debate in this area flourishes in the fertile ground of inconclusive evidence. A brief allusion to some characterizations of American politics should be sufficient to illuminate the confusion in our views of the parties.

There are indications that the parties of Lincoln and Jackson, the elephant and the wild jackass, are different. Remember the sharp division between Republican Goldwater's conservatism and Democratic Johnson's liberalism in the 1964 election. However, no sooner have we noted this sharp difference between the candidates of the two parties than we are reminded of a point of similarity: Johnson was reelected president and pursued the type of Vietnam policy that Goldwater had espoused during the campaign. Specific examples of this type can be provided ad infinitum, providing ammunition for both those who argue that the parties are different and those who see nothing but confusing similarity.

The differences between the parties are further lessened by differences within the parties. Marking the differences within, and thereby the similarities between, the parties are the common references to liberals and conservatives in both.

Contributing to actual policy differences within the parties, at both the elite and the commoner level, is the manner in which partisan affiliations are adopted and maintained. According to survey studies of the past twenty-five years, an individual's party affiliation is inherited from his parents and held with the same perseverance as his religious affiliation.[2] (At this writing there is much talk and considerable evidence of a growing independence of party labels, especially among the younger voters, which I tend to discount on two grounds. (1) Adoption of the Independent label has long been a personal style among a sizable minority of voters who then proceed to vote a party ticket—certainly this style is popular among the newer voters; and (2) the experience of additional campaigns, involving the need to make choices with little information about the candidate other than his party, will tend to draw the voter back to the party of his parents.) However, it is less evident that policy positions are equally well transmitted to the child.[3] Thus it is possible for partisan affiliation to be handed down from parent to progeny, whereas different policy positions are adopted by succeeding generations.

The party-policy confusion is enhanced by the persistence of party labels long after the original party-policy linkage has lost its meaning to the party loyalist. The linkage between the South and the Democratic party was tempered and hardened in the white-hot forge of civil conflict and continues despite policy differences between the southern and northern elements of the Democratic party. Northern Republicanism, the dominant political affiliation of the North after the Civil War, has continued to hold many of its original followers despite internal policy conflicts. For example, rather than reject their party along with their enemies within it, Republican agrarian populists of the late nineteenth century formed the Nonpartisan League; early in the twentieth century, the western progressives battled the eastern establishment within the fold of the Republican party. More recently, the Republican party has sought to keep afloat in the rising tide of urbanism by permitting its metropolitan candidates to tack toward the Left. Northern Democrats, dominating the urban sea, and spared in the past from serious internal divisions, are experiencing difficulties in fitting policy programs to the concerns of the urban majority. Problems are emerging in accommodating the black and white politics of inner metropolises to the white politics of outer metropolises, not to mention the division between the hard Left and the hard hats. Yet it is reasonable to predict that the Democratic party affiliation will withstand the centrifugal forces of policy differences.

Somewhat inadvertently I have adopted the tripartite division of American party adherents and elites that is so commonly used to denote regional-party aggregates: southern Democrats, northern Democrats, and northern Republicans (elected southern Republicans have remained a rare breed). The three-way division not only represents geography and party, but is a convenient way to describe politicians in terms of the mix of party and ideology. In the northern Democratic party the outlook is considered to be liberal, while among southern Democrats the cast appears more conservative. The northern Republicans appear to some to be more conservative than southern Democrats, while others feel they are so similar that they might well form a new party.

However, the classificatory utility of this neat regional-party trichotomy is severely limited because it clearly lacks precision. As mentioned before, urban Republicans are reputed to be more liberal than rural ones, so to treat all northern Republicans as peas in a pod is patently absurd. Nor are southern Democrats a monolithically conservative bloc; indeed so great is the variation among them that explanations for this variation have often been sought, usually with more optimism than success.[4]

In drawing out the varying impressions of the mixture of party, issue, and ideology, I have set the stage in darkness and confusion. This is deliberate, but also realistic, for there are no clear assessments of the role of party in the decisions arrived at on the various policy questions that make the national scene. In the "play" that follows, I work hard to ascertain such order as does exist.

In this work, I rely principally upon an examination of what politicians *do* (in Congress) rather than upon what they say they are going to do. *This distinction between action and rhetoric is important because much of the confusion concerning the presence and meaningfulness of party differences is produced by too much attention to campaign speeches and too little attention to policy decisions.* To put it bluntly, when politicians are competing for votes they want to be all things to all men, whereas when they are forced to make policy choices in the councils of government they have to take sides. Consequently, the record of official choices provides the firmest foundation for an analysis of political cleavages in the body politic.

The examination of the role of party, as revealed in the public voting records of the House and Senate, begins with a look at party as a predictor of policy positions on the five policy dimensions. Subsequently, measures of the level of conflict (or the distance) between the parties on each of the dimensions will be presented along with estimates of the cohesion within each of the parties.

Party as Voting Predictor

A fortune awaits the person who can exact a toll of twenty-five cents for every time a political scientist repeats that tiresome truism: Party is the best single predictor of voting in the United States Congress.[5] I have no quarrel with its accuracy, only doubts as to what it means, beyond the most superficial level. At this level, it means that a division along party lines is more frequent than a division along any other lines, such as regional, racial, or economic lines.

The truism concerning party as the best predictor is refined at times to denote areas in which party influence appears strongest. According to one fairly comprehensive study these include foreign trade, monetary and fiscal policy, conservation, health and welfare, government economic intervention, agriculture, housing, education, government regulation, labor, and un-American activities. This excludes public works, states' rights, taxation, business claims, veterans' affairs, foreign affairs, and foreign aid, among others.[6]

Although there have been numerous efforts to analyze and specify the role of party with respect to particular policy concerns, the results are frustratingly ambiguous. Part of the problem arises from the classification of roll calls into narrow and subjective definitions of content, with no criteria of classification shared by different researchers. Consequently, there is poor comparability from one study to the next. Another aspect of the problem is that the impact of party, or at least what appears to be the impact of party, may actually change over time. Consequently, researchers looking at different time periods come up with different issues as party related.

It is my position that some of these problems of classification and analysis may be substantially lessened by using measurements of general policy dimensions that can be compared across studies and time. These policy dimensions are based on the congressman's own classifications of individual legislative proposals which will be the same for different researchers thereby reducing researcher bias. Furthermore, the level of generality of the dimensions, as represented in the policy concepts that are their foci, increases their chances of persisting through time. This permits an examination of the role of party, whether it is a stable or a changing factor through time. It is with respect to the policy positions of congressmen on five such general policy dimensions that we assess the success of party as a predictor of policy positions.

Statisticians have provided a simple summary measure that reflects our ability to predict scores on one measure from scores on another. Values vary from 0 to 1, as predictability goes from nil to perfection. Thus, the more important the influence of party on voting, and therefore the better we can predict a congressman's policy position from his party affiliation, the higher will be the value of this measure of predictive capacity, with a maximum value of 1. The bar graph in Figure 6 shows the variation in the effectiveness of party as a predictor across the five policy dimensions; it also permits a comparison between the House and the Senate.

Our ability to predict policy positions on policy dimensions, using party as the predictor, is measured through the use of a coefficient of correlation known as the Pearson product moment r. The greater our predictive capacity, the closer this coefficient comes to 1.0, its maximum value; to the extent that party is less useful as a predictor, the coefficient drops toward 0, the minimum value. When the correlation between party and policy becomes

Figure 6
Party as a Predictor of Voting on Five Policy Dimensions

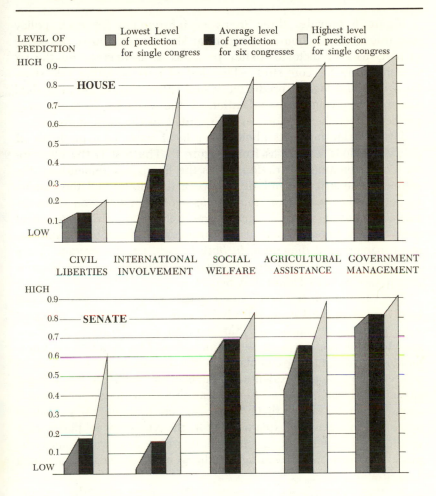

0, it means we could have done just as well in predicting policy positions from a congressman's blood type.

Figure 6 provides three items of information for each policy dimension in each house. The central shaded bar shows the value of party as a predictor of policy positions as an *average* for the six Congresses in the core study. The slashed bars on either side show the *lowest* and *highest* predictive values calculated on the individual Congresses, giving some indication of the variation in party as a predictor over the six Congresses included in the core study.

Two interlocking facts about the role of party as a predictor of policy positions leap at us from Figure 6. The first is the clear indication of enormous variation across the five policy dimensions; the second is the striking similarity between the House and the Senate. In both bodies *party is a consistently strong predictor* on three dimensions, social welfare, agricultural assistance, and government management. Note that party is the strongest predictor on the government management dimension *in both houses.* On the average, party is a weak predictor on the international involvement and civil liberties dimensions in both House and Senate.

The variation in the predictive capacity of party on international involvement in the House and civil liberties in the Senate interferes with the simple conclusion that partisan considerations are consistently irrelevant to these two dimensions. The variation on international involvement, particularly in the House, to be explained in a later chapter on presidential influence, is based on the relative capacity of Democratic and Republican presidents to get their party's congressmen to follow their leadership on foreign policy. I have developed no general explanation for the variation in party as a predictor of Senate voting on civil liberties. Nor would such explanations have much bearing on the general conclusion to which I am drawn.

At this juncture, let me rejoice once more over the striking similarity in the data on the House and the Senate. This strongly suggests that the factors affecting the variations in party-as-predictor across the five policy dimensions originate in a political community that embraces both houses of Congress. Furthermore, I would argue that Congress registers the effects of forces emanating from the far reaches of the political system and that the similarity in the behavior of the two houses results from the simple fact that both are representative of the same national constituency.

Let me train this view of the behavior of senators and representatives on the finding that party is most effective as a predictor of policy positions on the government management dimension. This means also that party differences are the greatest on this dimension. Therefore, in response to the question, Are there really any differences between the parties? the answer is in the affirmative where the government management dimension is concerned. Look to the House, look to the Senate, and look to the political activists across the country. Granted, the evidence comes only from Congress; we can only speculate about the views of activists among the partisan supporters of the members of Congress. But consider this as part of the speculation: During the twelve years of the core study many new members were recruited to Congress who apparently shared the same party differences in points of view. If they had not, the predictive capacity of party would have dropped and eventually disappeared. Remember also that the party tie to the government management dimension continues in the Ninety-first Congress, meaning that there are even more recruits from the political activist segment of the population who maintain the party cleavage on the government management dimension.

But why have I not been singing the praises of party as a predictor of policy positions on social welfare and agricultural assistance? Quite simply because the record on these dimensions is distinctly less impressive. So while party is an important predictor on the social welfare and agricultural assistance dimensions, the government management dimension deserves a special niche in the party-predictor hall of fame.

Thus, it is abundantly clear that the old refrain "party is the single best predictor" should be sung only when one is sure what policy tune is being played. Let me make another point. The finding that party is a good predictor does not automatically generate the inference that party is a causal agent. We have yet some distance to travel before we can begin generating causal statements. I am not being hesitant because of any support for the perverse philosophical position that causality can never be inferred. My only concern is that more evidence is needed before we can make a case either for or against party influence on a given dimension.

The search for evidence of the influence of party continues with another look at the same data from another perspective. Here the measures are of *party conflict* and *party cohesion*. The analysis will be restricted to the House of Representatives, as will be the case for subsequent analyses that involve a more detailed investigation.

There are several reasons for conducting certain detailed analyses on the House only. Most stem from the larger membership of the House, which provides a more accurate representation of the national constituency. Results are more reliable because there is less chance that general patterns will be obscured by idiosyncracies in the behavior of individual members. Nevertheless, the inclusion of both the Senate and the House in the analysis of various aspects of congressional behavior is often useful, not only for comparative purposes, but as a way of cross-validating the findings on each. The Senate contribution is greatest when the analysis is fairly gross, for the reasons of size given above.

Party Conflict and Cohesion

The measure of *party conflict* that I am using is the magnitude of the difference between the mean or "average" policy positions of the members of each of the parties on each of the dimensions. (Scale scores range from 1, for high support to 3 for low support.) For example, the mean scale score position of all Democratic representatives on civil liberties is 1.89, whereas the mean score position for the Republicans is 1.83, a difference that is quite small and gives no indication of party conflict on this dimension. It is expected that parties that are in conflict over policy questions will be some distance apart in their policy positions—hence the conflict.

An equally uncomplicated measure of *party cohesion* reflects the amount of variation in policy positions within each of the parties. The greater this variation, the less the evidence of party cohesion. The technical name for the measure of variation within the party is the *variance*. So much for the technical discussion.

Both the conflict between parties and the cohesion within them are illustrated in Figure 7. In an effort to maximize the visual impact, the distance between the parties on each dimension is directly reflected in the distance between the party markers along the scale; the cohesiveness of each of the parties on each dimension is indicated

Figure 7

Party Cohesion and Party Conflict on Five Dimensions
(variance within parties and differences in party means: average,
Eighty-third–Eighty-eighth Congresses)

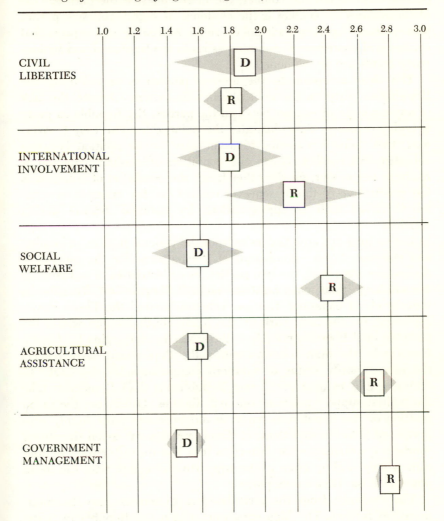

by the horizontal spread of each party marker—the less the spread (the more compact the party marker), the more cohesive the party.

The general pattern of conflict and cohesion is as would be expected: The higher the conflict, the more cohesive the parties. One of the reasons for conflict is the existence of highly cohesive parties some distance apart in their policy views. Moreover, one expects that conflict will contribute to cohesion as ranks are tightened and within-party bonds are strengthened.

The clear exception to the general pattern is provided by the Republican party on the civil liberties dimension. Despite the lack of any evidence of conflict between the parties, the Republican party is highly cohesive. This illustrates the point, otherwise easy to overlook, that there is a degree of asymmetry in the relation between cohesion and conflict. Given the condition of conflict, cohesion is likely to be present; on the other hand, the condition of cohesion is less predicative of the presence of conflict, as, for example, on consensus issues such as appropriations for national defense during wartime.

Let us turn our attention now from the general pattern of conflict and cohesion to an examination of the patterns for the individual dimensions. As noted, the two parties, as collectivities of individuals, are similar in their mean positions on civil liberties but dissimilar in their levels of cohesion. The low cohesion among the Democrats is explained, for the most part, by the North-South division within the party on civil liberties, notably with respect to civil rights for blacks. Conversely, the high cohesion within the Republican party reflects the mini-minority status of southern congressmen in the GOP. In addition, it is evident that fewer Republicans than Democrats take the highest support positions on civil liberties. Otherwise, the mean position of the Republican party should be much more highly supportive of civil liberties than the Democratic party, given the strong southern contingent in the latter. As it is, the mean for the Republicans is only slightly more in the supportive direction than the mean position of the Democratic party.

The evidence from the civil liberties dimension may be interpreted as follows. The high consensus within the Republican party, or high cohesion if you wish, would normally be read as evidence of party influence, with the cohesion a function of party leadership or shared partisan attitudes. I see no reason to make an exception in this case. As for the Democrats, it is clear that at the national level party influence is nil.

So we see that the evidence from this view of the data is different from the evidence generated when we were looking at party as a predictor of policy positions. There the indication was that party was not a factor on the civil liberties dimension, whereas here we can conclude that party is punchless only in the case of the Democrats.

On the international involvement dimension, the evidence from the two perspectives on the data gives consistent support to the inference that party is not an important factor in the policy decisions of congressmen. There is little difference between the positions of the two parties (less than a fifth of the length of the scale), and there is low cohesion within the parties.

It will be recalled that in the party-as-predictor analysis, party makes a good showing on the social welfare and agricultural assistance dimensions, but is particularly impressive on the government management dimension. The evidence on cohesion and conflict follows the same pattern. Both parties are highly cohesive on the government management dimension, *and* they are far apart. They are nearly as far apart on the agricultural assistance dimension, but neither is nearly so cohesive. On the social welfare dimension, the parties are closer together than on the other two dimensions, and less cohesive.

Whatever the final conclusions regarding the role of party in the decisions made by congressmen on the five policy dimensions, it is obvious that the impact of party can not be studied without attention to the policy content. It is clearly meaningless, in other words, to use the level of party cohesion and conflict as the basis of a statement about the predictive capacity of party for *all roll calls* taken in a session of Congress.

As an aid to comprehension, let me briefly review the evidence on party cleavage on the five policy dimensions, without presuming an explanation for the presence or absence of cleavage. Partisan cleavage is strongest on the government management dimension, a dimension concerned with business-government relations, the level of public spending, and the public versus the private development of our natural resources, among other things. The parties have been divided on these issues for the last hundred years. The partisan cleavage, while apparent, is less strong on the social welfare and agricultural assistance dimensions; let me note in passing that these are questions on which constituency forces, urban and rural particularly, are more likely to be effective, providing some counterbalance to party. Finally, there is the lack of partisan cleavage on civil liberties and international involvement. The lack of cleavage on international involvement is consonant with the inappropriateness of partisan conflict over matters of national interest. On civil liberties, the absence of party cleavage may be attributed to the dominance of the North-South division on these issues.

With this view of American policy cleavages and partisan divisions in mind, let us turn to the view offered by an analysis of the role of ideology in American politics.

In Search of Ideology

The widely accepted view that political ideology is a minor ingredient in the mix of American politics offers little hope for the search for ideology in congressional decision-making. On the other hand, continuous references to conservative and liberal properties of persons, places, and programs do not permit an offhand dismissal of ideological influence on policy decisions. I assume that most of us can agree that the two major ideologies, or pretensions to ideology, in American politics are conservatism and liberalism.[7] This assumption is made with reference to the *pervasiveness* of ideological beliefs in these United States rather than to the quality of the belief configurations as ideological forms. That is to say, Marxism may, from the philosopher's point of view, be of higher quality as an ideology, but it clearly lacks adherents in this country.

Whatever one thinks of conservatism and liberalism as ideologies, as logically interrelated sets of beliefs about the political order that derive from a limited number of values and premises about the characteristics of human beings, there remains evidence of opposing orientations to politics that deserve consideration as work-a-day guides to policy decisions. Central aspects of conservatism are experience (tradition), stability, and the prudent use of power. The liberal values imagination, change, and broad distribution of power resources while not being averse to centralization of the employment of power. The conservative is wary of this centralization while he may be much less concerned about the existence of scattered power centers that control domains of human existence within which power

resources are not broadly distributed. The conservative values existing institutions as the products of experience and questions the
liberal's optimism regarding the capacity of the human imagination
to change those institutions in ways that will benefit the individual
and the society. The liberal favors the use of government to amelio-
rate the ills of society; the conservative looks upon the growth of
government as an unnatural and even malignant phenomenon. To
the liberal, government is good; to the conservative, good government
is limited.

The two philosophies converge in their support for individual
rights and liberties. In a political culture that has placed a high
premium on individuality, certainly in word if not in deed, the proponents of either ideology have little choice but to include a strong
commitment to individual rights and liberties in their ideological
programs. To do otherwise would be to seek an annulment of the
Declaration of Independence.

Before going further, I must protect myself against charges of
political naïveté by indicating my awareness of the strong possibility
that a political ideology is not simply a statement of abstract principles applied to concrete problems but serves as well to rationalize
self-interest. Nor is there really any reason to argue that an ideology
is such only if it meets the standard of moral selflessness or if it is a
product of an objective analysis of what the society needs in the
way of a political order. For our purposes, the importance of an
ideology lies in its capacity to reinforce behavioral patterns and in
its status as a causal antecedent of behavior.

I also want to make it clear that the ensuing analysis does not
depend upon either a highly formalized and precise definition of
ideology or complete and incontrovertible statements of conservatism
and of liberalism. Certainly, this is not at all critical to our understanding of the ideologically colored motivations that may affect
congressional policy positions. Few politicians, indeed few persons
of any description, possess either the talent to develop, or the desire
to abide by, a clearly formed ideology.

The ideologies of conservatism and liberalism in the United States
clearly are lacking in adherents whose political beliefs form a neat
bundle wrapped in tight arguments. In fact, this view is already supported in this study by the observation that it makes little sense to
order American citizens on a single liberal-conservative continuum
bounded by the extreme ideologues of the two opposing orientations.

Instead of one dimension of voting in Congress, the evidence is supportive of five dimensions. However, these observations and findings do not preclude the possibility that a sizable proportion of our citizens and congressmen *do* behave in a manner consistent with the liberal or conservative ideologies.

In the following analysis the policy positions of the members of the House on the five policy dimensions are reviewed in search of evidence supportive of the proposition that ideology is a force in congressional policy-making—a force that affects some congressmen much more than others. The investigation is undertaken with respect to House voting because the larger membership of this body provides a broader base on which to form conclusions concerning the policy cleavages in the political system. In a smaller body such as the Senate the effects of individual differences can too easily fragment the general pattern of association between policy cleavages and the ideological expectations regarding those cleavages.

Although I have no intention of forcing an ideological structure, I think it may be helpful as a first step to relate the policy stances of representatives to those we might expect of liberals and conservatives. This will give us some idea of the potency of ideology. The second step in the analysis makes use of an inductive procedure in which the patterns of policy positions on the five dimensions are all identified, without preconceptions concerning the patterns.

Liberals and Conservatives

Most can agree, I think, that the liberal congressman is expected to take a high support position on social welfare, agricultural assistance, government management, and civil liberties. Similarly, it is anticipated that the conservative representative will stand in opposition to the liberal representative on the first three of these dimensions, while joining hands with the liberal member on the civil liberties dimension. Granted, current popular conceptions, particularly those held by the more radical Left, may place the conservative in opposition to civil liberties, being for law and order and all that; but the conservative ideology has long contained a strong commitment to individual privileges and liberties.

It is less clear what the position of the liberal or the conservative member should be on international involvement. For these are ideologies primarily adapted for domestic politics. Views concerning a world order as opposed to a national order often seem to follow from belief systems that apply primarily to international relations and our participation in them. The ambivalence I give expression to here is consistent with common references to a liberal-internationalist or a conservative-isolationist posture, with the hyphenation indicating a linkage but not a fusion of two systems of political values, beliefs, and attitudes.

For the time being, we shall treat support for international involvement as a liberal position and link international restraint with the conservative positions. One thing makes this linkage less tenuous than it might be: support for international involvement is in large measure support for foreign aid and excludes the question of defense. Thus, the liberal ideology as expressed in an activist position on all five policy dimensions is a commitment to government activity as a means of providing for the general welfare at home and abroad. The conservative consistently questions the utility of government as a means of effecting this end and sorely regrets the squandering of national resources on something far short of a sure thing. Finally, both ideologies come down on the side of civil liberties, thereby standing foursquare behind Thomas Jefferson and the Declaration of Independence.

Format of Analysis

The analysis is based on voting in the House in the Eighty-fifth and Eighty-sixth Congresses, 1957–1960. It includes all representatives who served in either or both of the Congresses, except for a few who did not vote often enough to be scored on all five dimensions.

One reason for using two Congresses is to increase the reliability of the ideological sorting and labeling. The analysis uses averages of the scale score positions earned by individual congressmen in the two Congresses, on the grounds that two measurements are better than one. However, not all congressmen served in both Congresses; some served in the Eighty-fifth only, others in the Eighty-sixth only. They were included in the analysis even though their single scores may be somewhat more lacking in reliability; this seems reasonable in that the broadening of the base thereby achieved (from something less than 435 members to 501) more than compensates for the loss in measurement accuracy, and at a low additional expense.

It is true that I could perform the analysis on all six Congresses in the core study. However, the high degree of stability in the policy positions of individual congressmen over time means that a further extension of the time span of the analysis would be highly redundant and characterized by a high research *cost:benefit* ratio.

The first step, after calculating the mean scores, was to assign each representative a low or high support position on each dimension. Although somewhat arbitrary, the classification of low and high supporters is adequate to the search for evidence of different ideologies, within the tolerances established for this particular analysis. Just as one may make some errors in sorting out little potatoes and big potatoes, without doubting the existence of little and big potatoes so long as there emerge sizeable piles of each, so one may make errors in classifying individual congressmen according to ideological configurations without doubting the existence of those configurations that are well represented.

The second step of the analysis consists of identifying all of the individually different policy profiles exhibited by the representatives. A policy profile is a shorthand designation for the particular combination of low and high support positions taken by individual congressmen on the five policy dimensions. The maximum number of profiles that can appear, given five policy dimensions, is thirty-two.

Policy Profiles:
Liberal and Conservative

The number of representatives who show a policy profile that accords with my preliminary definition of a liberal ideology—a high support position on all five policy dimensions—is just short of one-fourth of the House members included in the analysis, 121 out of 501. All are Democrats and almost all are from the North, with an additional few from Texas and the Border states.

Conservatives, as defined by a low support position on every dimension with the exception of civil liberties, are clearly outnumbered by the liberals. According to my definition, there are 57 conservatives. All are Republicans and two-thirds of these are drawn from the swatch of states forming the greater Midwest, beginning with Ohio and carrying westward to the Rockies and northward to Canada.

The combined total of conservatives and liberals is 178, just a shade in excess of one-third of all the representatives included in the study. If we exclude the Border and Southern states in order to identify the more homogeneous political culture of the North, the conservative and liberal ideological components loom larger, constituting nearly half of all northern representatives. By the same token, over half of the northern members make political decisions that cannot be accounted for by references to conservatism and liberalism.

Further support for the use of the conservative and liberal tags can be generated by excluding the international involvement dimension from the two policy profiles designated as conservative and liberal. Since reasonable doubt exists anyway concerning the appropriateness of extending either ideology to matters beyond our borders, it behooves us to at least investigate the organizing capacity of liberalism and conservatism with regard to positions on domestic policy dimensions.

Excluding the international involvement dimension, the number of conservatives increases from 57 to 129, and the liberals number 139 instead of 121. Thus, instead of slightly more than one-third of all representatives displaying liberal and conservative policy profiles, we now find slightly more than one-half doing so. Again, if we restrict our attention to northern representatives, three out of four fit under the ideological umbrellas, compared with one out of two when international relations is included.

Even though we may not be able to agree on this redefinition of the two ideologies, I think we can agree that it is understandable that the conservative and liberal labelling persists, given the number of congressmen to whom the labels can be applied without doing them a serious injustice. Nor should we overlook the interlock of party and ideology: all conservatives are Republicans and all liberals are Democrats.

I cannot argue either that "ideology lives!" in American politics or that it is the stillborn procreation of fertile fanciful minds. The evidence gap is too great. It is much more within my capacity to argue that the evidence displayed thus far suggests the existence of a set of powerful forces that cause individuals to adopt particular combinations of policy positions while rejecting numerous other combinations. This does not imply that ideology is the ordering force, but that the ordering forces are strong enough to produce patterns of policy positions that entice and give credence to the ideological labels, liberal and conservative.

As a corrective to the view of the patterning of congressional policy positions that is developed when specifically looking for ideology, let us now inspect all the policy profiles that exist among the representatives in the two Congresses under study.[8] We will try to keep an open mind and a clear vision, so that we may see the individual policy profiles as they are, rather than as we might like them to be. This approach involves much less prejudgment of the data than in the prior search for policy profiles that fit a conception of ideology.

The Big Nine

As stated earlier, given five policy dimensions on which high and low support positions are defined, there are thirty-two possible profiles. However, *nine* of the profiles account for 436, or 87 percent, of the 501 representatives in the analysis. The distinctiveness of these nine profiles is underscored by the fact that the incidence of the least popular of the nine is twice that of the most popular of the remaining profiles. Thus, our initial focus is on the Big Nine.

These nine profiles are nicely distributed, three to a customer, among the three regional-party groupings referred to earlier: northern Democrats, southern Democrats, and northern Republicans. Furthermore, each profile is nearly always exclusively identified with only one of the three groupings. The importance of the three regional-party groupings is apparent also in the fact that, in general, the profiles within each regional-party grouping are more similar to each other than to profiles from different groupings.

The concentration of congressmen in just nine configurations of policy positions on the five dimensions, and the further sharp division among the three regional-party groupings, greatly simplifies our descriptive task and augurs well for a comprehensible interpretation. We shall first consider the substance of the nine policy profiles, in relation to their location in the political geography of the United States, by describing the profiles associated with each regional-party grouping, northern Democrats, northern Republicans, and southern Democrats. Subsequently, there will be a brief review of Border state representatives to see where they fit into the scheme of things.

NORTHERN DEMOCRATS

The liberal profile, consisting of high support positions on all five dimensions, describes approximately two-thirds of the northern Democrats. An additional one-fifth of the northern Democrats deviate from the liberal profile solely on the basis of a low support position on agricultural assistance. Equally restrained in their deviation from the liberal norm are the one-tenth who take high support positions on all but the international involvement dimension. This leaves less than one out of 20 who fails to fit into either of the three major policy profiles among the northern Democrats. (See Table 1.)

Since the designation "northern Democrat" is almost synonymous with liberal Democrat, it is the deviants from the liberal norm who are most interesting. We turn to them while keeping in mind the predominance of the straight liberal profile.

The deviation that many observers might have anticipated is that resulting from a low support position on agricultural assistance.[9] Given the strong urban base of the northern wing of the Democratic party, it is perhaps more surprising that as few as a fifth balked at government support of rural interests to the point where they are classified as low supporters. That the urban interest comes into play is clear from the roster of states that contribute representatives to this deviant

Table 1
Policy Position Profiles: Members of House of Representatives *

REGIONAL-PARTY GROUP: POLICY PROFILES	PATTERNS OF LOW AND HIGH SUPPORT POSITIONS ON FIVE POLICY DIMENSIONS **										PERCENT OF GROUP
	LOW SUPPORT					HIGH SUPPORT					(%)
Northern Republicans											
Hard-line conservatives	GM	SW	AA	II	—	—	—	—	—	CL	27
Internationalist conservatives	GM	SW	AA	—	—	—	—	—	II	CL	35
Eastern moderates	GM	—	AA	—	—	—	SW	—	II	CL	22
Southern Democrats											
Dixie populists	—	SW	—	II	CL	GM	—	AA	—	—	44
Dixie welfare populists	—	—	—	II	CL	GM	SW	AA	—	—	16
Dixie liberals	—	—	—	—	CL	GM	SW	AA	II	—	17
Northern Democrats											
Liberals	—	—	—	—	—	GM	SW	AA	II	CL	65
City liberals	—	—	AA	—	—	GM	SW	—	II	CL	22
Isolationist-liberals	—	—	—	II	—	GM	SW	AA	—	CL	9

* Nine major profiles organized by three major regional-party groupings.
** GM = Government Management; SW = Social Welfare; AA = Agricultural Assistance; II = International Involvement; CL = Civil Liberties.

group: Connecticut, Maine, New Hampshire, Vermont, Massachusetts, New Jersey, New York, Pennsylvania, Illinois, Ohio, and California. On the other hand, it is important to note that liberal orthodoxy prevails in Massachusetts, New York, Pennsylvania, Illinois, Ohio, and California—all of the larger urban states—although each contributes one or more members to the deviant group. To those who wonder why Maine, New Hampshire, and Vermont, the somewhat legendary paragons of pastoralism, oppose agricultural subsidies, let me offer the fact that the commodities involved, such as grains, cotton, peanuts, and tobacco, are not grown for sale in great abundance in these three states.

The second set of deviants among the northern Democrats are those who draw the line on international commitments. These are few in number and are scattered across states with a history of isolationism: the Midwestern, Plains, and Mountain states.

Briefly summarizing, for purposes of future reference, there is a huge set of liberal northern Democrats, a respectable minority of city liberals who defect on agricultural assistance, and a small number of defectors to the liberal-"isolationist" camp.

NORTHERN REPUBLICANS

The hard-line conservatives, those taking a low support position on everything but civil liberties, constitute slightly more than a fourth of the northern Republicans. The representatives displaying this policy profile make their homes in the core Midwest. Six states—Illinois, Indiana, Michigan, Ohio, Wisconsin, and Iowa—contribute 34 of the 53 members in the hard-line conservative group.

The largest bloc of northern Republicans, 70 strong, deviates from the hard-line profile by taking a high support position on the international involvement dimension. A quartet of adjacent states, New York, Pennsylvania, Massachusetts, and Ohio, produce over one-half of the northern Republicans deviating from the hard line with respect to international relations. In the states of Michigan, California, and Washington, this profile is the most popular one without being the majority profile.

The smallest of the three major profile groups among the northern Republicans is also the most deviant from hard-line conservatism. Members of this group take a high support position on both social welfare and international involvement in addition to civil liberties, while saying nay to only government management and agricultural aid. The membership of this group includes about one-fifth of the northern Republicans, and is drawn almost entirely from the North-eastern states; 38 of the 44 members of this group come from east of the Ohio River. The only other states contributing members to this eastern moderate wing of the Republican party are Michigan, Iowa, Minnesota, California, and Washington. It is fair to guess that within this sector of northern Republicanism reside those who boosted the presidential candidacies of Willkie in 1940, Dewey in 1944 and 1948, and Eisenhower in 1952, while shunting aside Republican conserva-tive leaders such as Robert Taft of Ohio.

The three major profiles in the Republican party describe the voting patterns of 84 percent of the northern members of the party of Lincoln. Yet not one of these profiles includes a high support posi-tion on agricultural assistance, even though the Republican party has a strong rural base! (A further 6 percent, not described by the three major profiles, also show low support.) This finding, together with the finding that most northern Democrats have high support scores on the agricultural assistance dimension, poses an apparent anomaly.

Before attacking this anomaly, it is only fair to point out that almost two-thirds of those not included in the three major profiles (that is, 10 percent of the northern Republicans) *do* take a high support position on agricultural aid.[10] But this still remains a pretty weak showing.

The regional origins of those Republicans who do support agricul-tural subsidies go a long way toward explaining the lack of more general Republican support. These Republicans come from west of the Mississippi, particularly the Plains states of Nebraska, Kansas, Minnesota, and the Dakotas. These are also the states that produce the grains (wheat, oats, corn, etc.) that are under the subsidy pro-gram. Furthermore, they produce them for sale. States east of the Mississippi may produce the same grains, but not for sale; instead, grains are fed to livestock that end up in the meat trays at the local supermarket. Furthermore, many "feeder" farmers are buying the grains produced on the great plains. Consequently, for them there is no advantage, and even a disadvantage, in having price supports for agricultural commodities. This is comparable to the argument used previously to explain the resistance of Maine, Vermont, and New Hampshire Democrats to the price support program reflected in the agricultural assistance dimension.

But let us return to the northern Republican voting patterns across the five policy dimensions. As already mentioned, three policy profiles dominate, accounting for 84 percent of the members. In contrast to the northern wing of the Democratic party, where the orthodox liberal configuration is clearly dominant, none of the three northern Republican profiles accounts for much more than a third of the membership, and the smallest includes over one-fifth. Clearly, the northern Republicans are more divided among themselves than are the northern Democrats.

The three groupings within the northern Republican set have been referred to as the hard-line conservatives, the internationalist-conservatives, and the eastern moderates. Members of all sets take a high support position on civil liberties. This is the *only* high support position taken by the hard-line conservatives. The internationalist-conservatives are one step removed from the hard-liners in also supporting international involvement. And the eastern moderates are found on the high support side of the social welfare question, in addition to supporting international involvement and civil liberties.

In general, the farther east one goes in the Republican party, the greater is the deviation from hard-line conservatism. This is no particular surprise in view of recent election results. For example, it is clear that the 1964 Goldwater vote, a vote for a hard-line conservative, declined as one moved toward the eastern seaboard. Indeed, Goldwater is alleged to have had dreamy visions of that part of the country breaking off and drifting out to sea.

SOUTHERN DEMOCRATS

The southern Democrats are the representatives coming from the southeastern perimeter, the Gulf and Atlantic states beginning with Virginia and sweeping around to the "independent" state of Texas, plus Arkansas. The Border states of Oklahoma, Tennessee, Kentucky, West Virginia, and Maryland will be considered later.

Among the southern Democrats the three major profiles are designated as Dixie liberal, Dixie welfare populist, and Dixie populist. The Dixie populist profile is by far the most popular, characterizing nearly one-half of all the southern Democrats. Dixie populists join with their northern Democratic colleagues in supporting the government management of the economy and natural resources; in addition they support the programs of agricultural assistance. On all other dimensions—international, welfare, civil liberties—Dixie populists oppose government activity.

The populist designation comes from the nineteenth century

agrarians, both North and South, who sought to use the government to battle the strong eastern business interests, hence the tradition of support for government management of the economy. The members of the populist movement, and their descendants and close relatives, have not been reluctant to call upon the government for their portion of the kind of subsidy that undergirds the railroads, keeps the merchant marine afloat and the airlines in the sky, and primes the industrial pump. Another aspect of this populism has been something less than overwhelming sympathy for the problems of the urban areas, partly as a function of economic self-interest but also resulting in part from the ethnic and religious differences between the inhabitants of rural and urban areas. Moreover, the populist tradition has been isolationist. And, of course, the Dixie component of the Dixie populist policy profile is the low support position on civil liberties.

Dixie populism is dominant in the states of Mississippi, North Carolina, and South Carolina; it is also well represented in Arkansas, Georgia, Florida, Louisiana, and Texas.

The small band of Dixie liberals (15 members out of the 88-member southern Democratic contingent) takes a low support position on but a single dimension, civil liberties. In all other respects they resemble northern Democratic liberals. The strongest support for Dixie-style liberalism is found in Alabama. This will come as more of a surprise to those who think of George Wallace as a typical Alabama product than to those who think of Senators Hill and Sparkman. The rest of the Dixie liberals are spread thinly across the South, with Arkansas and Texas providing the strongest support.

The third group of Southern Democrats, equal in size (small) to the Dixie liberals, is the set of Dixie welfare populists, who view international involvement with a jaundiced eye but support government management, social welfare, and agricultural aid. Of course, they provide little support for federal activities in support of civil liberties. These representatives are quite widely scattered, although a third of them do come from the large Texas delegation, but none originates in the Dixie populist states of Mississippi and the Carolinas.

One state in the South has not been mentioned thus far because most of its representatives are of a different political breed than that represented in the strains of Dixie populism, liberalism, or welfare populism. This is the state of Virginia, the home of the late southern conservative, Senator Harry Byrd. Its representatives display a conservative profile, with nearly half taking a low support position on four of the five dimensions, the exception being the agricultural assistance dimension (think tobacco!). One member of the delegation even rejects this form of government activity. None of the Virginia delegation is a Dixie liberal and only one out of nine makes the Dixie welfare populist cut. In short, the Virginia delegation resembles no other delegation in the South and has a strongly conservative cast.

The *common lines running through the profiles of the southern Democrats,* with the exception of a majority of the Virginia delegation, are *opposition to government activity in civil rights and support for government management and agricultural assistance.* Slightly to the left is the distinct minority of welfare populists who also support social welfare. Of equal size, and similar minority status, are the Dixie liberals, who differ from northern liberals on only one dimension, civil liberties.

Border States

Ignored to this point have been the representatives from the Border states of Oklahoma, Tennessee, Kentucky, West Virginia, and Maryland. These states normally present problems in classification, North versus South, and for that reason they are treated separately. However, the delay in their examination has been for another reason, the possibility that after reviewing the policy profiles of the three major regional-party groupings it may be possible to assign the Border states to either North or South. We shall look first at the Border Democrats, then the Border Republicans.

DEMOCRATS

Maryland and Oklahoma Democrats have policy profiles of the northern variety, no question about it. West Virginia and Kentucky representatives are only slightly less northern in their behavior: West Virginia has one Dixie welfare populist, and Kentucky sends two Dixie liberals to Congress. Tennessee representatives, however, behave just like the Southern democratic delegations. On the basis of this information, I have to divide the Border states, four to one, in favor of the North.

REPUBLICANS

The number of Border Republicans is small, ten to be exact. Of these, only one takes the position on civil liberties that is expected of Southern representatives—he hails from West Virginia. So there is really no basis for changing the four-to-one North-South division of the Border states effected with the review of Border Democrats.

The North-South partitioning of the Border states seems further justified by the absence of any unique policy profile particularly suited to their condition. Which is perhaps to say that the Border state condition is no longer unique and that the aftermath of the struggles of the Civil War period is now a part of history. To put it most clearly, Tennessee representatives act like southerners, while Oklahoma, Maryland, West Virginia, and Kentucky appear to have been integrated into the political culture of the North, if not in the manner of their politics, certainly in the policy positions of their representatives in Congress.

Bypassed in this description of policy profiles, because of their small number, have been the Southern Republicans. When they do surface, they conform to the regional norms on civil rights and look like the more conservative northern Republicans in other respects.

Despite my efforts to keep detail to a minimum, a bit more information has been dispensed than can be readily comprehended in a quick sweep of the mind's eye. Although the detail may be of interest, given numerous popular conceptions about the politics of different states, somewhat more general observations may be in order.

The Big Nine in Review

It was pointed out earlier that, at the most general level, each of the big nine policy profiles is almost exclusively identified with a single regional-party grouping. Furthermore, the profiles within a regional-party grouping are more similar to each other than are profiles drawn from different groupings. These observations point to the homogeneity of policy profiles within the three regional-party groupings—northern Democrats, northern Republicans, southern Democrats—while extending recognition to a smaller measure of variation within the groupings.

The association of regional and policy variations should come as no surprise to political historians, for these are echoes from a not too distant past when sectional, or regional, divisions were a standard and highly salient aspect of American politics. Nor have regional differences been forgotten in latter day ruminations on American politics, but they *have* become more an undertone than a major theme, with the exception of the North-South division on civil rights for blacks.

Thus, at the general level *we find the policy expression of the most salient regional division in American politics in the civil liberties dimension. This dimension cuts the Democratic party in two.*

The policy dimension that most clearly separates Democrats from Republicans is the government management dimension. Indeed, the separation of the two parties is strikingly sharp; there is very, very little overlap in the policy positions of Democrats and Republicans. This point needs special emphasis in order to burn through the fog of ideological obfuscation generated by references to liberal Republicans and conservative Democrats, the latter from the South. On the dimension of government management it is very rare to find a southern Democrat who is more conservative on this dimension than the most liberal Republican.

The government management dimension, then, as a party dimension and the civil liberty dimension as a regional division are the keys to the major differences among the three regional-party groupings. The government management dimension divides the two parties; the civil liberties dimension bisects the Democratic party and conceivably robs this party of its strength as a national force. Although their impact is of smaller magnitude the other three dimensions contribute to the definition of the nine policy profiles.

Actually, the agricultural assistance dimension does little to disturb the oneness within the three regional-party groupings. The three policy profiles in the southern Democratic wing are not differentiated on this dimension, nor are the three main policy profiles in the northern Republican party, although there is a small troop of dissidents within the Republican ranks that can be counted on to support agricultural assistance. It is only among the northern Democrats that the division on the agricultural assistance dimension is of major proportions; it cuts out a subset of 41 northern Democrats who oppose agricultural assistance enough to separate them from the main body of their wing of the Democratic party.

Even with the effect of the agricultural assistance dimension on the northern Democrats, if one looked only at the three policy dimensions just reviewed—government management, civil liberties, and agricultural assistance—one would come up with a fairly tidy trichotomy of American politics: northern Democratic liberalism, Dixie populism, and Republican conservatism.

However, complexity is introduced by two policy dimensions that underlie the issues raised by the problems associated with two major twentieth-century developments: world power status for the United States and the massive impact of industrialization and urbanization on the American way of life. The international involvement dimension is most effective in fragmenting the trichotomy of regional-party policy profiles. In each of the three regional-party groupings there is a policy profile that is separated from the other two policy profiles by the international involvement dimension. Its power to divide is least among northern Democrats, where about 10 percent support constraint on international activities; it is somewhat more effective among southern Democrats where about 20 percent favor involvement, in opposition to their fellows; and the divisiveness of this dimension comes into full play in the northern Republican group, where a third earn low support scores while their colleagues line up in support of their Republican president, General Dwight David Eisenhower.

The divisions along the dimension of international involvement bring us back to a consideration of region. In both northern party groups, support for international activism increases as one moves from the interior of the country toward the eastern and western coasts. While it is true that a larger proportion of interior Republican representatives favor international restraint than is the case among interior Democrats, the modern version of pre–Pearl Harbor isolationism finds adherents in both parties in heartland America.[11]

In the South, which once had a reputation for internationalism, international activism has declined in favor.[12] As we shall see later when we look at presidential influence, the support for international activism in the South is particularly low under a Republican administration, the condition that existed for the two Congresses on which the analysis of ideological configurations is based. Of the one-fifth of the representatives who continue the older Southern tradition, even under a Republican president, most come from Alabama, Arkansas, and Texas; only in Alabama, however, are they in the majority. Whereas the coastal-interior pattern of policy cleavage on the international involvement dimension in the North is so traditional as to require little explanation, there is no handy explanation for the distribution of points of view within the South.

The fifth dimension, social welfare, adds further to the fragmentation of the policy profiles among members of the House. It sets a quarter of the northern Republicans at odds with their brethren and divides the southern Democrats nearly in half. Only the northern Democrats keep their ranks closed in tight formation on this dimension. As with international involvement, there is a regional cast to the divisions on social welfare within the regional-party groupings. Among the northern Republicans, those taking a supportive position with respect to social welfare are drawn almost entirely from east of the Ohio River. Federal social welfarism is not for the hardy Republican pioneers of the middle and far West.

The center of opposition to social welfare policies in the South lies in three adjacent coastal states, Virginia, North Carolina, and South Carolina, and in the state of Mississippi. The opponents of social welfare are in undisputed command of these four state delegations. However, the regional mold is cracked in the South in that Mississippi is some distance from the first three states. Furthermore, in traveling by mule train from South Carolina to Mississippi one has to cross the state of Alabama, which sends a delegation to Congress as dominated by social welfare supporters as the first four states are by opponents.

The Wide-Screen View

This wide-screen view of the American political scene, drawn from the perspective on Capitol Hill, is complex enough to prove interesting, yet it is neither so complex nor so fluid as to be incomprehensible. An element of order is provided by party on three of the policy dimensions but not on the other two. This finding will not satisfy those who yearn for the programmatic party.

There is more than a hint of ideology, but it too fails to produce the sense of order so devoutly sought by earnest ideologues. By one definition of liberalism and conservatism, restricting the scope of each to domestic politics, about one-half of the nation's representatives and three-fourths of those representing northern states appear to be following the dictates of either conservatism or liberalism.

What, then, do we conclude regarding the roles of party and ideology? Neither is powerful enough to bring the simplest of order into American politics, yet the effects of neither can be denied. Party is strongly associated with the cleavage on three dimensions and promises to emerge as the prime mover on at least one, if not two, of these three.

Ideology, as a source of policy positions and as a mechanism of reinforcement of policy view, needs further investigation. We simply can not ignore the fact that one-half of the members of the House can be classified as liberals or conservatives on the basis of their positions on four domestic policy dimensions. I find it hard to reject the existence of two political orientations, one liberal and one conservative, which predicate policy positions on a number of domestic questions. Granted these orientations are not the products of profound thought, for they lack anything approaching an elaborate and soul-stirring structure of ideas and beliefs.

Nevertheless I do offer the proposition that there are those individuals, *liberals*, who are inclined to support federal government activity on a variety of fronts, without close inspection of specific programs, in the belief that federal government action is needed to solve or mitigate most problems. Federal government action is the most appropriate because most problems have their origins and distribute their curses at more than the local level. For example, in the absence of federal programs, sister states must bear each other's sins as their sons and daughters exchange residence in search of opportunity.

There are others, *conservatives*, who are inclined to oppose most forms of federal activity as too costly and of dubious merit. Problems are best left to private initiative or to local governments more knowledgeable of their origins and possible solutions. The federal government is too big, beyond citizen control, and unresponsive to the pressures acceded to by state and local governments.

In short, there are general points of view on the efficacy of federal government action that play a major part in reactions to policy proposals. To refer to them as ideologies is a bit presumptuous, and even outrageous to the committed ideologue, but to reject them as influential orientations may be equally unreasonable. The liberal and conservative philosophies are adopted by one-half of the members of Congress, as reflected in their policy actions; they can not be ignored in a hurried effort to write off the existence of "ideological ways" of thinking and acting.

The conclusion that will probably enlist the support of most political observers and participants is that citizens of these United States are still too bound by local orientations and too independent in their policy choices to be organized into regimented legions of ironclad ideologies or submerged in the ranks of disciplined parties. They may be *affected* by party loyalties and ideological points of view, but they are not *controlled*. With due homage to this "red, white, and blue" image of American politics, let me back off to the position that an ordering of representatives on five policy dimensions is the most that can be claimed. It is in this perspective that the remainder of the analysis is conducted.

References

1. American Political Science Association, Committee on Political Parties, "Toward a More Responsible Two-Party System," *American Political Science Review* 44 Supplement (September 1959), (New York: Holt, Rinehart & Winston, 1950), especially pp. 56–65; Austin Ranney, *Doctrine of Responsible Party Government* (Urbana: University of Illinois Press, 1954).

2. This is my interpretation of evidence such as that presented in Angus Campbell, *et al.*, *American Voter* (New York: Wiley, 1960), pp. 146–167.

3. Robert D. Hess and Judith V. Torney, *Development of Political Attitudes in Children* (Garden City, N.Y.: Doubleday, 1967); M. Kent Jennings and Richard G. Niemi, "Transmission of Political Values from Parent to Child," *American Political Science Review* 52 (March 1968), pp. 169–184.

4. One of the more successful analyses is Thomas A. Flinn and Harold L. Wolman, "Constituency and Roll-Call Voting: Case of the Southern Democratic Congressman," *Midwest Journal of Political Science* 10 (May 1966), pp. 192–199.

5. Studies on which this observation is based are numerous, from A. Lawrence Lowell, "The Influence of Party upon Legislation," Annual Report of the American Historical Association, I (1901), pp. 321–543, to Julius Turner, *Party and Constituency: Pressures on Congress,* revised by Edward V. Schneier, Jr. (Baltimore, Md.: Johns Hopkins Press, 1970).

6. Turner, *op. cit.*, pp. 103–104.

7. Treatises on conservatism and liberalism in America include Clinton Rossiter, *Conservatism in America,* 2nd ed. (New York: Random House, 1962); Allen Guttmann, *The Conservative Tradition in America* (New York: Oxford University Press, 1967); Louis Hartz, *Liberal Tradition in America* (New York: Harcourt Brace Jovanovich, 1955); Russell Kirk, *The Conservative Mind* (Chicago: H. Regnery, 1960).

8. For a similar analysis see Charles D. Farris, "A Method for Determining Ideological Groupings in Congress," *Journal of Politics* 20 (May 1958), pp. 308–338.

9. See David Mayhew, *Party Loyalty Among Congressmen* (Cambridge, Mass.: Harvard University Press, 1966), pp. 12–56.

10. *Ibid.*

11. For an extensive discussion see Leroy N. Rieselbach, *Roots of Isolationism* (Indianapolis, Ind.: Bobbs-Merrill, 1966).

12. Charles O. Lerche, "Southern Congressmen and the 'New Isolationism'," *Political Science Quarterly* 75 (September 1960), pp. 321–337; Malcolm E. Jewell, "Evaluating the Decline of Southern Internationalism Through Senatorial Roll Call Votes," *Journal of Politics* 21 (November 1959), pp. 624–646.

6

Policy Representation: Party and Constituency Influence

In the tradition of American legislative politics, the legislator has the responsibility of representing his constituency and promoting its interests. However, the constituency interest is seldom so clearly defined, or so politically potent, that the legislator's policy options are severely limited. Instead, the role of constituency representative can provide the congressman with a sense of freedom so aptly described by the poet Robert Frost as "a feeling of being loose in the harness." The collar of constituency constraints seldom chafes, while the harness of office establishes the legitimacy and enhances the effectiveness of the individual legislator's own political pull. For we must not forget that legislators are not simply representatives of various clienteles; they are also individuals who view the legislative office as an opportunity for advancing their own policy objectives.

Despite the latitude of decision accorded the representative, the sense of constituency responsibility certainly remains in most cases. Actually, extensive research indicates that the constituency looms larger in the congressman's calculations than need be, leading to a greater attention to constituency views than would be necessary to avoid serious political repercussions. The most salient finding is that the constituents' knowledge of their representative and his activities is insufficient to serve as a controlling mechanism.[1] It is likely, therefore, that the norm of constituency responsibility, as internalized by the legislator, is more important for representation than the capacity of the voters to enforce responsibility through constant surveillance and the threat of reprisals at the polls.

Compared with the high standing and impeccable credentials of constituency responsibility in the American political system, party responsibility is of dubious pedigree. Representatives in legislative bodies in this country are seldom publicly lauded for their service and allegiance to party. Indeed, most legislators feel the need, at one time or another, to assert their independence of party.

Given the acceptance of the norm of constituency responsibility among legislators, it is understandable that the role of party should be played down. For it is often the case that the policy requirements of party at the national level are in conflict with local constituency interests. Or perhaps it is more correct to say that the variation in constituency interests impedes the development of nationally acceptable party policy positions. Nor should one overlook the advantages that accrue to the representative, in terms of his freedom of action, through an insistence upon the duty to consult constituency before party. Adding weight to this argument is the need of the congressman to run for reelection.

There are indications, nevertheless, that partisan bonds are treasured more in the halls of Congress than they are in the broader expanse of American politics. This is reflected in comments by individual congressmen to the effect that going along with the party is desirable, although not always possible.[2] It may also be inferred from the party cohesion displayed on a substantial proportion of roll calls, suggesting a level of intraparty unity and interparty conflict that is more than sufficient to contradict the cynical view that party differences are negligible.[3]

That party bonds are treasured in two large bodies such as the Senate (100 members) and the House (435) is quite understandable; it would be odd if it were otherwise. Party is a link with the past and with the constituency, and it provides a basis for establishing new friendships and working relations in the confusing whirlpools of Washington politics. Accompanying this informal intrapartisan interaction is a more formal arrangement of party officialdom in a loose party organization. The party organization's dispensation of rewards and privileges can only serve, however slightly, to augment the level of partisan cohesion that arises out of the camaraderie of the natural grouping. However, I would place a greater premium on the natural affinity between legislators of the same party as a source of party cohesion than I would on the formal party organization.

The relative influence of party and constituency on policy decisions, viewed in a context in which they are competing with each other, is the ultimate concern of this chapter. The relative impact of party and constituency will be assessed on the five policy dimensions, using a means of analysis that makes the most of the analytic advantages of a longitudinal study.

Party Influence

The difficulties confronting an attempt to pinpoint the effect of party on the decision-making process of the individual in Congress are a bit more challenging than I would prefer. There is, first of all, no easily interpretable and definitive set of documents that state the party program; nor is there any statement of a party ideology, nor even a set of discrete party policy views, for either the short or the long term. Attempts along these lines occur every four years at the national conventions, and on occasion party leadership groups outside of Congress may suggest a program. In neither case do senators and representatives line up for instructions. The clearest example of the closest thing to a party program is provided for the "in" party by presidential messages to Congress; the "out" party may send off public relations signals promising alternate policy programs, but somehow the subsequent signals always seem to weaken and fade away, like a well-tutored old general.

Even in the instance of the presidential party, it is far from self-evident that the president's program is obligingly accepted by members of Congress as a legitimate expression of *party policy* aspirations. Rather, I suspect it is accepted as the president's program more than as the unifying policy statement of the party.

Nor is the president necessarily the party leader in more than name in the eyes of the members of Congress; this applies especially to the party in Congress. Indeed, with the powerful figures of Congress in mind, I suggest that, in comparison with their long play on the national political stage in the "Washington Theatre," a presidential administration may appear to be no more than the guest performance of a traveling celebrity. It draws a good crowd, but doesn't last long. This is especially true since the establishment of a "union" rule, the Twenty-second Amendment, put a two-act limitation on the presidential performance. Even if the president is called back for the second act, interest is likely to fall off before the act is finished. Everyone knows the star will not be around for the third act to resolve the dilemmas posed in the first two. In this staging of Washington politics, the role of the president as a highly influential party leader in Congress is a bit more difficult to fit into the script than is commonly recognized.

In the discussion of party influence to follow, I make a distinction between two broad classes of party influence. The first is concerned with party as a life-long factor in the formation, modification, and maintenance of policy attitudes; beginning in early childhood and persisting through the present. The second broad class of party influence includes those instances in which a member of Congress seeks out, or accepts, the counsel of another person in arriving at a policy decision *because* the other person is a fellow partisan.

Party Colleagues as Source of Policy Cues

The influence of party that is present when one member seeks the advice of another member, or a nonmember, *because of a common party affiliation* is the easier of the two sources of party influence to describe. So I will begin with it.

The partisan cueing of members may take place at every point in the decision process. Cues may be given immediately prior to the casting of the roll-call vote. Or the cueing may occur at a very early stage of the policy evaluation, as when individual members look to party leaders, interest-group leaders influential in party circles, and fellow colleagues to stake out policy positions on proposals when they are little more than half-baked offerings. Half-baked or well-done, one senses this process after the submission of presidential proposals that exude an unfamiliar aroma suggesting an uncommon policy recipe. Eager reporters are put off as congressmen, even august senators, plead the need for more time to study the proposal. This evokes an image of congressmen retiring to their offices and poring over the relevant documents with members of their staff. An image evoked by the cue-taking theory is that of a form of retirement where the pouring is more likely to be of refreshments for trusted companions, telephone conversations with others, consultation of the oracles through the media, and reflections on simpler days. (But perhaps this image of congressional behavior borrows too heavily from fantasy and political fiction.) To make the same point in less fanciful terms, we frequently are informed that "party lines are forming on the president's proposal."

The impact of party leadership in this cueing process is not clear. Such leadership as manifests itself appears to be highly dependent on the persuasiveness of formally designated party leaders rather than upon their organizational positions. Leadership is provided also by the policy and political expertise of the ranking party members on key committees, which implies a shift in leadership as the policy focus shifts, as from taxes to defense.

Contributing to the ambiguity in the concept of party leadership as an important source of policy cues to party members is the image of the party leader as a consensus manipulator. Thus, a party leader may find it useful to spend at least as much time looking back at his troops to assess their policy field positions as he does in marching forward on a new policy front.[4]

However, the disappointment over the failure of parties to operate as rational, strongly programmatic organizations, with highly centralized leaderships, should not lead us to reject the influence of party in Congress. It is not to be denied that there is the party influence that is effected in congressmen's looking to the president from their party, or deliberately opposing the president because he is from the other party. There are also party effects in the desire of members to fall in line behind the positions of party leaders, whoever they are, with respect to the issue in question. There is the additional more diffuse desire of the member "to belong," and party offers a warm shelter in out of the cold. In general, the party standard always has strong potential as a rallying banner.

In sum, the partisan-based policy cue is an aspect of the decision process that is well recognized and accepted. It is, however, immensely difficult to measure with any level of precision, given the multifarious ways that party counsel may affect a member's decisions.

Partisan Policy Attitudes

Much more complex and difficult to describe is the performance of party as a source of personal policy attitudes (but one component in the congressman's decision mechanism). This form of partisan influence, the second broad category specified earlier, may have begun while today's congressman was still in possession of most of his baby teeth and was solely dependent upon his family for orientations toward politics and politicians. At an early age, these orientations are of the simplest form, but not necessarily of a transient quality. With maturation, the political orientation fills out into a multifaceted view of the political environment, although there is great variation in the number of facets developed by different individuals. However, the extent to which the political orientation learned in youth includes partisan policy attitudes, as well as partisan identifications, is not clear. The recency of attention to early political learning, as a field of study, does not permit judgments in this respect.

The process of political learning, so often referred to with respect to the preadult period, is actually a never-ending process. Therefore, if there exist what may be identified as partisan attitudes and beliefs regarding public policy, organized into an ideology or existing as discrete entities, the potential for party influence through political learning continues throughout the life of the individual. Congressmen, because of the greater likelihood of their sustained exposure to partisan agents including party elites, as compared with the much less involved citizen at large, are people for whom the potential for partisan policy influence is maximum.

In brief, the influence of party may be a long-term affair. To the extent that policy differences among affiliates of different parties exist in one generation, these differences are available for transmission to the next generation. Also, to the extent that active partisans and leaders, in and out of Congress, share policy attitudes, individuals recruited into the top levels of activists and leaders are exposed to a partisan policy orientation. Finally, the continuously high level of fraternization among affiliates of the same party, *relative* to the lower level between affiliates of different parties, serves to encourage the commonality of policy views within parties.

It is important to recognize that the processes of attitude formation and convergence described above do not by any means ensure national party policy unity. Given the societal scope of American parties and their success in attracting affiliates from a potpourri of regional, religious, economic, and class groupings, it is unrealistic to expect a high level of commonality on very many policy questions. Remember also that American national parties are often referred to as loose aggregations of state parties. Consequently, while the representative is articulating the wishes of his party constituents at the state and local levels, he may be contributing to party disunity at the national level. Only on certain issues can one expect a common party point of view that is shared across the country and is a source of high party cohesion within the Congress.

In wrapping up this discussion of party influence, let me comment briefly on the proposition that partisan voting cohesion in the Congress is greater than might be predicted from the intraparty level of policy agreement. One basis for arguing this proposition is research that indicates the importance of partisan giving and taking of cues among congressmen.

Conditions under which the partisan influence in Congress is enhanced are the following: First, the influence of party through cue-taking expands as the constituency pressures decline. This may seem obvious unless one recognizes the possibility that party need not move in to fill the vacuum left by constituency. Second, partisan cues are more likely to be taken when the congressman's decisions are less visible. The lesser influence of party on the more visible decisions is attributed to the danger of relying upon partisan cues when there is a possibility that groups and individuals opposing the partisan position may have the matter brought to their attention.[5] Low visibility attends voting in committee, floor votes on which an individual record of yeas and nays is not kept (when only the division of the vote or the success or failure of the motion is reported for public inspection), and issues that the media judge insufficiently newsworthy.

This commentary on the conditions under which partisan influence is enhanced may appear to call into question my earlier statement that the policy positions of individual congressmen, measured on the basis of roll-call votes, can be assumed to be the ones they take at other stages in the legislative decision-making process. Since roll calls are more visible than other decisions, perhaps they are less partisan than nonrecorded votes and, thereby, somewhat unrepresentative. However, let us not be too hasty. In the first place, systematic evidence in support of the greater level of partisan cue-taking on less visible votes is not available. In the second place, there is variation in the visibility of roll-call votes, so that the full set of roll calls may be only slightly more visible than decisions in other legislative contexts.

Finally, there is the argument that roll-call votes bring out a partisan element not observed elsewhere because the roll-call vote can be used to build partisan campaign issues. Thus, in arguing back and forth, I still come down in support of the assumption that policy positions measured on the basis of the roll-call votes are highly reflective of positions more generally expressed and acted upon.

Constituency Influence

Compared with the complexity of partisan influence, the functioning of constituency influence might appear to be much more straightforward. It is not. The first problem is understanding what is meant
by constituency. The second problem concerns the properties of the
constituency that the legislator is expected to represent. The third
problem is to specify the manner in which constituency exerts its
influence.

Representation of Whom?

The constitutional arrangements of the country and the individual
states provide a legal definition of constituency as the set of individuals who have the legal right to vote for a legislative representative upon reaching the age of competence, recently set at eighteen.
The legal right to vote is established by the individual's place of legal
residence within the boundaries of an areally defined legislative
district.

A more realistic alternative in defining constituency, where "realistic" implies the individual representative's capacity to perform the
representational function, is to limit the constituency to *the subset
of voters who supported the representative in the last election.* Given
the usually strong correspondence between the party affiliation of
the voter and the party of the candidate he chooses, this constituency
would be composed, for the most part, of the representative's party
brethren plus a smaller set of voters to whom he has a particular
appeal.

Redefining the constituency to include no more than the subset
of voters who supported the representative in the last election makes
the task of representation a much more manageable one, although
still sufficiently difficult to prevent boredom from setting in. Three
points are offered. (1) Since the congressman's supporters are
drawn in large part from members of his own party, less diversity
is expected in their policy views than in the full constituency including all parties. (2) Voters supporting the representative because
of his policy positions, apart from those implied in a partisan preference among candidates, are likely to vary less in their policy views

than the full set of constituents making choices in terms of policy. (3) After as well as during the election the representative will have more contacts with his supporters than with his opponents, providing him an opportunity to get to know the views of his followers. These three points, together, mean a greater exposure of a representative to a less heterogeneous set of constituent-voters than will be the case for the representative vis-à-vis the legally defined constituency. Consequently, given this more realistic definition of constituency, the level of representation can be substantial, even though the representative possesses no superhuman powers.[6]

The injection of a shot of realism into the definition of constituency is an effort to immunize the representational form of government against the debilitating disease of disgust with its malfunctioning. This disease flourishes when impossible standards of performance are set for the mortal beings who take on the role of representative. Dissatisfaction with the lack of representation is not restricted to legislative bodies. It may also develop with respect to executive, judicial, and administrative institutions.

It so happens that legislative bodies, from city council to United Nations Assembly, have come in for more than their share of criticism. Certainly, not all of this criticism is directed at a lack of representation. It is based as well on what appears to be undignified and irresponsible behavior, for example, dalliance in the face of year-end fiscal obligations and junketing at the taxpayer's expense. And there is the general, vague, uneasy sense that only the lean, dry hands of the saintly ascetic can pass through the public till without a little of the green adhering.

More serious, however, is the dissatisfaction that is focused on the legislature's failure to represent the people, as when Congress is criticized for its domination by old men with dried roots and fossilized attitudes. Representation is the legislature's claim to power, as the English House of Lords can well attest.

These definitions of constituency may be irrelevant to the individual voter's evaluation of the representative body. John Q. Voter may be interested in only one representational relationship, the one between the representative and himself. It is not his concern if the legislator fails to represent this or that constituency, so long as he represents John Q.

However, it seems likely that John Q's evaluation of the quality of representation provided by the elected representative is consistent with the terms set by the realistic definition of constituency. My argument is that most voters accept the defeat of their preferred candidate as a temporary loss of representation. Consequently, there is no representational relationship subject to evaluation; that judgment is for those whose man won. Although this does not preclude John Q. Loser from being represented by the opponent of his candidate, such representation is a bonus and not a regular payment of the representational system.

Stated in the baldest terms, the implication of this discussion of constituency definitions is that legislators are expected to represent the subset of constituents who voted for them on the Big Day. Given the overwhelming importance of party affiliation as a basis for choosing among candidates for office, and given the long-term exposure of most candidates to the people and views of a single party, the expectation is that the legislator will represent his partisan followers best. The empirically based, but nonetheless normative, argument is that such partisan representation is the most we have a right to expect of the representational system.

Representation of What?

The definition of the congressman's constituency, who belongs to it and who does not, leaves us with the problem of considering the properties of the constituency to be represented. In the introduction to this work, the focus was placed on political representation. Given the principal orientation of this book, the policy orientation, representation is further defined *as the congruence of the policy requirements of the constituency with the policy decisions of the representative.* This definition of representation will be referred to as *policy representation.*

Trimming the substance of representation down to the solid red meat of policy representation slices off a number of delicacies that constituents may savor in their representative. Such delicacies include distinguished appearance, an air of honesty and sincerity, the right family, the right party, the right color, the right sex, the right nationality, the right religion, and the rare smile. Indeed, it may well be the case that these properties of the representative are of much more immediate concern to constituents. Nor do we need to assume that attention to these properties will necessarily diminish policy representation. When the choice provides some match between characteristics of the constituent and those of his representative, it may mean a common background and life experience, and thus shared attitudes.

The definition of policy representation as the congruence of the policy requirements of the constituency with the policy decisions of the representative includes the phrase, *policy requirements of the constituency*, whose meaning is far short of being self-evident. False hopes of clarification are raised by redefining policy requirements as the policy formulations and positions that are consistent with the *interests* of the constituency. This is just a step backward in the same definitional quicksand, for now what is the meaning of constituency interest?

Reference to the interests of the constituency raises the problem of who is to specify that interest. Is it to be defined by one whose role it is to assess this interest, such as the representative, or by a self-appointed arbiter, such as the editorial writer for the *Daily Bladder?* Or, as implied before in defining the constituency, do we accept the individual constituents' policy demands as they might express them in a letter to a congressman, in a conversation, or in response to a public opinion poll? A surprising number of allegedly democratic individuals have little if any use for this option. The undemocratic view here is that "the people" can't be trusted to use good judgment. Another view, informed by somewhat more objective evidence, is that the individual citizen has not the inclination, and if he has the inclination, has not the time, and if he has the time and inclination, has not the access to the necessary information to make policy judgments that are consistent with his self-interest.

The preference for an "objective" evaluation of constituency interests, consistent with but also sometimes in opposition to constituency policy views, is not only undemocratic; it prohibits an evaluation of the performance of the representational function other than by a number of observers with an equal number of definitions of the constituency interests. In short, how does one decide that the representative's policy decisions are inconsistent with the interests of his constituents? There is no way that I know of or could even imagine.

One can, however, obtain measurements of constituency policy requirements when these are equated with the policy views of the constituents.[7] These measures will be plagued by some degree of unreliability, as is your bathroom scale. There will also be arguments over their validity. After all, ascertaining the policy views of con-stituents requires a more sensitive measurement apparatus than is needed in the census-type study of marital status, occupation, and race. So there are going to be problems, but they are not prohibitive. We know how policy views are measured when, for example, the re-sults of an attitude survey are reported. Subsequently, we can dis-count the results because the methodology is deficient, or accept them when the method of measurement appears valid and reliable.

Linked to the question of the validity and reliability of the mea-sures of constituency policy attitudes is the objection that such atti-tudes are nonexistent with respect to many of the questions on which the congressman must make a decision. Obviously, it is absurd to attempt to measure what does not exist.

I am more than happy to grant the point that it would be futile to measure representation as the match between the preferences of congressmen and the preferences of constituents on *specific* policy proposals. With the exception of policy concerns of the most imme-diate importance to him, the ordinary citizen would be at sea. It is not just that the legislation is so complex and technical, for this property of legislation can set many congressmen adrift as well, but that the policy concerns of individual citizens are not oriented to that level of specificity. The individual voter may favor assistance to the farmers, but he would be unprepared to vote on a particular form of such assistance, because he is not perennially exposed to dis-cussions of the legislation as is the congressman. This experience is most useful in decision-making because it helps to answer the central questions: What does the legislative proposal involve? What are its implications? Who is likely to be benefited by it? Given the answers to some of these questions the congressman, even though he is no expert himself and does not devote his time to studying the legislation, can still find some basis for a decision that accords with his view of his policy responsibilities. It is an oversimplification, but the congress-man can be viewed as a professional decision-maker who has devel-oped a strategy of decision-making that suffices without technical expertise, and whose policy decisions are to be compared to the policy positions of his lay clients. This comparison must necessarily be at a general, nonspecific, nontechnical level.

It is my view that *it is feasible to compare the policy position of the representative to that of his constituents on a broad policy dimen-sion* such as social welfare. Thus, the policy dimension theory states that each congressman develops a policy position, on each of several policy dimensions, that reflects his policy responsibilities to a variety of groups and individuals, including himself. This policy position is equivalent to a general attitude toward welfare policies that he adopts for his performance of his congressional role. It is this general attitude of the congressman, his position on a policy dimension, that can be compared to a similar general attitude among the citizenry. Whereas we can not expect the ordinary citizen, or even the extraordinary one, to have attitudes on the myriad policy questions posed to the legislator, it is reasonable to expect constituents to have attitudes toward such general policy concepts as are the focus of this study. Although the constituent can not evaluate a foreign aid bill, he can have an attitude regarding the appropriate level of international involvement. This level is not set with any precision, but then the decision criteria of policy-makers are not all that discriminating either.

It is quite common to refer to some regions, such as the Midwest, as being isolationist and to others, such as the Eastern Seaboard, as being more internationalist. Such references to the attitudes of the inhabitants of a region toward the desired level of international involvement are specific examples of the property of constituency opinion that is comparable to the positions of individual congressmen on a policy dimension. In short, it makes sense to think of an ordering of *both* constituents and congressmen on general policy dimensions, with positions ranging from low to high support for the policy concept that is the policy substance of the dimension.

The Manner of Constituency Influence

There are two general forms of constituency influence. The first form comes through the congressman's internalization of the political orientations of the constituency in which he now resides and probably has resided for many years. The second form of constituency influence is effected through the congressman's perceptions of the needs and demands of his constituents. These perceptions are a conscious attempt to assess constituency attitudes, whereas the attitudes of the congressman that are a product of his constituency origins are an effortless expression of constituency viewpoints. Of course, everyone knows that the congressman's attitudes, whatever their derivation, are likely to affect his perception of the attitudes of others, and vice versa. However, this does not preclude each from making some independent contribution to his behavior as a legislator seeks to represent his constituency.

The form of constituency influence that is effected through the legislator's internalization of the political orientations of his constituency results in "involuntary" representation; this is a concept developed in an earlier paper.[8] Representation of the constituency is involuntary in that it occurs without a conscious effort by the representative and is something over which the representative exercises little control, as in the case of breathing or the beating of his heart. The constituency orientations are an integral part of his being. They are operative in his personal political attitudes, in his cognition of the political environment, and in his views on a variety of nonpolitical matters, some of which become intertwined with his politics.

The feature of involuntary representation that distinguishes it from the representation that comes about through a voluntary self-conscious attempt to heed the press of constituency forces is its unconsciousness. Indeed, the orientations that result in involuntary representation affect the congressman's conscious efforts to represent the whole constituency, or any part of it, because they are a part of his perceptual apparatus. Where the internalized political orientations are drawn from a segment of the constituency, such as represented by his fellow partisans in the constituency, they may interfere with his conscious effort to represent the full constituency. It is not just that the congressman sees what he wants to, a voluntary act, but that his angle of vision is blocked by the blinders of his particular orientations.

The full meaning of involuntary representation can perhaps be brought out another way. It is more than what is implied when the congressman says, "I don't have to talk to my constituents to know what they would do in my place; I know!" This is only the part of the involuntary representation that he recognizes. The other part, perhaps a larger part, is effective when he takes a policy direction without being conscious that it represents the thinking of his constituency on the issue involved. Yet involuntary representation *is* present in the way the congressman thinks about the issue.

The second form of constituency influence is exerted both through the sending of signals from the constituency to the attentive congressman and through the existence of the constituency, and all its properties, as objective facts of the congressman's environment. In the first instance, the congressman is the target of policy directives from his constituents. These are communicated by letters, telegrams, signed petitions, delegations to the congressman's office, editorial comments, and other means by which constituents seek to impress upon the congressman the fact of their existence, political awareness, and potential for delivering the vote.

In the second instance, where constituency exerts its influence simply by being there, the legislator is the active agent, seeking information about changes in the constituency, utilizing information on the major societal groups (occupation, region, religion, ethnicity, race) that he has stored up during his tenure as a member and representative of the constituency—in general, making sure he understands his constituency and that it doesn't "slip away from him." Congressmen use mail questionnaires to poll constituents and ascertain their positions on current issues. It is undoubtedly true that the poll serves the additional, and possibly even more important, function of assuring the constituents that the congressmen care. Nevertheless, I would be greatly surprised to hear of the congressman who wasn't just a bit curious about the results of the poll.

Congressmen also use holidays and long weekends to return to their constituency to keep in touch, as well as to remain visible, as well as to get away from Washington. Again this may be less effective in deepening their understandings of constituency desires than in forestalling the potential opponent's criticism that he is neglecting his constituency. However, it can not be summarily dismissed solely as a public relations gambit.

When constituency influence is put in terms of the existence of the constituency, not as a pleading, petitioning, demanding body, but as an objective fact in any representative's environment, my image of the constituency is that of a somnolent giant usually oblivious to the representative's existence. However, this giant has certain tender spots that must be protected from the prodding opponent who would like to arouse the giant and turn its wrath on the negligent representative. To guard against this eventuality, the representative must constantly reexamine the otherwise placid constituency to locate the tender spots and provide the needed protection against the pesky opponent.

It would be incorrect, however, to suggest that slipping past the "incumbent" guard and activating the giant is an easy matter; the unseating of congressmen unexplained by other electoral factors is not that common.[9] And I rather suspect that the lack of success in waking the giant is due as much to the deepness of the giant's slumber as to the hovering care of his servant-representative. Nevertheless, the congressman rests less easily with the notion of a giant in deep sleep than does the detached observer. It all depends upon where you are sitting, in the lap of the giant or at a safe distance.

The point of this metaphor, in terms of constituency influence, is that various elements within the constituency can be activated into potentially damaging electoral activity against the congressman; for that reason an accurate perception of their policy requirements is of relevance to the congressman's behavior. This is easy in some cases, such as the one in which the representative of a cotton and soybeans constituency is called upon to legislate on farm price commodity supports. It is less easy when the same representative must legislate on foreign policy. Whereas on the matter of commodity supports the rankest outsider might perform adequately as a representative, it is hard to think of an outsider being given this responsibility on foreign policy. And why is it absurd? Because only a resident of the constituency could know or involuntarily express its attitudes on international involvement. This, of course, is the whole point of a representational system that emphasizes the constituency responsibility of a representative in residence.

In the next section the focus shifts away from the understanding and defining of party and constituency influence to the problems arising in the measurement thereof. This will not be a lengthy section, given my desire to move rather quickly to the results of an assessment of the influence of each on the five dimensions of policy.

Measurement of Party and Constituency Influence

Measuring Party Influence

Normally, researchers are forced to make a long inferential leap, and a backward one at that, from the existence of partisan alignments in legislative voting to the presence of partisan forces. Partisan-based attitudes are not identified and measured; they must be inferred. Although "simulators" have attempted to include partisan cue-taking as a factor in the congressman's decision process, their measurement of cue-taking is itself based on behavior. Hence, the partisan quality of the cue-taking must, once again, be inferred from the record of the voting.[10]

The difficulty of inferring party effects from the existence of a partisan alignment is in separating the effects of party from those of other factors in the decision process. Apropos of the current chapter, the confusion of party and constituency influence has bedeviled research on legislative behavior for some time.

Consider a division of either house on an urban question: A majority of one party is opposed to the majority of the other, a commonly accepted indicator of party voting. The vote division also follows urban-rural lines; the rural-based representatives tend to oppose, the urban-based representatives to support, government activity in solving the urban problem. The simultaneity of the partisan and the urban-rural alignments on the vote is possible because urban constituencies are inclined to elect Democrats, while rural constituencies elect Republicans.

What can one conclude with respect to this particular alignment? Is it a party division resulting from opposing partisan-based attitudes, current partisan political strategies, or some other partisan factor? Or does the vote division reflect only the conflicting needs of urban and rural constituencies, with the partisan alignment a causally meaningless by-product?

Measuring Constituency Influence

The measurement of constituency variables, in contrast to the measurement of party variables, creates problems of another sort. Here a number of measures are available, but they are of limited utility.

Among these near worthless measures are those that characterize entire constituencies in terms of census-type information: occupation, race, ethnicity, urbanization, industrialization, education, age, home ownership, indoor plumbing, and so on, ad nauseum. Such information is not totally useless. But it is less useful for political scientists than for sociologists, who are less concerned about the linkage between personal attitudes and behavior and more concerned with behavior tendencies that are associated with class, occupation, status, education, and other properties of the social milieu. For most political scientists, the causal linkage between demographic characteristics and the policy requirements of the constituency is too extended, and too weakened by the battering of other factors, to provide a good basis for explaining the congressman's voting behavior.

We need measures of the crucial intervening variables: the policy attitudes of the constituents and the attitudes and constituency perceptions of the congressman. Unfortunately, these measures are costly to obtain. I know of only one study that had the requisite resources, and that study was restricted to a little more than a hundred House districts and a sparse sampling of constituents from each district.[11] So it's back to the drawing board. But not necessarily back to census characteristics of constituents. We shall avoid them, at least for a time, by turning to an analysis of party and constituency influence that parlays the passage of time into an exemption from some of the party and constituency measurement problems.

Party Versus Constituency

Before going into the analysis, let me pay my respects to those who have struggled with the same problem but have been considerate enough to leave it unresolved. One writer would interpret party differences as an expression of constituency differences; [12] when the members of the two parties divide on an issue, the division is attributed to differences in the constituencies they represent. The theory of *constituency primacy* also applies to those instances in which differences within the parties are related to the differences in the constituencies represented. The primary objection to this theory, offered by another writer, is that one can show numerous instances in which there are party differences despite similarities in constituencies, suggesting that party has an independent effect on legislative behavior.[13]

None of these studies can be considered conclusive, because none has very sensitive measures of either constituency or party influence. For example, the party differences observed across apparently similar constituencies may actually reflect differences among the allegedly similar districts that are not reflected in crude indicators of constituency characteristics. It is my hope that my analysis design skirts some of these measurement problems.

Design of Analysis

The influence of party and constituency on the five policy dimensions is examined for the Eisenhower Congresses, the Eighty-third through the Eighty-sixth, 1953–1960. The policy position score assigned to the representative of a constituency in the Eighty-sixth Congress is compared with the score assigned in the Eighty-third. *If party influence is effective in producing differences in policy positions, one would expect a partisan turnover in the representation of a constituency to produce a change in the policy representation provided.* On the other hand, *where constituency forces are dominant and partisan influence is nil, one would expect no change in policy representation when a particular seat in Congress passes from one party to the other.*

The preceding paragraph greatly oversimplifies the analytic framework within which party and constituency influence are measured. This simplification is for the reader who is interested only in the results and wants to skip over to them. For the more critical reader I have the obligation to lay out the analytic framework in more detail.

The Eighty-third and Eighty-sixth Congresses were chosen for comparison because they represent the longest time span within the time frame of the study during which there is no change of tenancy of the White House, Eisenhower having served throughout the eight-year period. Moreover, there were minimal changes in the boundary definitions of congressional constituencies in the House, in contrast with the redistricting that took place between the last two Congresses in the core study, the Eighty-seventh and Eighty-eighth. Both considerations are important. If the constituency to which a representative is responsible—*here constituency refers to the legal definition* —experiences no boundary changes, it is reasonable to consider constituency influence to be a constant over the eight-year span. Similarly, it is very useful to be able to treat presidential influence as a constant throughout the period, as opposed, for example, to the confusion resulting from a partisan turnover of the White House, when effects of presidential influence on congressional behavior would become hopelessly confounded with the more general influence of party.

I am not so naïve as to maintain that constituency and presidential sources of variation in congressional behavior are totally absent over the eight-year period. I do believe that they are minimal. This belief is strengthened by remembering that policy positions on policy dimensions are general positions. Such general policy positions are less critically affected by minor changes in the political environment than are positions on specific questions.

Party and constituency influence are investigated by looking at the changes in scores associated with each of three different conditions as regards the occupancy of each constituency seat over time: (1) The *same person* holds the seat in both Congresses, referred to as the *holdover* condition. (2) *Different persons from the same party* serve the constituency in the two Congresses, the *person turnover* condition. (3) *Persons from different parties* occupy the seat in the two Congresses, the *partisan turnover* condition.

The effects of party and constituency on congressional behavior are measured within the framework of the following argument: It is proposed that over the period on which change in the policy position scores is observed (1953–1954 to 1959–1960) the effect of constituency influence is to limit this change. In the context of this analysis constituency is as legally defined: citizens residing in an electoral district (the state, for Senators). It would be inappropriate to the current analysis to use the more realistic definition of constituency, because this constituency changes with the occupancy of the seat, particularly in the condition of partisan turnover.

If party is to be considered as an influence on the policy positions taken by congressmen, one expects a change in the policy representation of a constituency when a *partisan turnover* occurs. We would expect to find, in the partisan turnover condition, that congressmen in the Eighty-sixth Congress take different policy positions from those of their predecessors in the Eighty-third Congress.

Why, then, consider the other two conditions, *person turnover* (without a change in party) and *holdover?* Answer: In order to fend off the very appropriate criticism that the change taking place as a result of a partisan turnover may be no greater than the change that would have occurred if the same person had served throughout or if different persons from the same party had held the office on the two occasions. Thus, support for the party influence proposition is dependent on evidence that partisan turnover produces more change than the other two conditions.

There are four reasons why congressmen in two Congresses occupying the same seat may have different scores. (1) Measurement error can produce differences in scores where no differences in policy positions exist. The other three reasons involve changes in policy positions. (2) A change in an individual's policy position occurs. (3) Different persons take different policy positions because of differences among individuals. (4) Members of different parties take different policy positions because of party differences.

Moving across the three conditions, from holdover to person turnover to partisan turnover, the likelihood of change in policy position scores increases, reflecting an increase in the number and impact of factors that can contribute to change in policy position scores. In all conditions, measurement error is a factor. In the person turnover condition, it is expected that, on the average, *inter*person variation in behavior will be greater than the *intra*person variation in the holdover condition. Finally, in the partisan turnover condition, not only is a different person representing the constituency, but he comes from a different party.

Thus, *if* partisan differences in ideology or policy attitudes are influential in congressional decision-making, the change in positional scores associated with partisan turnover should be greater than that in the other two conditions. On a policy dimension where partisan influence is high, it is also to be expected that the change associated with person turnover will be only slightly greater (if any) than the change occurring in the holdover condition. For if partisan influence is strong, two persons from the same party should behave in much the same manner, consistent with the partisan norm.

Before moving on to the results of the analysis, let me refer to an earlier point. The longitudinal format skirts some of the measurement problems usually associated with measuring the relative influence of party and constituency when several measures are taken of constituency characteristics and their effects on behavior are compared with that of party. As noted earlier, the constituency measures leave a great deal to be desired and may underestimate constituency influence. Furthermore, in the statistical procedures (correlation, regression) used in studying congressional behavior at a single point in time, constituency influence becomes intertwined with partisan influence.

In the present analysis, constituency influence is measured in terms of the stability of the policy positions recorded for representatives serving the same constituency over a period of time. Without actual measures of the sources of influence within the constituency, we can still seek to answer the question: Is congressional behavior highly stable over time as is expected where constituency influence is strong? Or is the policy representation of a constituency highly variable over time, thereby implying the weakness of constituency relative to other factors? As regards party influence, do we find that policy representation changes while constituency is held constant and party incumbency varies (from Republican to Democrat or vice versa)?

The effectiveness of the longitudinal analysis for assessing the relative influence of constituency and party derives from the semi-experimental properties of the design of analysis. Social scientists, unlike physical scientists, are forever plagued by their incapacity to conduct experiments in which the effects of one factor are held constant, permitting observations of the effects of another factor, which is allowed to vary. Given the capacity to move across time *in the present study, the experimental design format is simulated by holding constituency constant while varying party.*

Results

The assessment of the amount of change in policy representation that occurs in the three conditions, *holdover, person turnover,* and *partisan turnover,* involves the calculation of an average change score for the set of constituencies subject to each of the conditions. This change score is based on the differences in the scores for the Eighty-third and the Eighty-sixth Congresses, as computed on the individual constituencies. For example, if the congressman serving the First District in Ohio had a score of 2.75 in the Eighty-sixth Congress and the congressman serving the same district in the Eighty-third Congress had a score of 2.50 on a particular policy dimension, the difference in scores would be .25. The average change scores for the three conditions is based on such differences for the subset of constituencies included within each.

Figure 8 presents the findings for all five policy dimensions for both the House and the Senate. There are clear differences between the policy dimensions in the relative influence of party and constituency. The partisan influence is strong on social welfare, agricultural assistance, and government management, as indicated by the change when a partisan turnover takes place. The partisan influence is unmistakably less important on the dimension of international involvement, in both houses, and for civil liberties in the House. In the Senate the partisan influence on civil liberties is also less, but the difference is not a sharp one.

Before moving on to the more precise analysis of the influence of party relative to that of constituency, let us look at the degree of

Figure 8
*Policy Position Changes on Five Dimensions:
Eighty-third to Eighty-sixth Congresses*

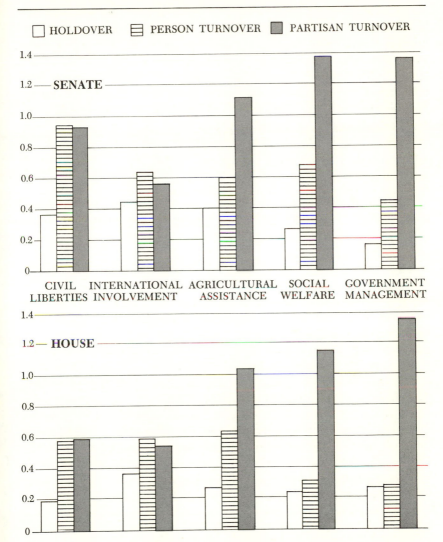

stability in the policy positions of the holdover congressmen. They exhibit the smallest change in scores on all five dimensions in both houses. The average change in scores for holdovers in the House varies from a low of .18 to a high of .35 across the five dimensions— a small change in comparison to the total range in scores of 2.00. In the Senate, the average change among holdovers shows more variability across dimensions, from a low of .16 to a high of .45. The slightly greater change among holdovers in the Senate is consistent with the commonly held view that senators are less bound by constituency constraints.

The high degree of stability in the policy positions of individual congressmen serving across the eight-year span was anticipated by earlier evidence on the stability and continuity of congressional behavior, measured in a different way. When viewing the high stability in the policy positions of congressmen serving continuously across the period of study, we should not forget that the stabilizing influence of individual resistance to change is aided by the *constant* effect of constituency influence and the *constant* effects of party constraints.

Our understanding of the effects of party and constituency is furthered, as noted earlier, by comparing the person turnover and partisan turnover conditions. If party influence is present on a dimension, it is expected that a partisan turnover will produce more change than a person turnover.

To improve the quality of this comparison, the amount of change in each condition is shown in ratio to the amount of change in the holdover condition. This takes into account the fact that the part of the change in scores that is due to measurement error will vary across the five dimensions because the measures of the several dimensions are not equally reliable. The ratio calculation also takes into account the variation in policy positions that occur on the several dimensions as a function of individual behavior changes.

Partisan Versus Person Turnover: Party Influence

The comparison between the amount of change occurring with a *partisan turnover* and that resulting from a *person turnover* is shown in Figure 9. Two dimensions, international involvement and civil liberties, show just as much change whether there is a partisan turnover or a person turnover, suggesting that the crucial component is the change in personnel rather than the change in party. I want to underscore this finding with respect to the civil liberties and international involvement dimensions by posting the reminder that it applies to both the House and the Senate.

The clear absence of partisan influence on civil liberties and international involvement stands in sharp contrast to the clear presence of party influence on the other three dimensions: government management, social welfare, and agricultural assistance. There is, in addition, no doubt that partisan influence is most clearly effective on the government management dimension: In the House the amount of change with a partisan turnover is five times that with a person turnover; and in the Senate there is three times as much change when the seat shifts between parties.

This shift on the government management dimension that occurs with a partisan turnover may be even better appreciated if we look at the change in absolute terms (Figure 8). The average change in policy representation is equivalent to moving nearly three-quarters of the length of the scale! *In effect, in both House and Senate a partisan turnover produces a reversal in the government management policy positions of representatives serving the same constituency.*

These findings, when added to the earlier ones showing a persistently strong correlation between party affiliation and policy positions on the government management dimension, go a long ways toward affirming basic attitudinal differences between the parties on policies concerning government management of economic and natural resources. Remember also that our analysis includes new members of Congress, thus implying a penetration of these partisan differences into at least the substrata of political activists from which members of Congress are recruited. These partisan differences in behavior reflect the traditional alignment of the Republican party with the business community and the ideology of free enterprise, and the Democratic party's support for the intervention of the federal government in economic affairs.

The lesser impact of party on social welfare and agricultural assistance is clearly discernible, particularly in the case of agricultural assistance. In the latter case, the lower profile of party is understandable in view of what may be relatively well defined constituency policy constraints. To illustrate: On the agricultural assis-

Figure 9
Party Versus Constituency Influence on Five Dimensions:
Partisan Turnover Change Compared to Person Turnover Change

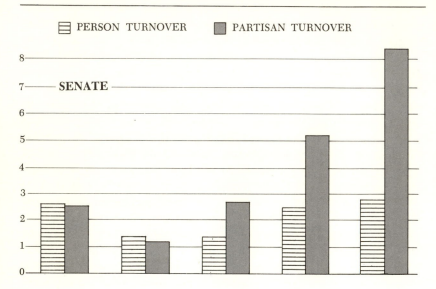

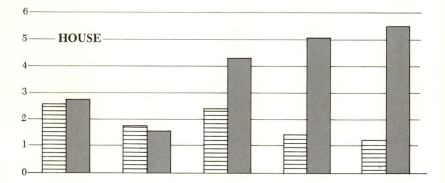

tance dimension 20 percent of the partisan turnovers in the House produce a change in scale positions *less than or equal to 0.4;* in contrast, only 5 percent of the partisan turnovers involve so small a change in position on the government management dimension.

Partisan influence on social welfare is a step below that on government management. The explanation is similar to that for agricultural assistance, but I want to defer this discussion to the final chapter on patterns of influence.

Implicit in the description of changes in policy representation has been the assumption that whenever partisan influence is effective it results in a change in policy positions that accords with common conceptions of party stances. Thus, on the three policy dimensions where a partisan effect is observed (government management, social welfare, and agricultural assistance) a turnover featuring a Republican replacement of a Democratic representative is expected to produce a shift toward less support for the policy concept. In point of fact, individual deviations from this expectation are extremely rare. On the government management dimension, out of 100 partisan turnovers only 4 show a shift in policy representation in the unexpected direction. And in these 4 cases the change was 0.4 or less, the kind of change that may easily result from errors in measurement. Hard as it may be to believe, the uniformity of partisan turnover effects is even greater on the dimension of social welfare. On the agricultural assistance dimension there is a slight exception to the pattern in the persons of a few Republicans who replace Democrats and provide significantly greater support for agricultural assistance.

To summarize briefly, the change observed in the partisan turnover condition may be interpreted as change in the predicted direction. Substantively, this means that *the replacement of a Republican by a Democrat will shift the policy representation of a constituency from less to more support for government management of the economy and control of natural resource development, to more support for federal government social welfare activities, and from lower to higher support for agricultural assistance programs.* Of course, the converse holds as well.

This assessment of the impact of party on policy representation is supported by the behavior of the Eighty-ninth Congress, which was elected to office in the Lyndon Johnson Texas-style victory in 1964. As a result of this victory the Democratic majority in Congress was increased considerably; the Democrats occupied 68 percent of the seats, thereby outnumbering the Republicans by slightly more than two-to-one. This strong Democratic majority provided the votes for the passage of a large number of programs, increasing the involvement of the federal government in matters associated with the government management and social welfare dimensions, commonly combined and referred to as liberal domestic legislation. In light of the evidence of this study I am disposed to be very skeptical of the thesis that it was President Johnson's mastery of legislative skills, or his famous "treatment," or his ear glued to the telephone that produced the legislative output. The opposition was simply outnumbered, not outfought, nor outthought. I would grant only that some minimum leadership was required, analogous to pointing the finger at the policy target.

In my eagerness to sort out the five policy dimensions according to the relative influence of party and constituency, I passed rather casually over the finding of no partisan influence on international involvement and civil liberties. In one sense this finding should occasion no surprise. Public views on both civil liberties (particularly civil rights) and international involvement have long been characterized as regional phenomena, implying a strong constituency influence.

Despite the fact that congressmen and other political leaders have underwritten the norm that foreign policy should not be a partisan affair, it still comes as a surprise to discover that a partisan turnover yields no more change in policy representation than does a person turnover. However, this does not eliminate the possibility that *the change in policy representation occurring with a partisan turnover may still be in a direction consistent with the partisan change in the seat, whereas the direction of the shift in a person turnover is unpredictable.* To follow the lead provided by the other dimensions, one might expect a Republican replacement of a Democrat to produce a move toward less support for international involvement. This expectation finds little support. Granted, there are shreds of evidence to be used by the internationally minded Demophile; however, the slight imbalance indicating Democrats to be more activist in international affairs is insufficient to support the inference of a partisan effect.

The absence of a partisan direction in the policy changes on the civil rights dimension is even clearer. There *is* the interesting phenomenon that nearly all the new congressmen are more supportive of civil liberties than their predecessors! This is true whether the seat goes from one party to the other, or the same party maintains control.

The apparent shift toward a stronger civil liberties position could be more show than substance. It is possible that the new representatives are no more civil libertarian than the old. The differences in scores may have arisen because the members of the earlier Congress were faced with policy decisions on legislation that was more aggressively civil libertarian than the policy proposals considered at the later time. Consequently, the new representatives could favor more of the legislation than their predecessors even though their positions on the dimensions were no different. Only the scores would be different. However, if such were the case, we would expect the holdover congressmen also to appear more civil libertarian in the later Congress. This is clearly not true.

One alternative interpretation is that new congressmen are truly more sympathetic to the civil rights movement, and to civil liberties in general, than those who served before them from the same constituencies. This trend among the recent additions to the congressional corps is in step with the country as a whole during these years, toward a greater support for the rights of blacks.

If this conclusion regarding civil liberties is correct, it supports the view expressed in the introductory chapter that Congress reflects the "effective" political forces in the nation. Thus, even during the fifties when Black Power existed in the form of Negro aspiration, the emergence of the blacks as a more potent political force altered the outlook of Congress through the infusion of new blood.

Thus we see illustrated the mechanism by which Congress alters its collective point of view: through the entry of new members rather than the conversion of continuing members. This dovetails nicely with my interpretation of the success of the Johnson administration in securing the passage of liberal domestic legislation. I don't rule out the possibility that Congress changes its policy stance as its holdover members change their minds. But the stability of personal policy positions observed previously casts serious doubt on the expectation that old members will adopt new positions.

A POINT OF METHODOLOGY

In this place, let me address the doubting Thomases who

object, quite correctly, that the comparisons among the three conditions—holdover, person turnover, and partisan turnover—are not just comparisons between three different conditions of seat occupancy over time but also between different types of constituencies. Implication? A measurement of the effect of a partisan turnover that is based on a distinctive subset of constituencies can not be generalized to the universe of congressmen serving the national set of constituencies.

The estimates of the effect of a partisan turnover might be quite different if one looked at this in relation to the changes in policy representation that occur for the person turnovers in the same set of constituencies instead of comparing the partisan turnover in one set of constituencies with the person turnover in another set. Unfortunately, given the large number of one-party constituencies, there simply are not enough constituencies in which both conditions are operative in the eight-year period under study.

The proper perspective on the foregoing analysis, in my view, is as follows: Given the subsets of constituencies falling into each of the three conditions, holdover, person turnover, and partisan turnover, *a comparison among policy dimensions* reveals different levels of party, personal, and constituency influence. This evidence alone is not sufficient to support the case that partisan influence is absent on international involvement and civil liberties and present on social welfare, agricultural assistance, and government management. However, it is a very powerful supplement to evidence adduced from other aspects of the full analysis concerning partisan and constituency influence.

Conclusions

A brief review of the analysis of the relative influence of *constituency* and *party* may sharpen the point of a rather long chapter. *Constituency influence* appears to be strongest where it is least expected, on the international involvement dimension. The change in policy representation, calculated as an average of the effects of partisan *and* person turnovers, is clearly least on this dimension in both houses. As we shall see later, the pattern of influence on the international involvement dimension is a complicated one and has some of the wrappings of an enigma.

Constituency also appears as an important influence on the civil liberties dimension in that it is clearly stronger than the party influence, if the latter exists at all. This conclusion is based on the finding that a partisan turnover contributes no more to a change in policy representation than does a person turnover. In other words, there is no evidence that the addition of a partisan change component to the personnel turnover adds to the amount of change observed in the policy positions of succeeding representatives.

The influence of *party*, relative to that of constituency, increases as we go to agricultural assistance, from there to social welfare, and then to government management. The government management dimension appears to be the kind of policy dimension on which partisan unity is a national phenomenon, on which the parties are clearly divided, and one where constituency influence is sharply dampened.

References

1. Donald E. Stokes and Warren E. Miller, "Party Government and the Saliency of Congress," *Public Opinion Quarterly* 26 (Winter 1962), pp. 531–546.

2. Randall B. Ripley, *Party Leaders in the House of Representatives* (Washington, D.C.: Brookings, 1967), p. 198.

3. Julius Turner, *Party and Constituency: Pressures on Congress*, revised by Edward V. Schneier, Jr. (Baltimore, Md.: Johns Hopkins Press, 1970).

4. Randall B. Ripley, *op. cit.*, and *Majority Party Leadership in Congress* (Boston: Little, Brown, 1969); Charles O. Jones, *Minority Party in Congress* (Boston: Little, Brown, 1970); Ralph K. Huitt, "Democratic Party Leadership in the Senate," *American Political Science Review* 55 (June 1961), pp. 333–344.

5. Lewis A. Froman and Randall B. Ripley, "Conditions For Party Leadership: Case of the House Democrats," *American Political Science Review* 59 (March 1965), pp. 52–63.

6. Evidence of the better representation of the congressman's supporters is provided by Warren E. Miller, "Majority Rule and the Representative System of Government," in E. Allardt and Y. Littunen, eds., *Cleavages, Ideologies and Party Systems: Contributions to Comparative Political Sociology* (Transactions of the Westermarck Society, 1964), pp. 343–376.

7. This approach to the study of representation is taken by Warren E. Miller and Donald E. Stokes, "Constituency Influence in Congress," *American Political Science Review* 57 (March 1963), pp. 45– 56.

8. Aage R. Clausen, "A Theory of Involuntary Representation," seminar paper (typescript), University of Michigan, 1958.

9. In general, the unseating of incumbents is the exceptional phenomenon. See, for example, Richard Witmer, "Aging of the House," *Political Science Quarterly* 79 (1964); Nelson W. Polsby, "Institutionalization of the U.S. House of Representatives," *American Political Science Review* 62 (March 1968), pp. 144–

168. Furthermore, there is evidence that much of the turnover that does occur is a function of electoral determinants unrelated to constituency reactions to the performance of their representative. See Angus Campbell, "Surge and Decline: A Study of Electoral Change," *Public Opinion Quarterly* 24 (Fall 1960).

10. Cleo Cherryholmes and Michael Shapiro, *Representatives and Roll Calls* (Indianapolis, Ind.: Bobbs-Merrill, 1969); Donald R. Matthews and James A. Stimson, "Decision-Making by U.S. Representatives: A Preliminary Model," Sidney Ulmer, ed., *Political Decision-Making* (New York: Van Nostrand Reinhold, 1970), pp. 14–39.

11. Miller and Stokes, *op. cit.*, pp. 45–56.

12. Lewis A. Froman, *Congressmen and their Constituencies* (Skokie, Ill.: Rand McNally, 1963).

13. Thomas A. Flinn, "Party Responsibility in the States," *American Political Science Review* 58 (March 1964), pp. 60–71.

7

Roots of
Policy Orientations

The study of the roots of the policy orientations of members of Congress is greatly facilitated by the high level of stability found in the policy positions over time. This stability enhances our chances of understanding the origins of the policy positions for two reasons. In the first place, there is simply less to explain than would be the case if legislators were constantly changing their positions. More importantly, however, the stability in the legislators' policy positions suggests that *the roots of the policy stances are firmly and deeply imbedded in the political soil that nurtures and supports the congressman.*

Not only have we found a high degree of stability in the policy positions of individual members, there is also a moderate to high degree of stability in the positions held by different members from the same party holding the same congressional seat. In other words, a common constituency origin and the sharing of a political affiliation work together in limiting the range of positions taken by different occupants of the same seat.

It appears, then, that the roots of congressional policy orientations are solidly implanted in the constituency soil. Therefore, the major effort of analysis is to explain the variations in the policy positions held by congressmen representing *different* constituencies, with little need to be concerned with variations in positions held by different occupants of the same seat from the same party. Of course, we must remain concerned with the impact of a partisan turnover.

In the analysis thus far a number of sources of policy positions have been considered—region, party, constituency, ideology, and the president—but there has been no detailed analysis of the effects of each of these. It has been shown that party differences are large on some policy dimensions and virtually nonexistent on others. Constituency has been shown to vary in its impact across the dimensions. The impact of region has been noted in the analysis of policy profiles and ideology, but at a fairly general level.

This chapter continues the study of the effects of constituency, party, and region. However, it includes also a very important addition to these three factors, one that cuts across all three. This variable will be called *state party*, expressive of the fact that there exist 100 state parties across the 50 states in the Union, considering only the Democratic and Republican parties.

Sources of policy positions that will not be explored in further detail in this chapter are ideology and presidential influence. The role of ideology is left pretty much to surmise and speculative inference since I have no independent test of its paternal status. All we have to go on is a remarkable resemblance between the policy profiles of a large number of congressmen and the profiles of the well-known ideologies of liberalism and conservatism. As for presidential influence, the next chapter is devoted to that topic.

One question that may arise in the reader's mind, and quite properly so, is: What ever happened to pressure groups? Here we are discussing the forces affecting the policy positions of congressmen, and not even a nod of recognition has been made in the direction of pressure groups, alias interest groups, alias special interest groups, alias lobbies. First of all, it should be recognized that the reward offered for the heads of the villainous pressure groups has been greatly decreased in the last few years. The latest word is that the legislator, at the national if not at the state and local level, is not the helpless and corrupt tool of the all-powerful interest groups that he was once made out to be. It has nearly gotten to the point where the poor lobbyist representing the group interests has become a pitiable figure, beseeching the congressman's ear, plying him with favors without the slightest guarantee of any return, while running the risk of being scolded and scorned like a common cur! I stretch the point here to emphasize the sharpness of the rejection of the image of the congressman's policy decision as nothing more than a mechanical response to the balance of pressure-group forces bearing upon the point of decision.[1]

The more skeptical view of the change in the congressional image may be that the helpless tool is now seen as the willing tool, in an atmosphere of genuine cooperation. However, the prevalent view is, I think, more like this: Most congressmen occupy seats that are virtually sinecures—over 70 percent of the seats in the House, for example. Their political organizations are personal pieces of political property on which reliance may be placed in repeated elections. These organizations will certainly involve interest groups on whom the congressman is at least partially dependent and with whom he is probably in sympathy, such as a labor union organization in an industrial district. Other interest groups must *go to* the congressman and win his favor to the point of getting a hearing. As his incumbency becomes well-established, however, the congressman becomes more independent of even his most consistent backers, for they need him as much as, or more than, he needs them. On the other hand, the congressman is probably sufficiently sympathetic to the views of those groups who most consistently support him that his own policy preferences will seldom be the cause of a falling-out.

Another reason for not giving special attention to the influence of interest groups is that much of this influence is compatible with, and integrated within, the general measures of constituency, state, or region. This is not to deny that a sharper articulation of the role of interest groups as policy clients of the congressman is possible. On the other hand, that is not an easy task; the strength of interest groups is difficult to measure. The data are hard to come by, particularly at the congressional district level, a territorial division of political consequence that is seldom used as a data collection and display unit.

Finally, I can ignore interest groups, as such, with some measure of impunity because I am not concerned with legislative battles over single pieces of legislation. The focus here is on a general policy position that affects particular decisions but is not represented by any one such decision. It is my assumption that the congressman's response to interest-group pressures, over a variety of policy decisions, is consistent with his general policy position. Furthermore, these policy positions do not seem to be greatly affected by transient political forces such as interest group pressures at particular points in time; if this were the case the earlier observations on stability would not have been possible. In sum, my argument is that interest-group views are incorporated into the congressman's general policy position and reflected in the measures used in this study to explain that policy position.

Sources of Policy Positions: A Strategy for Analysis

In the presentation of the policy dimension theory that occupies a central position in this study of congressional decision behavior, the stress has been upon stability rather than change, upon simplicity and generality rather than complexity and specificity. The import of the evidence has been in the same direction. This emphasis is about to be carried over into an analysis of the sources of the policy positions held by members of Congress. It will be argued, and shown, that most of the variation in the policy positions held by different congressmen is associated with a few major contours of the American political landscape: *party* as an important political affiliation of constituents and representatives; *region* as a geographic-political classification of Senate and House constituencies; *state* as a major political subsystem inclusive of Senate and House constituencies; and two characteristics of American work and life style, *occupation* (blue-collar percentage of the work force) and *urbanization*.

It is my thesis that most of the difference in the policy stances of congressmen are related to these major aspects of American society and politics and, in a statistical-analytic sense, can be accounted for thereby. This relatively cautious, yet not entirely modest, statement deliberately avoids the imputation of causality to these major aspects. The properties of the congressman and his constituency to which I relate his policy positions are not causal factors; rather they are the outstanding features of the political landscape, which summarize and contain the more numerous set of specific causal factors.

A good example of what I mean concerns a finding that regional differences are strongly evident in the policy positions of senators and representatives. This does not permit the inference that region is the cause of the members' policy positions. For region is a composite of a number of characteristics that describe the constituencies located within a region and a number of factors that have affected the congressman's policy orientations (how he looks at and responds to policy matters). The inference drawn from this study, when regional differences in policy positions occur, is that some of the things that make regions different also cause the behavior of members of Congress from different regions to diverge.

Support for the thesis that congressional policy positions can be comprehended with reference to a few general aspects of our society and its politics is dependent upon the identification of differences in the origins and environments of congressmen that bear rather directly upon their policy views. This implies a need to get at differences among congressmen, and the forces affecting them, that are political differences; or if you prefer, the need is to measure policy-relevant differences in the factors that determine congressional policy positions and decisions.

Census-Type Constituency Measures: A Poor Strategy

Unfortunately, political or policy-relevent variables or factors are difficult to measure, at least in a precise and direct manner. In view of this difficulty, one option that has been pursued by countless studies, and with relatively little success, has been that of using economic-sociological characteristics of constituencies.[2] Sometimes these indicators—including everything from ethnic background to leaky plumbing—are scooped into the analysis with little thought as to their ability to distinguish between constituencies in terms of policy interest and persuasions.

There are several problems with such efforts to account for differences in the policy positions of congressmen. The first problem is that most constituencies are so heterogeneous that the variation *within* constituencies makes it virtually impossible to find any characteristic, or even any combination of characteristics, that can clearly represent this heterogeneous mass by some summary index value or values. The second problem is that only in the pure world of Marxist theory, the day before the outbreak of the revolution when class conflict reaches its peak, do economic and class conditions predicate political attitudes; therefore, leaky faucets, level of income, and the occupational structure of a constituency are less than adequate predictors of policy differences between constituencies.

Let me illustrate these two points with the example of the congressman representing what has been referred to as a blue-collar constituency. While it is true that such a congressman is more likely to take policy positions attuned to the interests and views of blue-collar workers than will a congressman representing a white-collar suburban district, or a corn-belt constituency, the differences are seldom as sharp as one might think, or as highly related to the proportion of blue-collar workers in the work force. One reason for this is that electoral districts, even congressional districts, are relatively heterogeneous. A district that is heavily blue-collar, comparatively speaking, also contains businessmen, professionals, and a variety of white-collar workers, from shoe salesmen to bank clerks. Furthermore, not all blue-collar workers are millhands and factory workers; there are also the trades (carpenters, plumbers, bricklayers, wheelwrights) which may, because of their semiprofessional character and income, have economic interests and political attitudes at variance with those of the semiskilled and unskilled workers.

It is, therefore, unreasonable to expect measures of the characteristics of entire constituencies to be keenly reflective of the differences between constituencies. The same type of problem bedevils political pundits who try to make sense out of election returns when relying upon measures of the ethnic, racial, religious, and economic composition of election districts, be they states or precincts. The variation *within* districts is simply too great relative to the variation *between* districts.

The third problem with the census-type indicator approach is that it characterizes the entire constituency, or at least this has been the general practice. Yet it is more realistic to think of the congressman as representative of only those of his constituents from whom he derives most of his electoral support.

As an illustration of the inefficacy of economic-sociological characteristics as predictors of congressional policy positions, I report the results of an examination of two such measures: urbanization of constituency [3] and blue-collar percentage of the work force in the constituency.[4] Both of these variables will be used in the later analysis, but in a different way. The question here is: How much of the variation in the policy positions of senators and representatives can be explained (in a statistical sense) by urbanization and occupational characteristics of constituencies?

Explanation *in a statistical sense* refers to the extent of similarity between the ordering of congressmen on measures of policy dimensions and the ordering of congressmen as regards the urbanization of their constituencies, or the percentage of the work force that is blue-collar. The degree of similarity in the orderings is translated into a statement of covariation, and we end up talking about the proportion of the variation in one variable that is associated with the variation in the second variable. It is at this point that reference is made to the proportion of the variation in one variable (policy positions on a dimension) that is "statistically explained" by the variation in a second variable (urbanization of the congressman's constituency).

Although we can talk about the proportion of the variation in the congressmen's policy positions that is statistically explained by our knowledge of the congressmen's party, or certain constituency features, or by regional differences, social scientists often stop short of equating the statistically based explanation with a causal explanation. It is clear that causality can not be inferred solely from statistical findings; it must be buttressed by knowledge of causality drawn from other sources. We might find, for example, that there is a similarity in the ordering of congressmen in their strength of preference for a flavor of ice cream and their support for social welfare legislation. In a statistical sense the variation in flavor preference is explaining a certain percentage of the variation in positions on social welfare, but one would be extremely reluctant to infer a causal explanation. We are on somewhat firmer footing when attributing causality to the relation between urbanization of a congressman's constituency and his support of social welfare legislation. It is generally recognized that welfare programs are directed more toward urban areas, even if one uses the broad concept of social welfare used here, from education to poverty relief. Also we recognize a political tradition of urban liberalism and rural conservatism that has an existence independent of the particular interests involved in a piece of legislation. Nevertheless, our attribution of causality is very vague, for it refers to various constituency properties that are not measured directly.

With respect to the analysis at hand, the foregoing digression on statements of causality from statistical results is less than crucial. The percentage of the variation in the policy positions on the five dimensions that is statistically explained by our two constituency variables is quite low. This was my expectation in view of my low regard for such constituency measures. Figure 10 gives the per-

Figure 10

*Percentage of Variation in Policy Positions Explained
(statistically) by* Urbanization *of Constituency*

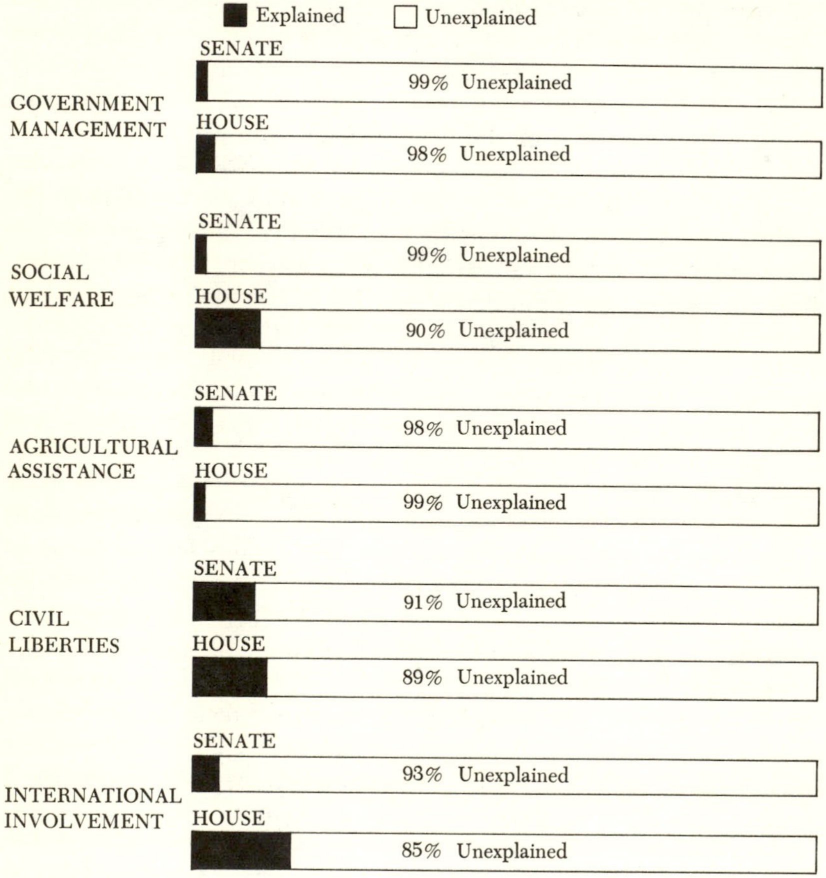

■ Explained   ☐ Unexplained

GOVERNMENT MANAGEMENT

SENATE — 99% Unexplained

HOUSE — 98% Unexplained

SOCIAL WELFARE

SENATE — 99% Unexplained

HOUSE — 90% Unexplained

AGRICULTURAL ASSISTANCE

SENATE — 98% Unexplained

HOUSE — 99% Unexplained

CIVIL LIBERTIES

SENATE — 91% Unexplained

HOUSE — 89% Unexplained

INTERNATIONAL INVOLVEMENT

SENATE — 93% Unexplained

HOUSE — 85% Unexplained

centage of variation explained by the *most* effective of the two variables, urbanization. The data are given for all five dimensions in both houses, with the percentage of variation explained by urbanization being an average across the six Congresses of the core study. It seemed unnecessary to repeat the dreary demonstration for the weaker of the two variables, percentage of work force that is blue-collar.

The strongest showing of urbanization appears in the House on the international involvement dimension where 15 percent of the variation is explained; urbanization does less than half as well on this dimension in the Senate. Indeed, urbanization never explains more than 15 percent of the voting behavior on a dimension, and often as not explains 1 to 2 percent, which is to say no percent at all. Emphasizing the weakness of summary measures of the properties of entire constituencies, is the distinctly weaker showing when the constituency is a senator's state; the same problem encountered at the district level is simply magnified—the constituency is too heterogeneous to be easily represented by measures such as urbanization or blue-collarness.

The curious reader may be wondering at the reasons for such differences in the impact of urbanization as do occur across the policy dimensions. But let us skip them for the moment; they will be discussed at a later stage of the analysis. The only issue here is the utility of measures of constituency properties as predictors of congressional decision-making behavior; this issue stands resolved against such utility. Let me assure the reader that the weakness of constituency characteristics as predictors of congressional behavior is well illustrated here and further documentation is readily available. Let me also point out that urbanization is generally one of the more powerful constituency variables, so the illustration is not biased in favor of the general conclusion.

Party, Region, and State: A Good Strategy

The dismal performance of the constituency characteristics stands in sharp contrast to two studies of congressional voting (in the House) that have achieved a high degree of success in predicting the members' votes, using other kinds of information. These are computer-simulation studies wherein an attempt is made to simulate the decision processes of individual members. Given information on the member and his constituency as well as information on the content of the legislative motions, the member's vote on each roll call is predicted. The results have been dramatic, with prediction success at around the 85 percent level.[5]

In reviewing these studies rather closely, it appeared to me that the reason for the prediction success lay in the inclusion of three characteristics: party, region, and state. (One of the studies offers the observation that the cues the member received from other members of the same state party delegation were very important in the decision process.)[6] But the nature of both simulation models precludes an accounting of the contribution of these three variables to the voting decisions. Accordingly, the hunch that state, party, and region are major sources of influence in the policy positions of members of the Congress needs to be tested. Before engaging the analytic machinery, let us consider why region, party, and state may be so relevant to policy differences among congressmen.

PARTY

The party affiliation of members of Congress is a unique illustration of a political variable of the sort we need more of if congressional decision-making is to be more precisely understood than it is at present. I say that party affiliation is unique, because it is an important political characteristic of the congressman *and* it is easily available to the researcher. Seldom does that combination occur. There is little need, after the extensive consideration that has been given to party, to dwell further on the nature of the partisan influence.

There are two things that *will* be done with party in this analysis that have not been done in earlier parts of this study. First the effect of party will be more precisely specified; second, the effect of party will be looked at in relation to the other variables affecting policy positions, and its relative contribution will be assayed.

REGION: REGION PARTY

As the subtitle suggests, the effect of region will be assessed, but the assessment will be made in terms of region party. In other words, our inspection of regional differences in congressional policy positions will be conducted within each of the parties separately. No attempt will be made, for example, to compare all Midwest congressmen with all Northeast congressmen. Rather, the comparison will be made between Midwest and Northeast Republicans, and between Midwest and Northeast Democrats.

One reason for looking at regional effects *within* parties is that party differences are often so strong that regional differences can not be clearly noted when Republicans are thrown in with Democrats. More importantly, however, I think it makes good sense to give priority to the most politically relevant variable, party; subsequently, an investigation of regional differences within parties can be used to expose additional sources of influence on the policy-making process.

The region variable consists of eight regions.

Northeast:	Maine, New Hampshire, Vermont, Connecticut, Rhode Island, Massachusetts
Middle Atlantic:	New York, Pennsylvania, New Jersey, Delaware
East North Central:	Ohio, Michigan, Indiana, Illinois, Wisconsin
West North Central:	Minnesota, Iowa, North Dakota, South Dakota, Nebraska, Kansas
Mountain:	Montana, Wyoming, Colorado, New Mexico, Utah, Idaho, Nevada, Arizona
Pacific:	California, Oregon, Washington, Alaska, Hawaii
Border:	Missouri, Kentucky, Tennessee, Oklahoma, Maryland, West Virginia
South:	Virginia, North Carolina, South Carolina, Georgia, Florida, Alabama, Louisiana, Mississippi, Texas, Arkansas

The use of region in the description of policy differences follows in a long and sturdy tradition of political analysis shared by political historians, political scientists, journalists, and a few stray sociologists. Sometimes the regional differences are quite clearly understood, as in the case of race politics; at other times the sources of the recognizable differences remain a bit of a mystery, a condition conducive to overly facile explanation. A case in point is the 40-year-old generalization that it is the insular quality of life in the Midwest that leads to its "isolationism," while the exposed, cosmopolitan coastal existence produces the "internationalism" of the East and the Pacific West. Such reasoning hardly dispels any mysteries, although it has the staying power of a simpleminded idea anchored in a comfortable analogy. Nevertheless, the regional differences are there; they are persistent and sometimes quite substantial; and they should not be ignored even though they are imprecisely defined and measured by the traditional regional classification.

STATE: STATE PARTY

The strategy of using the fifty states of the Union as sources of differences in the policy positions of congressmen is not commonly employed; state party has been entirely overshadowed by region party. The one way in which political scientists have used state is in the designation of state party delegations—Idaho Democrats, Illinois Republicans—as subgroups of the political parties within the Congress whose members consult with each other on political and policy matters, either in formal caucus or in informal get-togethers.[7] The intrastate party consultation is deemed to be a natural outgrowth of some commonality in constituency interests and of an element of identification with the home state.

There is probably fairly general agreement, although precious little evidence, that the state delegations, particularly within each party, are inclined to be unified on matters of common state interest. Paradoxically, there is less agreement, but more evidence, on the extent to which interactions among members of a state party delegation lead to common policy decisions on matters where a common state interest does not exist.

Clearly, I do not have the kind of information needed to isolate the effects on policy decisions that derive from the individual's membership in a state party delegation. Instead, I incorporate this kind of group influence in a more general measurement of the influence of state party on the members' behavior. In this measurement, the level of policy agreement among members of a state party delegation is attributed to a variety of sources, which I can suggest but can not demonstrate. Given the relative inattention to state party as a source of policy positions in the literature on congressional politics, let me take a little time on this topic. First let me specify what I mean by state party.

State party refers to all citizens of a state who consider themselves to be party affiliates—Democrats, Republicans, Conservatives, Socialists—or can, without hesitation, express a preference for one party over the other. This definition is fairly inclusive. However, it does not preclude the strong possibility that the most effective citizens of the state party will be but a small subset of the party affiliates. On the other hand, this definition of state party does allow for the party influence that derives from the political orientations passed down through successive generations of partisan identifiers who are otherwise fairly lackadaisical in their activities as political partisans. John

Q.'s father, a lifelong Republican affiliate, may never have raised a finger in political affairs, yet he may have possessed a partisan political orientation that he passed on to his son. Consequently, the father served as an agent of partisan political socialization and contributed to the influence of state party.

Now attention to state parties may appear somewhat beside the point at a time preceded by a long-term trend toward the nationalization of political issues, away from the fractionalization inherent in local issues. A candidate for president can give the same speech in different states without fear of losing the attention of his audience, at least not on the grounds of local irrelevance, because the top issues are likely to be of widespread interest.

Looking at state party from the bottom up, it may also appear that state party is largely irrelevant to the member of the House representing a constituency that is but a subset of the state party constituency. Surely his policy orientation derives from this more locally defined base and from his long experience in relating to this more specialized constituency. Thus it would appear that the state party is really relevant only to the senator whose constituency, realistically defined, is the state party.

However, a deeper probe suggests that the local roots of policy orientations are not tidily confined within such arbitrary boundaries as those often used in defining House districts. A particularly apt illustration of this argument is the congressional district that slices through a metropolitan area, having no more justification for its existence than its equivalence in size to an equally unnaturally defined district. Indeed, it is the exceptional rather than the usual congressional district that makes any sense with respect to media patterns, existing communities, economic arrangements. Thus to talk about the congressional district as the context in which the congressman's attitudes and beliefs are formed may be to talk nonsense. Granted, it is possible that the congressman is a product of a part of his constituency and will thereby be representative of it. But grant also the possibility that the congressman is partly a product of a larger context than the constituency he represents. In particular, accord a hearing to the proposition that the American state provides a separable, bounded context in which the attitudes and values of the residents are formed and by which they are influenced.

There are several bases for the claim that the state, and particularly the state party, is an important element of the individual's political socialization and thereby a potent force in the process out of which the congressman's policy positions have emerged.[8] First of all, there is the state's unique historical experience as a distinct political entity that developed into a sense of state consciousness prior to admission into the Union; Alaska and Hawaii are recent examples of this more general pattern.

An additional point to keep in mind is that the organization of the federal government along state lines, with independent state jurisdiction over many important facets of the citizens' lives, to a degree unappreciated because of the attention drawn to the more dramatic functioning of the national government, have made states more than administrative areas. The primary and secondary educational system is a local and state jurisdiction, and in times of increasing costs, the higher education system is increasingly becoming a responsibility of the state government. The judicial and enforcement system is primarily effective within state boundaries. A variety of social welfare programs are conducted at the state level, although the federal government may provide a substantial portion of the funds. And the states continue to differ in their response to and utilization of federal programs, in addition to differing in their own programs.

Finally, and importantly for my argument of the state as a bounded context, there is the fact that the flow of communications provided by the mass media, as well as the pattern of media organization, is statecentric. Newspapers, radio, and television aim at audiences within state boundaries and draw their news from sources within the state as well as from national sources.

The distinctive aspects of the political, social, economic, and religious milieus of the different states have led to the development of state parties of distinctive character. Oregon Democrats are not the same as Texas Democrats, and are possibly even distinctive relative to the Democrats of the neighboring state of Washington. As the late V. O. Key, Jr., a leading expert on state politics, stated, "The states, as substantial political entities in the federal system, develop party structures which must be founded on the cleavages peculiar to each state. . . . Thus, in a group of Midwestern and Plains states, the Democratic party, if it is to exist at all as a statewide party, must ordinarily exist as a party different from the Democratic party of an industrial state." [9]

The implication of this view of the states and the state parties for the behavior of members of Congress is nicely stated in another passage from Key, "Modern political parties . . . rest on foundations of support by groups of voters. The composition, the interests, the passions and the aspirations of these blocs of voters tend to fix the style of politics and the policy orientations of the leadership echelons of the parties." [10]

Certainly, members of Congress may be regarded as members of the leadership echelons who are in communication with other state party leaders, official and unofficial, sharing information and views that contribute to a sharing of political attitudes. The members of Congress may have been attracted to the party because of its views as represented by the visible partisans in the state. In some states the candidates for Congress are recruited by the party. Hence there are many ways in which candidates for Congress may have been exposed to or drawn from the mainstream of state party politics.

In this description of the three variables—party, region party, and state party—there resides some potential for confusion concerning the relation of "party" to "region party" and "state party." All the reader need remember is that when the word "party" is used by itself without reference to state or region, the object of designation is the national party. In looking at the impact of "party," the focus is upon the party differences that can be observed at the national level. However, not all Republicans are exactly alike (nor all Democrats) raising the question, What accounts for intraparty differences? This is where region and state come in, as possible sources of differences within the parties.

Another source of differences within the parties is the difference in constituency characteristics. The two properties of urbanization and blue-collarness will be used to see if these constituency properties can account for some of the intraparty variation in policy positions.

In sum, after seeing how much of the variation in the policy positions of congressmen can be explained by party differences at a national level, attention turns to the power of the remaining four variables (region, state, and the two constituency properties) to explain the variation within each of the parties. Out of all this analysis will emerge a total picture of the roots of policy orientations among members of the United States Congress.

Two sets of analyses are described. Analysis I deals directly with the capacity of the five variables to explain variations in policy positions. One outcome of this analysis will be a rough idea of the relative importance of each of the five variables on each of the five policy dimensions. A second outcome will be a statement of the total proportion of the variation on the individual policy dimensions that is attributable to the five variables that reflect the major contours of the American political topography.

Analysis II focuses upon the character of, and meaning to be attached to, state party influence. This involves a study of the stability of state party delegation policy positions, and an assessment of the degree of similarity between the policy postures of the states' party delegations in the House and Senate.

Five Major Sources of Policy Positions: Analysis I

The proposition on which this first analysis leans is that the sources of variation in congressional policy positions are well reflected in the major contours of the American political scene. It is not necessary to become involved in an intricate and complex analysis, nor to become entangled in the spidery web of a computer simulation, to obtain a pretty fair working understanding of the forces related to the policy decisions made by congressmen.

The evidence for and against the general proposition is drawn from a close study of the Congresses of the Eisenhower Administration.[11] These are the Eighty-fifth and Eighty-sixth Congresses, the middle Congresses of the set of core Congresses on which the full study is based.

The study of all Congresses was rejected on the grounds of redundancy, given the high degree of stability in policy positions. The study of a pair of Congresses, as opposed to a single Congress, was dictated by the desire to have the study of one Congress to serve as a backup for the results observed on a second Congress. I am always a bit reluctant to rely heavily on a single Congress, whereas two Congresses producing constant results increases my confidence in those results many times over. The test of consistency was a severe one in the present case because the two Congresses bracket the 1958 election in which nearly fifty Republican House members were replaced by Democrats, meaning a substantial change in the composition of the House. Finally, the two Congresses were chosen from a single presidential administration in order to hold the presidential factor as constant as possible.

The study is confined to the House of Representatives; such will not be the case for the second analysis in this chapter. Once again, the House is chosen when the investigation becomes somewhat detailed because the small membership of the Senate greatly inhibits such an analysis.

Two different views of the sources of policy positions are presented. In the first, the focus is upon the total variation in policy positions on each of the policy dimensions and in each of the Congresses. The second view focuses on the sources of variation within each of the parties, to give us an idea of how much of the variation in the policy positions of Republicans (or Democrats) can be attributed to regional differences, how much to state differences, and how much to constituency differences.

Focus: The Whole Congress

The big picture that is projected from the analysis onto Figure 11 shows that a very large percentage of the variation in policy positions is associated with the five variables used in this analysis: party, constituency (two variables), region, and state.[12] On four of the five policy dimensions, the five variables, on the average, account for 85 percent of the variation, and never account for less than 76 percent. On the fifth dimension, international involvement, the variation accounted for drops to slightly above 50 percent, still a quite respectable showing as these things go.

Our relative inability to account for the differences in policy positions on international involvement in terms of the major contours of American politics, party, constituency, region, and state, is a failure that is remarkably easy to bear. And I take great pleasure in explaining why this is so.

The first reason stems from my persistent insistence that political activities and behavior can be expected to vary across domains and dimensions of policy. Furthermore, the deviance of the international involvement dimension fits nicely with a general pattern of influence

Figure 11

Percentage of Variation in Policy Positions Explained by
Party, Constituency *(urbanization, blue-collar % of work force),*
Region, *and* State

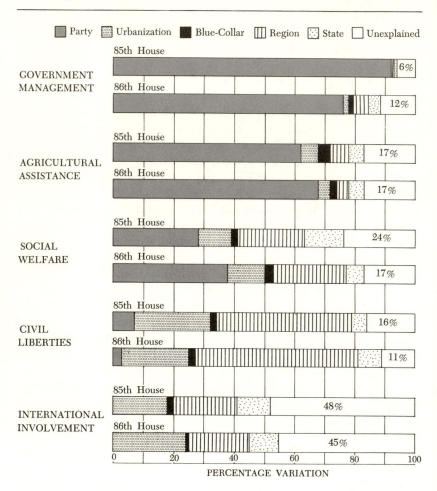

across the five policy dimensions. The other four dimensions are all domestic policy dimensions, where some combination of party, constituency, region, and state can be expected to have a substantial impact. Many of the issues on these dimensions strike close to the homes of most Americans and are concerns of long standing. Consequently, the policy cleavages on these dimensions have had time to form, have had the basis for formation, and have become major features of the political scene. In contrast, the questions making up the international involvement dimension are primarily of post–World War II vintage, and do not penetrate very deeply into the mass public consciousness. Thus, the roots of policy orientations associated with international involvement are not widely spread and securely fastened in the American political *terra firma*.

A second reason for my cheerful acceptance of the relatively poor showing on international involvement derives from my skeptical concern with statistical models of analysis that are highly successful in all applications. Unbroken successes in statistical analysis are, like a long series of winning poker hands, grounds for suspicion. Thus, the fact that the model of statistical analysis used here is not strikingly successful on the international involvement dimension means that the impressive results on the other four dimensions are not the artifacts of statistical sleight of hand.

THE DOMESTIC POLICY DIMENSIONS

Let us take a closer look at the relative importance of the factors affecting policy positions on the four domestic dimensions, returning to the international involvement dimension later.

On the government management dimension, taken as an average for the Eighty-fifth and Eighty-sixth Houses, party explains about 83 percent of the variation. This average drops to 64 percent on agricultural assistance, to about 31 percent on social welfare, and plummets to 4 percent on civil liberties. These data accord with earlier findings on the varying influence of party on the policy dimensions. So there is nothing new in these observations, except for some greater degree of specificity.

The interesting observation is that while party varies considerably as a predictor of voting, *when party falters other factors take up the burden!* It is true that the proportion of the variation in policy positions explained by the five variables working together is highest on the one dimension where party explains over 80 percent of the variation. But on the other three dimensions, where party effects diminish, the total proportion of explained variation does not decline commensurately. Hence, it is clear that congressional policy positions can be well comprehended in other terms when party is found wanting.

Let us turn from party to urbanization. As the analysis is set up, after party has explained all of the variation it can, urbanization of constituency is given its chance. The entry for urbanization, then, shows the percentage of the variation in policy positions *within* the two parties, summed across the parties, that is accounted for by the urbanization of constituency. It is clear, from these data, that urbanization increases in importance as party decreases, making its strongest contribution on the dimensions of social welfare and civil liberties. As observed in the analysis of policy profiles, urbanization is but weakly associated with opposition to farm support.

After party and urbanization have explained all the variation in policy positions of which they are capable, the second constituency variable, blue-collar percentage of the work force, is given its opportunity. Uniformly, this second constituency variable adds little. Its poor showing is due, in small part, to the fact that it is third in line and is forced to pick over what remains after party and urbanization have feasted.

Fourth in line, but much less overwhelmed by its adverse positioning, is the variable, region. Region is particularly effective on the social welfare and civil liberties dimensions, and actually dominates the latter.

Although last in the order of entry, state party manages to explain a surprisingly large percentage of the variation in congressional policy positions unaccounted for by the preceding four variables. Although the percentage of variation explained is as low as 3 percent, and never higher than 14 percent on any one dimension, this is a fairly impressive showing because it is achieved when there is little variation left to explain. It is analagous to mountain climbing, where the last thousand feet are the toughest.

In sum, the major sources of congressional policy positions on the four domestic policy dimensions are party, urbanization, region, and state. These vary, individually, in their effects from one dimension to the next. However, the strength of one compensates for the weakness of another, as we move from one dimension to the next, so that the end result is the explanation of a very high proportion of the variation in the policy positions on each of these four dimensions.

THE INTERNATIONAL INVOLVEMENT DIMENSION

The effective five-variable alliance breaks down on the international involvement dimension, where all five variables explain "only" about half the variation in policy positions. I put the word "only" in quotation marks because normally, in social science research, the ability to explain half of the variation under study is described in much more positive terms.

The three variables that account for nearly all of the explained variation in international involvement positions are urbanization, region, and state. There is no party effect, and blue-collar is typically ineffectual.

However, in the next chapter, I shall show that presidential leadership is a powerful force in congressional decisions on foreign policy questions. Indeed, if the effects of presidential influence had been built into the statistical model used in this analysis, the proportion of the variation explained would undoubtedly have been much greater, possibly even matching the performance on the four domestic policy dimensions.

In general, then, congressional alignments follow the contours of the American political landscape that express the politics of party, state, and region, and they reflect the conditions associated with varying degrees of urbanization and industrialization. More of the detail of this pattern accompanies the ensuing description of the sources of variation within the Republican and Democratic parties.

Focus: The Parties in Congress

The variation in policy positions within each party that is attributed to region, to state, and to the two constituency variables is the object of our attention now (see Figure 12). The percentage of variation explained by each variable is computed as an average for the Eighty-fifth and Eighty-sixth Houses. While considering the sources of differences *within* the parties, notice must also be taken of the differences *between* the parties, since interparty and intraparty variations are related: the greater the interparty difference, the smaller the intraparty differences. We shall look at each policy dimension in turn.

172   HOW CONGRESSMEN DECIDE

Figure 12

*Percentage of Within-Party Variation in Policy Positions
Explained by* Constituency *(urbanization, blue-collar %
of work force),* Region, *and* State

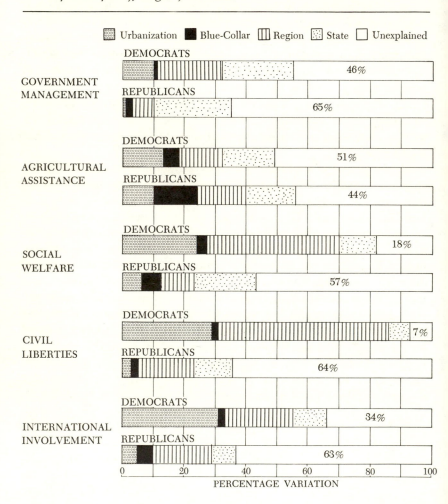

GOVERNMENT MANAGEMENT

The differences between the parties on the government management dimension are so great, accounting for 80 to 90 percent of the total congressional variation in policy positions, that it may appear to be a waste of time to talk about within-party differences. This is especially true when one recognizes that some part of the intraparty variation is due to measurement error and some to forces uniquely associated with a single term of Congress; in either case the resulting variation will elude our analytic net. Therefore, the chances of explaining very much of the intraparty variation appear slim from the outset. This pessimism is confirmed. In the Republican party nearly two-thirds of the variation in policy positions goes unaccounted for; we fare somewhat better in capturing one-half of the variation in the Democratic party.

Although the two parties differ in the amount of the intraparty variation accounted for by the four variables, the same two variables carry most of the load in both parties: region and state.

The regional variation within the Democratic party has both an east-west and a north-south slope. The southerners are least supportive of the government management of the economy and natural resources, while in the North the support for government management diminishes somewhat as one moves eastward from the Pacific.

The north-south slope appears again in the Republican party; among northern republicans there is a basin of low support stretching from the Hudson River to the Rockies, with rims of higher support for government management on the east and west coasts.

The regional pattern of support and opposition to government management that is observed within the two parties is understandable if one remembers that this dimension deals with, among other things, the preservation of natural resources, reclamation, and the development of public power (as opposed to private electrical power development). The Mountain and Pacific Coast states are concerned with conservation, cheap electricity through public power, and reclamation; not only are they concerned with these matters but, for historical reasons linked to geography, the depression, the drought, and the Roosevelt New Deal administration, they have been the beneficiaries of government activity. The same is true of the Border states, intimately affected by the Tennessee Valley Authority, another public power and conservation enterprise established in the traumatic thirties.

As regards the major source of intraparty variation on the government management dimension, the interstate differences, one should understand that the interstate differences across regions have already been absorbed in the regional differences. For example, while it is true that southern Democratic state parties are different in their policy positions from northern ones, this interstate difference is incorporated in the regional variation within the Democratic party.

In point of fact, the variation among southern Democratic state parties is a major source of the intraregional, interstate variation in the Democratic party. The nonmonolithic character of southern politics has been noted before.

The variation among Republican state parties is generally greater than among Democrats in the several regions. As in the instance of the variation in the policy positions of Democratic state parties, I will avoid conjectural explanations. The depth of analysis that would be required to illuminate differences in state parties is clearly not possible in the present analysis with its relatively broad national scope.

The overall picture with regard to the government management dimension, drawn in terms of party, constituency, region, and state, is as follows: The partisan division is the dominant factor in the differentiation of congressional policy positions. *The most conservative Democratic state party is more liberal than the most liberal Republican state party.* Furthermore, there are few individual Democratic congressmen who are more conservative than the most liberal Republican congressman. Such variation in policy positions as does occur within the parties is but slightly associated with urbanization of constituency and mostly attributable to regional and state variations.

AGRICULTURAL ASSISTANCE

On the agricultural assistance dimension party differences among congressmen at the national level account for about two-thirds of the variation in policy positions. Approximately a sixth of the total variation goes unexplained. This leaves a sixth of the total variation that is explained by within-party variations along constituency, region, and state lines.

The effectiveness of the two constituency characteristics, when viewed relative to their performance on the government management dimension, is quite strong on agriculture assistance. Notably, the impact of blue-collarness is greater on this dimension than on any of the other dimensions. This makes a great deal of sense in view of the inverse relation one would expect between the levels of farming and industrialization; as the latter rises, the support for assistance to agriculture drops.

The regional pattern in the two parties is perfectly consistent with expectations. As indicated earlier, the strongest support for agricultural subsidies emanates from those constituencies in which the major subsidy crops—wheat, corn, oats, barley, tobacco, peanuts, soybeans—are grown *for export*. This is precisely the case for the West North Central and Southern states. However, indications are that the regional groupings of constituencies are too gross to be highly effective in differentiating the policy positions of congressmen.

Interstate differences explain a larger share of the variation than does region. Although I have said that a thorough investigation of interstate variation is impossible in this study, in this instance I find it difficult to refrain from commenting on state differences. Consider the situation in the Northeast. Isn't it reasonable to find Maine and Vermont Republicans less opposed to agricultural assistance than Republicans from Connecticut, Massachusetts, and New Hampshire? It is a simple case of the more pastoral states set against the more urban, industrial ones. Similarly, among the Middle Atlantic states, it is Pennsylvania that is more supportive than Delaware, New Jersey, and New York. And the westernmost state of the East North Central region, Wisconsin, is more similar to the West North Central states than Ohio, Michigan, Indiana, and Illinois. Still, Republicans from Wisconsin are less supportive than Republicans from the West North Central region.

Yes, it is all ex post facto understanding. On the other hand there is an untortured quality in this interpretation of interstate differences.

In sum, there are two general sources of division on agricultural assistance policy. One is party, which accounts for about two-thirds of *all* the variation in policy positions. The paradoxical aspect of the party input is that it is the urban Democratic party that supports the farm programs, while the more rural Republicans stand in opposition. Of course, the rural southern wing of the Democratic party provides a large core of support for agricultural subsidy programs. There are also the Plains and Mountain wings of the party, particularly the wheat states, that support the subsidy program. However, the latter states send quite small delegations to Congress. This leaves

it up to the urban northern Democrats to provide the additional votes
necessary to support the farm program.

The second major source of division on the agricultural assistance
dimension, aside from party, is the degree of self-interest in the subsidy program. This is reflected in the power of the two constituency
variables to explain within-party variations in level of support for
agricultural assistance, and in the regional and state patterns of support for the farm program.

SOCIAL WELFARE

The social welfare dimension is distinct from the two preceding
dimensions in that the party differences among congressmen are much
smaller. Instead of explaining two-thirds of the variation, as in the
case of agricultural assistance, party explains about a third of the
variation on the social welfare dimension. This leaves plenty of elbow
room for the other four variables.

Within the Democratic party, urbanization and region account for
most of the differences in policy positions. However, interstate variations are also of importance; more so, clearly, than blue-collar percentage of the work force. In all, the four variables account for over
four-fifths of the variation within the Democratic party.

Republican variation appears less easy to pin down; only 43 percent of it is secured. In part, this is due to the fact that the total
amount of variation within the Republican party is less than in the
Democratic party. Consequently, a higher proportion of the variation
that does exist results from measurement error, individual idiosyn-
crasies, and transient political factors whose effects can never be
tallied. The higher level of Republican unity that prevails on social
welfare questions is understandable in view of the North-South division within the Democratic party that has been so effective in cleaving
the party. No regional division within the Republican party is in the
same league as a party-splitter. Indeed, on the social welfare dimension, region is way behind state party in accounting for the policy
differences among Republicans.

Substantial interstate variation in the Republican party is charac-
teristic of all the regions. For example, in the Middle Atlantic region,
New Jersey Republicans are more supportive of social welfare than
New Yorkers by about 70 points on a 200-point scale; within the East
North Central region, Ohio Republicans are 35 points less supportive

than Wisconsin Republicans; and the distance between Minnesota and South Dakota Republicans within the West North Central region is over 40 points. Not only are these differences substantial, but they conform to popular images of the Republican politics of these states.

Interstate, intraregion variations within the Democratic party are much less important. In most of the regions, uniformity is the rule. A sterling exception is the distinctly less supportive cast to the Tennessee delegation among the Border state delegations; remember that earlier I concluded that Tennessee is the most "southern" of the Border states. There is also substantial variation in the South. About 75 points separate the most supportive southern Democratic state party, Alabama, from the least supportive state parties, Virginia and Mississippi.

Social welfare politics in Congress may be characterized as follows. Differences between the parties are substantial at the national level but nowhere near those observed on agricultural assistance and government management. This is significant because there is some tendency in descriptions of American politics to peg the partisan differences on social welfare at the same level as the partisan differences on policies associated with the government management dimension. Part of the confusion arises from the failure to discriminate between the two kinds of policies.

Social welfare also provides an example of a dimension on which other variables compensate for the failure of party to explain (in a statistical sense) the variation in policy positions. The two constituency variables, plus state and region, account for all but 18 percent of the large variation in the policy positions of members of the Democratic party. Region, reflecting in large part the North-South division within the party, is the most effective variable. But level of urbanization, which is expected to be related to support for social welfare programs, is no shirker within the Democratic party.

Within the Republican party we find a higher level of unity, leaving less variation to be explained. Nevertheless, nearly half of the variation among Republican policy positions is explained, with state party making the major contribution, and region doing slightly better than urbanization and blue-collar.

The pattern of policy position variation in the two parties is highly congruent with the contours of American life and politics that are familiar to most of us. Congressional behavior on social welfare is understandable without the aid of cloakroom surveillance, without the need to unravel a Shakespearean tangle of intrigue, without amassing an army of variables to envelop the elusive quarry.

CIVIL LIBERTIES

National party differences on civil liberties are so small as to warrant no consideration. This means that the variation in policy positions on this dimension are contained within the parties. However, it is crucial that I point out that the variation in policy positions within the Republican party is no more than an eighth of that within the Democratic party. This difference between the parties helps to explain why a high percentage (93 percent) of the variation within the Democratic party is explained by the four variables used for this purpose, while a relatively low percentage (36 percent) of the variation within the Republican party is explained. For reasons specified earlier, when there is less variation to be explained, a higher proportion of it will be essentially inexplicable.

The major source of variation in policy positions on civil liberties within the Democratic party is, as everyone already knows, the North-South regional division. Second in importance, and explaining nearly all of the remaining variation that is accounted for, is urbanization. A portion of the explanatory power of urbanization is borrowed from the North-South division, since northern Democrats are elected from more urban constituencies than southern Democrats.

Within the Republican party, the small amount of variation that exists is apportioned between regional and state differences; the two constituency variables are unimportant. The regional differences among Republicans are of interest mainly because there is generally little known about such variations within the Republican party. A small part of the regional variation is due to the distance between southern and northern Republicans; it is a small part because, while southern Republicans take a civil liberties position that is light years away from their northern colleagues, there are so few of the former that this source of variation is limited in its total effect. In the North, the Northeast and Middle Atlantic representatives are most supportive of civil liberties and the Pacific Coast Republicans are least supportive. The remainder of the regions occupying the middle position are highly similar. The slightly stronger support for civil liberties in the eastern regions within the Republican party is consistent with the traditional abolitionist views of those regions.

The interstate variation among Republicans is approximately equal in magnitude to regional variation. This interstate variation is particularly noticeable within the West North Central region. Missouri Republicans are vastly more supportive of civil liberties than are those from South Dakota and Kansas; in between are the Republicans from Minnesota, Nebraska, and North Dakota. The higher level of support for civil liberties among Missouri Republicans is interesting because it indicates the "northern" character of a state that is sometimes treated as a Border state and sometimes thought of as having even stronger ties with the South than is suggested by the "border" designation.

In summary, the divisions on civil liberties are entirely comprehensible within a framework consisting of urbanization, region, and racial politics of a well-known variety. The additional contribution made by differences between state parties is not large, nor does it evoke a sense of déjà vu, for state politics are much less visible in this regard. This is particularly true when the category of civil liberties extends beyond civil rights for blacks.

INTERNATIONAL INVOLVEMENT

As in the case of civil liberties, the partisan differences on international involvement are insignificant. Such is the case under a Republican administration. In the last chapter it will be shown that partisan differences are to be expected when a Democrat is president. Thus, the differences in the levels of partisanship associated with international involvement vary as a function of presidential influence.

Not only are partisan effects absent, but the other four variables are relatively ineffective in accounting for positional variation on this dimension. Within the Democratic party 34 percent of the variation remains unexplained; the variation unexplained within the Republican party is 63 percent.

The primary difference between the parties is that urbanization is a much more powerful explanatory variable within the Democratic party. The association of urbanization with support for international involvement is of long standing. It has generated the view that urban residents are more cosmopolitan, less closely identified with their own quite heterogeneous community (less parochial in other words), and more aware of an interdependence with other nations.[13]

The regional differences within the two parties are substantial and of about equal strength, accounting for around 20 percent of the variation in policy positions. There is also a strong parallel between the two parties in the ordering of the regions on a continuum of support for international involvement. The most supportive regions in both parties are the Northeast and Middle Atlantic, followed by the Pacific and East North Central states. With very little distortion it can be stated that support for international involvement declines in both parties as we move to the Mountain and Plains states, to the Border states, ending up in the South.

However, the points in the orderings of the regions within the parties where the sharpest differences occur are not the same in the Democratic and Republican parties. In the Democratic party, the largest gap is between the Border states and the South, on the one hand, and the remaining regions of the North, on the other; in the Republican party the break comes between the three coast regions (Northeast, Middle Atlantic, Pacific) and the South and interior regions. Thus, it is in the Republican party that we find the greatest support for the parallel between the interior–coastal split and the old isolationist–internationalist split. There is a trace of this in the Democratic party but, in the main, northern Democrats of all regions are quite supportive of international involvement, even with a Republican president in charge of foreign policy.

Interstate variations in policy positions on international involvement exist but are not particularly notable in comparison with those observed on other dimensions. They are slightly greater in the Democratic party, particularly so within the Border region; for example, Maryland is much more proinvolvement than Oklahoma. In other words, Maryland is behaving like an eastern state and Oklahoma like a plains state. There is also, as usual, substantial variation in the South.

Interstate differences within the Republican party are fairly sharp within the interior regions. The West North Central states are nicely divided between three states strongly supportive of international restraint (Nebraska, South Dakota, and North Dakota) and three states taking more moderate positions (Minnesota, Kansas, and Missouri). In the Border states, coastal Maryland is highly supportive of international involvement, Kentucky and Tennessee share moderate positions, and Oklahoma and West Virginia Republicans come down hard against international involvement. Although these state differences occasion no surprise, indeed because of their fit with common conceptions, they give added meaning to the state parties' contributions to congressional politics.

More on the meaningfulness of variations in state party policy positions is to be said in the next section, Analysis II.

State Party: Analysis II

Earlier in this chapter, I went into some detail in describing my understanding of the effects of state milieus on the policy stances of members of Congress. Later it was shown that even after national party, urbanization and blue-collarness of constituency, and region had taken their turns at explaining the differences in policy positions among congressmen, state party inevitably accounted for an *additional* portion of these differences. This suggests that a differentiation according to state of origin is getting at differences between congressmen that are highly relevant to their differences in policy positions.

Furthermore, it is quite possible that the foregoing analysis has greatly underestimated the influence of state party, since state party was always the last variable to be entered into the equation used to explain variations in policy positions. Consider the effect of entering region into the equation before state party. To the extent that differences among state parties are geographically patterned, with contiguous states more likely to be similar than more spatially distant states, *any* regional classification of states that employs the criterion of contiguity will assign some of the variation between states to the region variable, even if region is a meaningless classification. The same argument holds for the effects of entering urbanization or blue-collarness of the constituency into the equation before state party. To the extent that constituencies within one state are generally more urbanized than constituencies within another, state differences will be commingled with differences in the level of urbanization. Even if differences among congressmen were due solely to state party differences, they would nevertheless "appear" to be associated with constituency differences.

Suppose the analysis is conducted employing a different strategy. Instead of state party coming last, let it be the first and only variable in the explanatory equation. Now let us see what percentage of the variation in policy positions may be attributed to state party. This is tantamount to proposing that the only factor in the development of policy orientations is the state party. In this formulation, for example, the national parties are treated as though they were loose aggregations of state parties with differences between the national parties being no more than by-products of the differences among state parties. Granted, this formulation is a bit extreme, for it contradicts the consensus that national party differences within the Congress are important factors in the decision process. Nevertheless, it is of interest to see how much of the variation in policy positions could be explained by a "state party theory" of congressional decision behavior.

Taking an average based on the Eighty-fifth and Eighty-sixth Congresses, the percentage of the variation in policy positions on each of the dimensions that is associated with state party is as follows: international involvement, 43%; social welfare, 77%; agricultural assistance, 83%; civil liberties, 86%; government management, 90%. In sum, on four of the five dimensions, excepting only international involvement, over three-fourths of the variation in the policy positions of members of the House is reflected in differences among state party delegations.

Looking at the data from another angle, we see that on four out of five policy dimensions *less* than one-fourth of the variation in policy positions is due to differences among members of state party delegations. In other words, *policy differences among representatives of different constituencies within a state party delegation are fairly minor.*

Favoring the state party variable is a point that was discussed at some length in the chapter on constituency and party: The congressman probably best represents those of his constituents who voted for him in the preceding election, and these are for the most part people of his own party. The state party variable has the advantage that it allows for the between-party differences within the constituency. It assumes the congressman is responding only to his party followers, whereas the constituency measures commonly employed are reflective of the entire constituency.

In short, the large proportion of the variation in policy positions associated with state party may be due to the fact that the congressman really does represent the state party, that this *is* the milieu in which his values, beliefs, and attitudes have been fostered. Accordingly, congressmen from different districts in the same state, but of the same party, are similar products of a common milieu, as regards their policy orientations. Citizens sharing a common party affiliation and residing in the same state, albeit different constituencies, will also be similar in their orientations.

Indeed, it may be that the congressman represents the central tendency in the state party regardless of the variation among constituents. This leads to the interesting proposition *that different persons (from the same party) representing a particular district will take policy positions that vary about the mean for the state party rather than about the mean for that constituency.*

While I think it is useful to present the "state party theory" and search for evidence to support it, it would be unwise to forget the counterargument: that differences among congressmen from different state parties are due mainly to national party differences, regional diversity, and constituency dissimilarities.

Whatever the precise nature of the causal relation associated with state party as a predictor of policy positions, I remain intrigued with the finding that there is so little variation among congressmen from the same party elected from the same state. The only policy dimension for which this is not true is international involvement.

Further analysis of the character and meaningfulness of the state party variable is conducted in answer to two related questions. (1) *Are the differences among the state party delegations reflective of differences in the policy preferences of state party constituencies, or are the differences between state party delegations more a product of the Washington congressional environment affecting the behavior of congressmen during a single term of Congress?* The latter is a distinct possibility as a function of interactions among members of a state party delegation with respect to the policy proposals arising during a congressional two-year term.

To the degree that differences in the policy positions of state party delegations are not the product of differences in state parties, but rather are differences that arise within the halls of Congress, it is to be expected that the policy positions of state party delegations will be subject to change over time. This change occurs as the congressional context changes from term to term, as individual members of state party delegations become more or less attuned to the wishes of their delegation colleagues, as new members replace old. In contrast, if the effective forces producing the policy positions of the state party delegation are the relatively constant ones of the state party constituency, it is to be expected that policy positions will be quite stable from one congressional term to the next.

My way of answering this question is to compare the policy positions of state party delegations in the Eighty-sixth Congress (1959–1960) with the policy positions in the Eighty-third (1953–1954). This is accomplished by computing a mean policy position score for each state party delegation, on each dimension, and then looking at the degree of similarity in the ordering of state party delegations in the two Congresses. This will be done for both the House and the Senate.

Question (2) is highly related to question (1) but gets at the meaningfulness of the state party delegation differences in another way, one that does not explicitly include the time dimension: *Are the differences in the policy positions of state party delegations in the House of Representatives mirrored by the differences between state party delegations in the Senate?* For example, does the Republican *House* delegation from Connecticut occupy a policy position that is similar to the Republican *Senate* delegation from Connecticut? A response in the affirmative is supportive of the interpretation that there is a state party constituency influencing and represented by the congressmen of both houses.

It is, of course, possible that the state party delegations in the two houses take the same positions because of extensive interhouse, intra-delegation consultation, and do so independently of state party influence. However, if we find *both* agreement between Senate and House delegations and stability in their positions, the case for state party constituency influence is greatly strengthened.

The examination of the state party phenomenon is based on the evidence presented in Figure 13, which includes data on the similarity of policy positions taken by state party delegations, both across time and across houses, for all five policy dimensions. Shown is the level of similarity relative to maximum similarity. The similarity refers to the ordering of state party delegations, from one time to the next, from one house to the other.

TIME 1 TO TIME 2

There is a high degree of similarity in the orderings of the state party delegations from time 1 to time 2 on all policy dimensions except international involvement. However, even on the international

Figure 13
*State Party Positions: Similarity (stability) Across Time and
Similarity Between Houses*

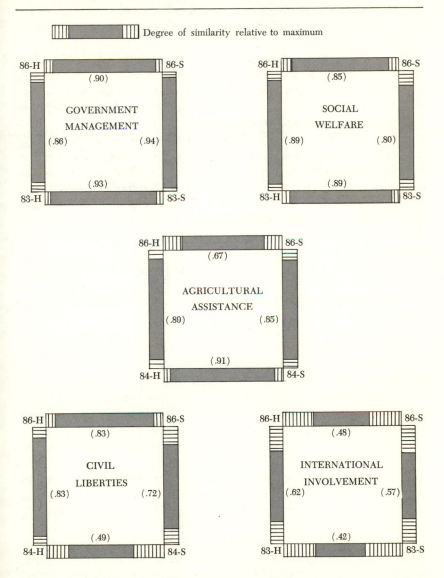

Degree of similarity relative to maximum

86-H ⸻ 86-S (.90) GOVERNMENT MANAGEMENT (.86) (.94) (.93) 83-H ⸻ 83-S	86-H ⸻ 86-S (.85) SOCIAL WELFARE (.89) (.80) (.89) 83-H ⸻ 83-S

86-H ⸻ 86-S
(.67)

AGRICULTURAL
ASSISTANCE
(.89)   (.85)

(.91)
84-H ⸻ 84-S

86-H ⸻ 86-S (.83) CIVIL LIBERTIES (.83) (.72) (.49) 84-H ⸻ 84-S	86-H ⸻ 86-S (.48) INTERNATIONAL INVOLVEMENT (.62) (.57) (.42) 83-H ⸻ 83-S

involvement dimension there is a moderate level of stability in the positioning of the state party delegations from one Congress to the next. (On civil liberties and agricultural assistance, it was necessary to use the Eighty-fourth rather than the Eighty-third Congress because not enough roll calls were taken to permit the construction of reliable scales.)

The stability of the delegation orderings means that the variation in the policy positions of individual legislators that was statistically explained by state party in the analysis of the Eighty-fifth and Eighty-sixth Congresses is due to real long-term differences between representatives of different state parties. The full import of these findings may elude us if we forget that the stability of the delegation orderings over time occurs despite three sources of change in the party delegation mean score over time. (1) The persons serving continuously may change their positions; (2) different persons may fill the congressional seats in the two Congresses; (3) different seats may constitute the state party delegation—this means that, in the House, different district constituencies may be represented in the Congresses at time 1 and time 2.

Our confidence in the meaningfulness of the state party delegation differences is enhanced to the extent that the same ordering of the state parties is found in both the Senate and the House on the individual dimensions.

HOUSE–SENATE COMPARISON

The correspondence between the orderings of the Senate and House state party delegations is remarkably high; again the exception is the dimension of international involvement, though there is a relatively poor showing on civil liberties for the Eighty-fourth Congress. The latter, as a singular instance on that dimension, may be due to the embryonic stage of the growing national debate on matters of civil liberties in the early Congress.

The exceptional character of the international involvement dimension, in terms of the lesser longitudinal stability and horizontal (across houses) similarity of the orderings of state party positions, provides a vantage point for a clearer view of the phenomenon under study. Recall that less than half of the variation in policy positions on this dimension could be explained by state party. Relative to the conditions on the other dimensions, this implies that differ-

ences within delegations are relatively greater than differences between delegations. We know also, from information on the position
changes in the holdover and the person turnover conditions over
time, presented in Chapter 6 (Figure 8), that such changes were
relatively large on the international involvement dimension. It appears that a fair amount of reshuffling of positions takes place
between Congresses, and that there are differences between party
delegations in the two houses, because the individuals constituting the
state party delegations are less constrained by the forces associated
with state party.

In my preparatory remarks, I offered the view that where we find
both longitudinal stability and horizontal similarity in the policy
positions of state parties, we are finding strong support for the causal
status of state party as defined in this chapter. State party emerges
as a very strong influence on government management and social
welfare, nearly as strong on agricultural assistance, weaker but still
moderately strong on civil liberties, and weakest on international involvement. In general, state party has demonstrated its right to a
hearing.

The most salient, and also the most serious, objection to the state
party thesis arises from the fact that the state party differences, when
calculated for the entire Congress, may borrow heavily on what are
essentially national party differences. The most forceful illustration
of this argument is provided by the government management dimension, where it is known that national party differences account
for almost nine-tenths of the variation in policy positions. Nevertheless, the state party theorist might argue that the state party had
chosen to incorporate a national party point of view in its policy
orientations on this one dimension. Hence, whatever the ultimate
source of the policy positions, it is the state party that makes the
choice of one position over the other.

Additional information on the stability, and the Senate-House
similarity, of the policy positions at state party delegations is given
in Table 2 in terms of *intra*party orderings. (The Pearson *r* was used
as the measure of longitudinal stability and horizontal similarity of
the orderings of state party delegations.) In general, state party is
supported as a source of influence even when we look only at the
differences between state delegations *within* each party.

Table 2
Longitudinal Stability and Horizontal Similarity of State Party Delegation Policy Positions

| | REPUBLICANS | | | | DEMOCRATS | | | |
| | 83RD* BY 86TH | | HOUSE BY SENATE | | 83RD* BY 86TH | | HOUSE BY SENATE | |
	HOUSE	SENATE	83RD*	86TH	HOUSE	SENATE	83RD*	86TH
GM	.02	.84	.35	0.14	.49	.65	.67	.72
SW	.12	.32	.45	0.45	.93	.72	.82	.81
AA	.65	.90	.86	0.65	.60	.66	.59	.53
CL	.68	.43	.28	0.31	.88	.83	.66	.90
II	.61	.70	.32	0.58	.55	.63	.52	.59

* The 84th is substituted, for reasons given in text, on the agricultural assistance and civil liberties dimensions.

Conclusions

The investigation of the state party explanation of congressional behavior is perhaps most significant for making the single point that *policy differences among members of a state party delegation are minimal on four of the five dimensions.* The one exception to this generalization is international involvement.

Further analysis is needed on the issue raised in this study: *Is it state party in whose shadow the congressman walks, or does state party serve mainly as a convenient way of expressing the constituency, regional, and party factors in legislative behavior?*

Before leaving this topic let me make one final point regarding the argument that senators and representatives from the same state can share a common political experience producing a common policy orientation. The point is that it is quite reasonable to expect the representative from a particular district within the state to reflect a state party orientation rather than a district policy orientation. Why? First, because the district is unlikely to coincide with a community, or even a community of interests, with which the representative can identify more easily than with the entire state party. Although the representative may desire to represent the constituency, it may be very difficult to get a fix on it. And, second, the representative is likely to represent those who elect him. These will be partisan followers, for the most part, and affiliates of the same party from different constituencies within the state are likely to have much in common.

Thus there is a high degree of commonality among members of the state party delegation, including the senators, for senators are likely to be supported by the same people who vote for their partisan fellows in the House, and they will respond to the same party milieu within the state.

But let us not lose sight of the original purpose of introducing state party into the analysis: It is one of a limited number of factors representing the major contours of American society and politics to be used in explaining the variations in the policy positions of congressmen. The other factors are national party, region, urbanization, and occupation (percentage of work force that is blue-collar).

The ability of this set of factors to explain congressional policy positions was remarkable on all of the dimensions except international involvement. On the four domestic policy dimensions the percentage of the variation explained, in the Eighty-fifth and Eighty-sixth Houses, varied from 76 percent on social welfare in the Eighty-fifth House to 94 percent on government management, also in the Eighty-fifth House. On the international involvement dimension, the level of explanation dropped off to slightly above 50 percent.

These dry percentages, when put together, are the basis for my contention that the variations in the policy positions of members of Congress can be understood in rather uncomplicated terms. Previously, we have observed that the policy positions were remarkably stable through many sessions of Congress. From those two sets of observations, I conclude that there is a reasonably comprehensible and enduring patterning of congressional policy positions on the four domestic policy dimensions. The pattern of cleavage is different on each dimension, yet the five factors, in different combinations, are sufficient to account for most of the variation.

I do not want to dwell upon the reasons why we have failed thus far to arrive at a better understanding of the variation in policy positions on international involvement. Some of these reasons have been given; furthermore, the next chapter, on presidential influence, contains a rather extensive treatment of this dimension.

To sum up the message of this chapter in a single boast: Tell me where a congressman lives and what party he belongs to, and I will tell you what his policy position is on each of the four domestic

190   HOW CONGRESSMEN DECIDE

policy dimensions! Certainly, I will be wrong on some occasions, because individuals have a way of exposing the error in the best predictions. However, the overall level of prediction error will be much less than that conjured up by the image of Congress as an enigma hidden in committee.

References

1. One of the most persuasive cases is made by Raymond A. Bauer, *et. al.*, *American Business and Public Policy* (New York: Atherton, 1963); also see Malcolm E. Jewell and Samuel C. Patterson, *Legislative Process in the U.S.* (New York: Random House, 1966).
2. For examples see Norman Meller, "Legislative Behavior Research Revisited: A Review of Five Years' Publications," *Western Political Quarterly* 18 (December 1965), pp. 787–789.
3. Urbanization measure on congressional districts is percentage urban minus percentage rural, based on data provided by "Congressional Quarterly Weekly Report, No. 5" (February 2, 1962), pp. 156–159. Urban areas contain a central city of 50,000 or larger, included are suburban areas containing a city of 100,000 or larger; suburban areas consist of closely settled areas contiguous to central cities; rural areas contain cities smaller than 50,000. The urbanization index for states is a weighted composite of the district indices.
4. Percentage blue-collar measure on congressional districts is based on data provided by "Congressional Quarterly Weekly Report, No. 29" (July 20, 1956), p. 853. The blue-collar definition includes craftsmen, foremen, machine operators, private household help, service employees, and all laborers except those who work on farms. The state measure of blue-collar is a weighted composite of the district indices.
5. Cleo Cherryholmes and Michael Shapiro, *Representatives and Roll Calls* (Indianapolis, Ind.: Bobbs-Merrill, 1969); Donald R. Matthews and James A. Stimson, "Decision-Making by U.S. Representatives: A Preliminary Model," in Sidney Ulmer, ed., *Political Decision-Making* (New York: Van Nostrand Reinhold, 1970), pp. 14–39.
6. Matthews and Stimson, *op. cit.*
7. John H. Kessel, "The Washington Congressional Delegation," *Midwest Journal of Political Science* 8 (February 1964), pp. 1–21; Alan Fiellen, "Function of Informal Groups: A State Delegation," *Journal of Politics* 24 (February 1962), pp. 72–91; Charles S. Bullock, "Influence of State Party Delegations on House Committee Assignments," *Midwest Journal of Political Science* 15 (August 1971), pp. 525–546; David B. Truman, *Congressional Party: A Case Study* (New York: Wiley, 1959); Barbara Deckard, "State Party Delegations in the U.S. House of Representatives: A Comparative Study of Group Cohesion," *Journal of Politics* 34 (February 1972), pp. 199–222.
8. The view of states as political subsystems of subcultures is presented in a review essay, Samuel C. Patterson, "The Political Cultures of the American States," *Journal of Politics* 30 (February 1968), pp. 187–209; Daniel J. Elazar, *American Federalism: A View From the States* (New York: T. Y. Crowell, 1966); and Ira Sharkansky, "The Utility of Elazar's Political Culture," *Polity* 2 (Fall 1969), pp. 66–83. The impetus for much of the research on state political systems was generated by V. O. Key, Jr., *Southern Politics* (New York: Knopf, 1949).

9. V. O. Key, Jr., *American State Politics* (New York: Knopf, 1965), p. 51.

10. *Ibid.*, p. 218.

11. Aage R. Clausen, "State Party Influence on Congressional Policy Decisions," *Midwest Journal of Political Science* 16 (February 1972), pp. 77–101.

12. Measurements of state party influence are obtained by means of a linear regression analysis (stepwise). This assumes interval level measurements. In the case of the nominal scales, region and state, this assumption is met by converting them into dichotomous (dummy) variables; dichotomous variables meet the interval level criterion of equal intervals by having only one. For example, the eight-region variable is converted into seven dichotomous variables. The first region is represented by a code of 1 for congressmen elected from it and a code of 0 for all other congressmen. The same code is applied for each of seven regions. A dichotomous coding of the eighth region is redundant since members of this region are uniquely identified as being members of none of the first seven regions.

The use of dummy variables in a regression analysis format is the equivalent of entering the nominal scale variables into an analysis of variance. Thus, the proportion of the variation in scale scores *explained,* statistically, by the seven dummy variables for region is the same proportion of variation that would be explained by region in analysis of variance.

In the analysis, congressmen are first sorted into Democrat and Republican subsets, then the regression model is applied within each subset. This has two advantages: (1) It exposes the interrelation of independent and dependent variables within each party; (2) it increases the precision of the analysis because it permits a different linear model to be fitted to each of the parties.

13. George L. Grassmuck, *Sectional Biases in Congress on Foreign Policy* (Baltimore, Md.: Johns Hopkins Press, 1951), pp. 107–111; Leroy N. Rieselbach, *Roots of Isolationism* (Indianapolis, Ind.: Bobbs-Merrill, 1966), pp. 114–120.

8

Presidential
Pull up
Capitol Hill

Presidential influence on Congress is a vast topic. It has some of the fatal allure of the female spider who kills her lovemate immediately after mating. For quite different reasons, the topic of presidential influence seems like one worth pursuing. It deals with the relation between the two branches of government most instrumental in the production of legislation, most important to the conduct of the daily business of government, and most responsible for the determination of our national commitments at home and abroad. However, the promise in the pursuit, and the potential inherent in the conquest, of this topic are, by the very nature of things, followed by the sudden death of any hope for immortality. The topic is simply too vast to be comprehended, much less researched, in any systematic and meaningful way.

The question of presidential influence on Congress, or the relative influence of each on the making of public policy, is often approached with one of two possible biases. One bias is the preference for a strong executive and a compliant Congress; the other bias is for a Congress that asserts policy leadership independent of, or in cooperation with, the president. Whatever course it follows, Congress is likely to be the object of criticism. Congressional leadership is characterized as obstructionism by proponents of executive powers; its compliance is seen by the friends of Congress as lack of initiative and political ineffectiveness.[1]

Whatever the observer's bias, the prevailing thesis appears to be that we have, today, a condition of presidential dominance, though with limitations. Consider the effects of the semiautonomous administrative agencies within the federal bureaucracy. Although most of these agencies appear in organization charts to be subordinate to the president, many operate under rules established by Congress and are beholden to Congress. Politically, most of these agencies are sensitive to the wishes of the members of Congress, particularly the relevant committees in Congress. It is not entirely clear, then, that legislation drafted as a part of the president's program, or an appropriation request put forward by an agency and subsumed under the president's budget, is an act of executive initiative. It may have developed out of a complex pattern of communications between congressmen, administrators, and the "interest" clients who are the potential beneficiaries of the new, or modified, program. Consequently, it may be misleading to infer that congressional influence is on the wane simply because the legislative initiative appears to originate in the executive branch.

Whatever questions I might raise about the validity of the thesis of executive dominance, it is only fair to say that there is a consensus today that congressional influence is on a steady decline relative to that of the president. And the main component of this argument is that the legislative initiative has been preempted by the president.[2]

In this view, Congress is a reacting organism; it only accepts or rejects alternatives provided by the president and "his" bureaucracy. The situation is analogous to that of the American voters—they can *choose among* candidates, but few put forth candidates. This effectively limits the voters' range of choice and is an abdication of influence to the initiators. Similarly, the president assesses the country's needs, sets the agenda, and solicits a congressional response to his own liking. *The president is the chairman of the Committee on Legislation in the United States government.* Or so they say.

It is one of the blessings of scientific research that its demands for evidence, systematically assembled and cautiously interpreted, prevent one from tackling the vast topic or what some may grandly refer to as the important question. With this said, let me narrow the scope of the inquiry to the topic of *presidential influence on congressional policy positions.*

Presidential influence on policy positions is unlike the other factors considered previously; the presidential factor is a highly changeable component of the decision equation for the simple reason that presidents serve for a fairly short duration. In contrast, the other factors bearing upon the congressman's decision processes are fairly constant for periods of time probably encompassing several presidential administrations. In this work, these other factors include party, constituency, region, state, and just possibly ideology.

Although left to the last, it should be clear that *presidential influence is a fullfledged member of the set of factors that should always be included in the study of the decisions made by individual congressmen.* In terms of the very early discussion of the policy dimension theory, the president is one of those elements in the congressman's political environment that the congressman must deal with in adopting his policy position on each of the five dimensions, along with constituency, party, and so forth.

One reason for pushing the presidential component of the congressman's policy position is that I think it would be unrealistic to ignore it. Furthermore, I am emphasizing the role of presidential influence in the determination of the congressman's general policy position on each dimension in order to provide a better understanding of my earlier refusal to assess the stability of congressional policy positions in terms of positions taken during different administrations. My view is that one can expect a high degree of stability in the policy positions of congressmen during the term of a single president, since there appears to be no factor affecting the congressman's general policy positions that is subject to appreciable change. However, when a new president assumes office there is a change in one potentially important factor in the individual legislator's policy calculations. Consequently, high stability in policy positions can not be expected across a changeover in the presidency. This is not to say that high stability across presidential terms will not occur, only that it would be perilous to take it for granted.

Expectations

Expectations concerning the depth and breadth of presidential influence on congressional policy positions are not at all well established in the literature. There is nothing matching the redundant profusion of research reports on the effects of party, constituency, ideology, and region. The one policy dimension about which expectations may be held, on the basis of solid research, is international involvement. Here clear evidence that presidential influence is operative was presented in a groundbreaking study by Mark Kesselman.[3]

Kesselman demonstrated that members of the House of Representatives move from previously held positions to support of a new president elected from their own party. The evidence is drawn from two turnovers: from Truman (Democrat) to Eisenhower (Republican) and from Eisenhower to Kennedy (Democrat). It demonstrated that representatives show more support for international involvement when the president is of their own party. This is consistent with expectations regarding the direction of presidential influence on this dimension given his role-defined responsibility for foreign policy and his need to have the tools for effective international involvement.

When we leave the field of foreign policy and enter the field of domestic policy, we are somewhat at a loss as to what to expect. It is certainly reasonable to anticipate that the president will engage the support of his fellow partisans and that he may even attract votes from the other party. The "president's position" would appear to be common knowledge in the Washington community. The *Congressional Quarterly*, the indispensable chronicler of Congress, regularly reports the president's position and publishes support scores showing each congressman's support of the man in the White House. Furthermore, congressmen are reported to have said that they like to go along with the president whenever they can. With all these indicators of the prominence of the president's wishes, our expectation would have to be that presidential influence is not restricted to the dimension of international involvement.

The Investigation

My investigation of presidential influence on congressional decision-making is a very simple operation; it consists of a measurement of the shift in congressional policy positions that accompanies a partisan turnover of the administration. Where such a shift occurs, there is a basis for inferring presidential influence.

The study embraces two partisan turnovers of the presidency, from the Republican Eisenhower administration to the Democratic Kennedy-Johnson administration, and from the latter to the Nixon administration. The mean position of each congressman in the last two Congresses of the Eisenhower administration is compared with his mean position in the first two Congresses of the Kennedy-Johnson administration to see whether there has been any change. (If the congressman has served in only one Congress of an administration, the score for that one Congress is used.) In addition, the position of each congressman in the last Congress of the Kennedy-Johnson administration (the Eighty-eighth) is compared with the one Congress of the Nixon administration for which a complete record is available at this writing (the Ninety-first). (Only the Eighty-eighth Congress was used in order to minimize the time span.)

The study skips over the Eighty-ninth and Ninetieth Congresses, since the main purpose of including the Ninety-first was to demonstrate the currency of the findings on the Eighty-third through the Eighty-eighth. I think this is no real problem, although it does mean that I am assuming no major shifts in the policy positions of congressmen during the administration beginning with Kennedy-Johnson in 1963 and ending with Johnson in 1968.

The examination of all five policy dimensions provides a broad-based test of presidential influence. It also gives us an opportunity to study relative levels of presidential influence on particular dimensions.

As it turns out, there are only two levels of presidential influence observed: some and none! The only policy dimension exhibiting any influence is international involvement; there is nothing approaching even mildly promising evidence of presidential influence on the four domestic policy dimensions. The lack of presidential influence on these four dimensions will be discussed briefly later; the discussion will undoubtedly make more sense after one has a greater familiarity with the analysis. Accordingly, we turn to a fairly searching examination of presidential influence on the international involvement dimension.

Presidential Influence: International Involvement

There is clear evidence of presidential influence in the finding that members of both the House and the Senate respond to a president *of their own party* by either retaining a constant position or moving toward a position of greater support for international involvement. For example, when a Democrat is in the White House, Democrats in the Congress are, collectively, more supportive of international involvement. Broken down to the individual level, three types of behavior are exhibited. There are (1) congressmen who are highly supportive of international involvement under *all* presidents, (2) congressmen occupying a range of positions from moderate to low support who *hold* their respective positions under different presidents, and (3) senators and representatives who *move* from a position of less to a position of more support when the new president is of their own party. In one sense, there are only two classes of congressmen, those who change their position on the international involvement dimension when there is a partisan turnover of the presidency and those who do not.

CHANGES IN POSITIONS OF INDIVIDUAL MEMBERS

The closer examination and demonstration of this phenomenon begins with data that demonstrate the pattern of stability and movement just described. Data are presented for each party and each house, first for the effects of the Eisenhower to Kennedy-Johnson turnover, in Figure 14(A), and second for the changes in position within each party and house during the Kennedy-Johnson to Nixon turnover, in Figure 14(B).

The scatterplot is used to show the relation between positions held by individual members before and after a turnover of the presidency. Each point in the plot gives, simultaneously, the positions of a single congressman on the international involvement dimension in both of the presidential administrations included in a single scatterplot. To find this position for each administration, simply draw two lines from a given point, one to each of the two axes and perpendicular to it.

To aid in the comprehension of the scatterplots I have denoted three zones on each. The zone occupying the diagonal, marked "no change," identifies the subset of congressmen whose positions do not change with the change of administrations. The width of this zone takes cognizance of minor changes in scores that probably do not reflect changes in actual positions. The two zones about the diagonal band include the legislators who have moved toward positions of increased or decreased support for international involvement as a concomitant of the presidential turnover.

Let us look first at the effects of the turnover featuring the retirement of President Eisenhower and the installation of the black-

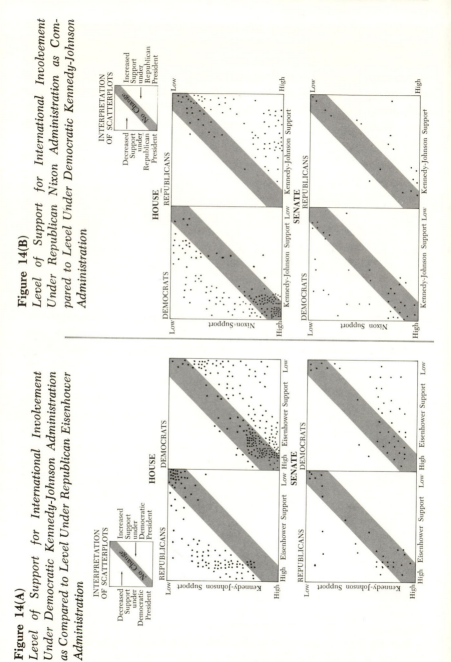

Figure 14(A)
Level of Support for International Involvement Under Democratic Kennedy-Johnson Administration as Compared to Level Under Republican Eisenhower Administration

Figure 14(B)
Level of Support for International Involvement Under Republican Nixon Administration as Compared to Level Under Democratic Kennedy-Johnson Administration

bordered Kennedy-Johnson administration. For both parties, in both houses, the phenomenon of stability and movement described earlier is sharply illustrated by these data. The Senate and House patterns are as similar as one could possibly expect. Democrats move toward a more supportive position when a Democratic administration comes into being, and the Republicans move to a less supportive position, since they no longer need to heed the call of a president of their own party.

Moving on to the Kennedy-Johnson to Nixon turnover (Figure 14B) we see the pattern repeated. Of course, the direction of change is reversed as Democrats move toward low support positions and Republicans shift back to more support—though we must not forget that some congressmen maintain their positions through different administrations.

When one's data display such perfect order, it is difficult to avoid the temptation of displaying them in another form, thereby allowing oneself the opportunity to dwell upon them a bit longer. Such is the latent function of the next analysis; the manifest function is to obtain a more complete understanding of the workings of presidential influence on this policy dimension.

CHANGES IN REGIONAL PARTY DISTRIBUTIONS

Distinct regional variations in policy positions on the international involvement dimension, *within* each of the parties, are found in this study as well as previous ones. Within the Republican party the gross regional pattern is one of relatively high support for involvement among the congressmen from the coastal states, compared with the level of support among interior Republicans. In the Democratic party the main difference is between northerners and southerners, the northerners being more supportive of international involvement. With these observations in mind, I have divided senators and representatives into four groups for the purpose of further analysis; northern Democrats, southern Democrats, coastal Republicans, and interior Republicans. Southern Democrats are those from the Border and Southern states; northern Democrats include the remainder. Coastal Republicans are those from three of the eight regions—Northeast, Middle Atlantic, Pacific; those from all other regions are considered interior Republicans.

For another perspective on presidential influence, let us now examine, not movements of individual members or the lack thereof, but changes in the distribution of congressmen along the continuum from high to low support, that occur with presidential turnovers. This will be done for each of the regional party groupings specified above, for both the House and the Senate. Given the earlier findings, it is anticipated that the distribution of the Republican regional groupings will shift toward the high support pole when a Republican takes over from a Democrat in the White House, and vice versa. Similarly, the center of gravity of the distribution of Democrats along the international involvement dimension will be closer to the high support pole under a Democratic president.

The current demonstration of presidential influence is significantly different from the former one in two ways. (1) Regional variations within the parties are taken into account; (2) all members of each of the five relevant Congresses are brought into the analysis (the Eighty-fifth through Eighty-eighth and the Ninety-first). Up to now only those congressmen who managed to serve in at least one of the Congresses before *and* one of the Congresses after each presidential turnover have been included.

In order to simplify the review of the results of this investigation, each of the parties will be viewed separately. Thus in Figure 15, the basis for the first description of findings, the distribution of policy positions for the two regional groupings within the Republican party is shown for the two houses. Figure 16 gives the same information for the Democrats. In both figures, distributions within each house's regional-party groupings are shown for the three presidential administrations, reading from left to right, Eisenhower, Kennedy-Johnson, Nixon.

Let us look first at the *Republicans.* The shifting of positions in response to presidential turnover is clearly illustrated by the interior Republicans in the House. Under the Democratic administration, nearly two-thirds of these Republicans take the least supportive position relative to international involvement, whereas only one-half occupy the low support position under the Eisenhower administration and less than a third do so under Nixon. By the same token, *none* of the interior Republicans are found at the high support pole of the dimension under the Kennedy-Johnson Administration whereas one-quarter of them move to that pole position under the two Republican administrations. Note that the same pattern of movement characterizes interior Republican Senators, only in a more subdued form.

Figure 15
*Distribution of Republican Senators and Representatives on
International Involvement Dimension (percentages taking
high to low positions)*

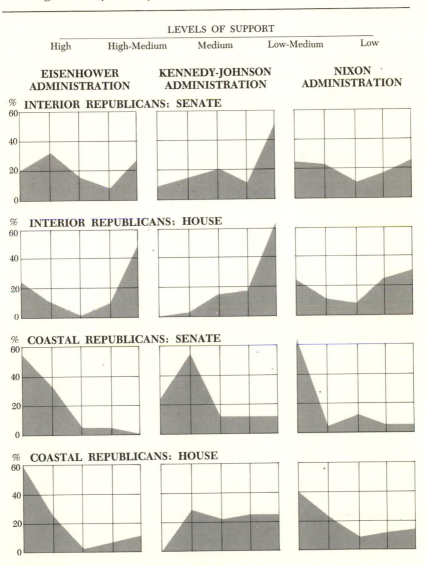

Whereas the center of gravity of the interior Republican distribution on this dimension is clearly toward the low support end of the continuum, the center of gravity among coastal Republicans is much more towards the high support pole of the continuum. Indeed, in the Senate the coastal Republicans are massed toward the high support pole regardless which party is in the White House. However, in the House, the coastal Republicans show a very strong movement away from the high support position when a Democrat is in the White House. When the Republicans resume the White House occupancy, the coastal House Republicans join hands with their Senate fellows.

Among the *Democrats,* it is the southern contingent that displays the greatest movement from one administration to the next (Figure 17). Southern House Democrats are particularly volatile; on balance, they are high supporters of international involvement during a Democratic administration and low supporters during a Republican administration. We also see a major shift in the policy positions of southern Democratic senators between the Kennedy-Johnson and the Nixon administrations, but a much less dramatic one after the Eisenhower administration pulls down its tents.

In contrast to the southern Democrats, the northern Democrats are a bit of a bore. They tender strong support for international involvement, whichever administration is in control. However, by acting as a nearly monolithic bloc in support of international involvement under a Democratic administration, the northern Democrats manage to conform to our general expectation that the president exerts a pull on his fellow partisans in the Congress in the direction of greater support for international involvement.

Contrary to what one might expect, Democratic senators in the North are slightly less supportive of international involvement than are representatives. This is not a function of institutional differences between the Senate and the House, because the general pattern is the opposite: Senators tend to be equally or more supportive of international involvement than their colleagues in the House from the same party and region. One possible reason for the odd pattern in the northern Democratic contingent is that, relative to the House, the Midwestern, Plains and Mountain states are overrepresented in the Senate. Since the latter regions tend to be somewhat less supportive of international involvement, the whole northern Democratic

Figure 16
*Distribution of Democratic Senators and Representatives on
International Involvement Dimension (percentages taking
high to low positions)*

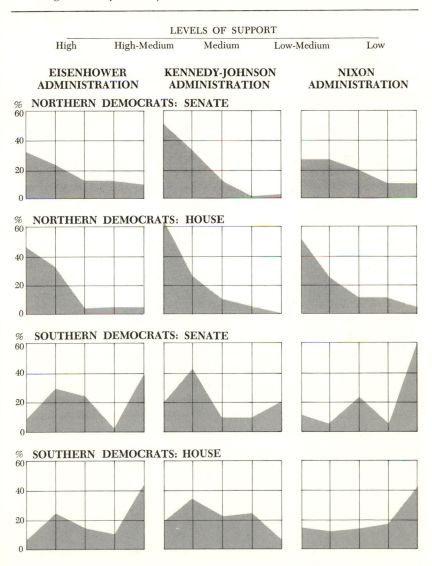

LEVELS OF SUPPORT

| High | High-Medium | Medium | Low-Medium | Low |

EISENHOWER
ADMINISTRATION

KENNEDY-JOHNSON
ADMINISTRATION

NIXON
ADMINISTRATION

NORTHERN DEMOCRATS: SENATE

NORTHERN DEMOCRATS: HOUSE

SOUTHERN DEMOCRATS: SENATE

SOUTHERN DEMOCRATS: HOUSE

Senate group appears less supportive than the northern Democratic House group.

Speculations aside, the Senate-House regional-party analysis shows the strength of the evidence in support of presidential influence. This influence is effective, and demonstrably so, in all of the eight conditions I have defined: two regions within each of the two parties within each of the two houses.

MEMBERS RESISTING PRESIDENTIAL WISHES

Throughout the greater part of this analysis and discussion of presidential influence on the policy positions of congressmen on international involvement, the emphasis has been upon the changes in policy positions accompanying a presidential turnover. There are, however some congressmen who do not change their positions. Some of the stable types are consistently highly supportive of international involvement and would have no reason to change position in response to presidential wishes, others are stable *and* do not follow their party's president's policy lead.

Congressmen who consistently vote *against* continuing or increasing international commitments, or take moderate positions fairly consistently are most interesting in comparison with those who provide little support for international involvement when their party is out of the White House but move to higher support positions when their party is in. What is the difference between these two sets of congressmen?

Although I can provide no explanation for the difference between congressmen who are responsive to presidential influence and those who are not, I can provide further information that confirms the meaningfulness of the distinction between the responsive and the resistors. This information is drawn from a study of representation conducted by Miller and Stokes on the Eighty-fifth and Eighty-sixth Congresses, 1957–1960.[4] In this study, members of the House were asked about their voting in the area of foreign affairs: "How much difference has the administration's position made to you in your roll-call votes—a great deal, a lot, some, little, or no difference?" When the answers to this question were related to the qualitative distinction between *Republicans* who persistently took low support positions on international involvement and those who moved to provide more support during the Eisenhower administration, this is what I found:

Difference Made by Administration Position

	GREAT	LOT	SOME	LITTLE	NONE
Responsive Republicans	6	2	3	1	3
Nonresponsive Republicans	1	1	1	1	8

Although the sample is small, being a subsample of a sample of representatives, and therefore subject to substantial sampling error, there seems to be little doubt that there is a real qualitative difference between responsive and nonresponsive Republicans. Two-thirds of the representatives whose voting behavior indicates no responsiveness to administration wishes report that the administration's position made no difference in their policy decisions on legislative notions; in contrast, only one-fifth of the representatives who change their policy positions report no administration influence.

Significantly, when the same question was asked of Democratic representatives there was an overwhelming denial of presidential influence. This is significant because these Democrats were serving under a Republican president; accordingly, there is no reason why they should be affected by the administration's position, at least not as a function of party loyalty.

THE POSITION OF THE PRESIDENT

The presumption built into this analysis of presidential influence on the international involvement dimension is that the president himself takes a position toward the high support pole. This presumption is based on evidence. Just as congressmen can be ordered on a policy dimension according to their votes on individual roll calls associated with that dimension, so it is possible to locate the president on a dimension according to the positions he has taken on the various roll calls. When this is done for each of the three presidential administrations, the president emerges as a strong supporter of international involvement.

It may not always be the case that the president will be out front in the support of international commitments, although the fact that foreign policy is his area of responsibility makes it highly likely that such will be the general pattern. It is in his interest to push for legislation and appropriations that will give him the instruments he needs to exert influence on the international level. Such would seem to be the case for the period of eighteen years covered by this study. Much of this legislation was concerned with foreign aid of a unilateral variety, and some was supportive of international agencies such as the United Nations and the International Monetary Fund. As such it was legislation that gave the president resources useful in international negotiations, resources that are likely to be sought by any president who is concerned that this country, and he himself, should be a force in world politics.

In this light, it is understandable that the presidents in the period under study should favor international involvement. Kennedy and Nixon made it very clear that theirs was a strong interest in international relations, and the conduct of their presidencies suggests that domestic policy was certainly of no more than equal interest. Eisenhower's attentions were naturally drawn to foreign affairs because this was his area of expertise and experience in the military service during and after World War II.

Johnson is the only one of the four presidents whose capabilities and interests were domestically oriented. However, his presidency enters into our analysis only to the extent that he has an impact on the Kennedy-Johnson administration. This impact is restricted primarily to the last one of the four years, when he, as a matter of fact, gave all appearances of playing out the presidential hand of John F. Kennedy.

Before going on to a brief discussion of the lack of evidence of presidential influence in domestic policy, let me assure you that I shall return to more general comments on the international involvement dimension in the concluding chapter.

Presidential Influence:
Domestic Policy

The apparent lack of presidential influence on the policy positions of congressmen on the four domestic policy dimensions may appear a bit strange at first glance. After all, as commented earlier, there is a great deal of attention given to the president's position on a wide variety of policy questions. Yet it seems from this analysis that presidential positions on domestic policy do not alter enough votes to cause any discernible movement within the congressional ranks.

Now if the findings had been uniformly negative across all policy dimensions, it would have been possible to shrug them off as the results of an inadequate mode of analysis. Or, to the glee of some detractors of quantitative techniques, it could be just another example of the eternal verity that "if you can count it, it isn't worth counting, and what counts can't be counted." However, the counting does add up to something on the international involvement dimension; indeed the sum of the count is very impressive.

There are several objections that may be raised against my conclusion that presidential influence is either trivial or nonexistent on the domestic policy dimensions. Let me spell some of these out, doing so in the context of a clear understanding of the meaning of presidential influence as analyzed here.

Most simply, I see presidential influence as a partisan gravitational force exerted by the president on the members of congress from his own party. This force pulls the congressman away from the position he would occupy in response to the more stable nonpresidential factors such as constituency, state, and region. When the president from the congressman's party leaves the White House, this force is removed and the congressman snaps back into his normal position, so to speak. Some congressmen somehow manage to escape the presidential gravitational field and retain their normal position. Then, of course, there are the congressmen who already occupy a position consistent with that of their party's president.

In the case of the international involvement dimension, the president's position is always at the high support pole, and his influence is always recognized as pulling congressmen in that direction. It is possible that on other dimensions Republican and Democratic presidents will be at opposite poles. No matter, this should still show up in movements in those directions as administrations change. For example, a strongly conservative Republican president taking over from a strongly liberal Democratic president should produce movement in the conservative direction among both Republicans and Democrats.

What happens if the president is a moderate in relation to his party colleagues in the Congress? Theoretically, we should see the party's congressmen converging toward the presidential position. What the members of the other party would be doing as a result of this new presidency would depend upon the character of the previous president from their party; whatever way this president had pulled them, there would be a return to their normal positions.

However, there are circumstances that diminish the importance of presidential influence on congressional policy positions. For example, if the party is highly cohesive *and the president's position is in accord with the party members' normal positions,* there is neither a need nor an occasion for the exercise of presidential influence.

The condition of party cohesion can be used as an explanation for the lack of any evidence of presidential influence on the government management dimension. The same clearly applies to the Republicans on the civil liberties dimension; and one would hardly expect a Democratic president with a liberal civil rights position to have much of an influence on the Democratic congressmen committed to the exclusion of the federal government from this field. So, for two of the four dimensions, the lack of presidential influence appears quite understandable.

Actually, the party cohesion on the two remaining dimensions, agricultural assistance and social welfare, may be high enough that few party members will be far enough out of line with their party's president to feel a strong compulsion to change their positions. The greatest opportunity for presidential influence would appear to be on the social welfare dimension among Democrats. At least a portion of the southern Democrats are clearly less supportive of social welfare than the main body of Democrats.

Even with the use of a microscope, I failed to detect any evidence of movement that went beyond the changes in scores one expects as a function of idiosyncratic factors affecting individual congressmen in individual Congresses and as a function of what has to be a very small amount of measurement error. There simply is no case that can be made for presidential influence on the social welfare dimension, even among southern Democrats. Nor is there any evidence of such influence on the agricultural assistance dimension.

The Many Facets of Presidential Influence: A Caveat

One major qualification must be presented before going on to concluding remarks. I recognize that presidential influence takes many forms that are not manifested in the current analysis. The president may, for example, "go all out" for only a few items of legislation of truly major importance, on which only a few roll calls are taken. Consequently, their effects are lost in the mass of votes on the more common, and recurring, items such as appropriations for existing programs. The president may also compel changes in legislation, formed or worked into shape in Congress, through recourse to the instruments of formal power (such as the veto) and political influence at his disposal.

But I need not go further in spelling out the limitations on my measurement of presidential influence. There are undoubtedly many willing hands more competent to do this task, both by training and inclination. I merely wanted it known that my view of presidential and congressional politics derived something from the capacity for peripheral vision.

Conclusions

Presidential influence has been recognized as a powerful factor in the determination of the policy positions of congressmen on one policy dimension. However, it appears to be effective only on congressmen of the same party as the president.

The policy dimension on which presidential influence is effective is international involvement, a dimension that the president has some reason to call his own. Let me add to this sense of proprietorship by offering the opinion that the legislation found on the international involvement dimension, in the Congresses under study, is concerned primarily with the *national interest* in international relations. The question being asked is: How can national resources best be used to maximize our political and economic advantage in a basically competitive international system? I make this point as strongly as possible to make it clear that this is not a dimension primarily concerned with the extent of United States participation in a world community.

Thus, the ordering of congressmen on the international involvement dimension does not go from the "isolationist, fortress-America-firsters" to the "antinationalist, one-world internationalists" who would prefer that the ultimate political and military power reside in some form of United Nations government. Rather it is an ordering that goes from those who seriously question the value of assisting others as a means toward helping ourselves and who prefer military strength over strong allies, since the latter may be here today and gone tomorrow, to those who feel that an active involvement in international affairs is an investment that serves the national interest.

Of course, everybody claims peace and national strength as his goals, but the proponents of international involvement are more likely to be sanguine about the possibility of avoiding conflict with the Russian bear and the Chinese dragon. It is interesting that President Nixon, an avowed anti-Communist but an international involvement *president,* is one of the relatively sanguine types, as his journeys to Peking and Moscow suggest. Perhaps the example of Richard M. Nixon, as a supporter of international involvement in the role of president, is the clincher in the argument that to support international involvement, as measured here, does not automatically imply support for internationalism as an aspect of a humanitarian one-world philosophy.

What all this boils down to is this: The international involvement dimension is concerned with the instrumentation of a foreign policy that is premised on the need for national survival and the search for national well-being, security, and power. As such, it encompasses mainly programs, such as foreign military and economic aid, that are desired by the president to enhance his prestige, strength, and flexibility in the conduct of American foreign policy. Therefore, it is inevitable that his position will be a strongly positive one as regards the legislation he is likely to have sponsored, in one way or another. Following this same line of thought, we can expect members of the president's party in Congress to support him even though they would not necessarily support the same policies were they presented by a president of the other party. Foreign policy is the president's responsibility, and members of his party will back him because he is their president.

Congressmen of the president's party who oppose him on foreign policy requests certainly must have strong reasons for doing so. Under a Republican president they are most likely to be ones from the Midwest and the Plains and Mountain states. During a Democratic administration, it is the congressmen from the Democratic South who are most likely to hang back when the president beckons, but they are not as numerous as the interior Republicans.

The interior regions, as we have noted before, have a long tradition of opposition to "foreign entanglements," to use George Washington's words. Such deeply implanted views are difficult to uproot. Furthermore, they are sustained by a particular view of history that is not easily dismissed as irrelevant and uninformed. They can point to allies who have become enemies and enemies who have become allies, when time spans of twenty-five years, or even less, are taken into consideration. For instance, since 1900 our relationship to Russia has changed from friend, to foe, to friend, to foe again, and might possibly be turning back to friend. Observations such as this on the alternating currents of sympathy and antipathy in relations with Russia, China, Japan, Germany, Italy, and Spain are all the more difficult to discount because of the hundred-percent fervor with which we have hated our enemies and embraced our friends of the time being. If alliances and conflicts between ourselves and other nations had consistently been viewed as temporary adjustments to an international environment, the commitments of national resources in behalf of the allies of today and the enemies of tomorrow might have been borne more easily. They could have been looked upon as costs involved in deriving short-term advantages rather than as long-term investments.

I am *not* spending this much time presenting an argument for the policy of restraint in international commitments because such is my own policy view. My policy views are neither relevant nor appropriate to this work. My reason for expounding this argument is that I think it is seldom that the "isolationist" point of view is sufficiently well recognized, or even well understood, by social scientists who are preponderantly favorable to activist foreign policy. In addition, it may make it easier for the reader to understand congressmen who reject "their" president's requests.

My final words on presidential influence, in this chapter, are addressed to the finding of presidential influence on the international involvement dimension and the absence of even a trace of such influence on the four domestic policy dimensions: government management, social welfare, agricultural assistance, and civil liberties. To a large extent the results of this analysis were inherent in the findings of the preceding chapter. The greater part of the variation in the policy positions on the four domestic policy dimensions was found, in the preceding chapter, to be accounted for by constituency, party, region, and state. Only about half of the variation on the international involvement dimension was explained by these factors.

The lack of success in explaining the variation in international involvement positions implies the existence of unmeasured factors that can account for an additional portion of the variation. There was good reason to believe that presidential influence would move into the existing void. Moreover, there existed the possibility that the presidential factor was counteracting the effects of the other variables. Consequently, a diminution of the influence of these other factors would occur. On the domestic policy dimensions, on the other hand, it appeared that the party and constituency roots of the congressmen's policy positions were so strong, explaining upwards of three-forths of the variation in policy positions, that there would be no opportunity for an effective exercise of presidential persuasion.

I must say that I am most strongly attracted to the proposition that presidential influence is a major force on the international involvement dimension for two reasons. First, this is an area in which the president is expected to provide leadership; and, second, foreign policy has implications sufficiently removed from the cognitive experience of the citizen that congressmen are not tightly constrained by perceptions of constituency demands. Therefore, a congressman may shift about a bit in response to executive requests without risking his political investment. And I rather suspect that those congressmen who do not respond to the president of their own party, and vote against his programs, do so more out of a personal conviction than out of concern for reprisals at the polls. This is not to deny the possibility that they are strongly influenced and supported in these convictions by political elites from their areas, such as the powerful metropolitan daily that serves their state. But let me come back to this point in the next and final chapter, dealing with patterns of influence.

References

1. James M. Burns, *Deadlock of Democracy* (Englewood Cliffs, N.J.: Prentice-Hall, 1963); Ernest S. Griffith, *Congress: Its Contemporary Role*, 3rd ed. (New York: New York University Press, 1961); David B. Truman, ed., *Congress and America's Future* (Englewood Cliffs, N.J.: Prentice-Hall, 1965), see especially pieces by Neustadt, Huntington, and Mansfield.

2. James A. Robinson, *Congress and Foreign Policy-Making*, rev. ed. (Homewood, Ill.: Dorsey, 1967).

3. Mark Kesselman, "Presidential Leadership in Congress on Foreign Policy," *Midwest Journal of Political Science* 5 (August 1961), and "Presidential Leadership in Congress on Foreign Policy: A Replication of a Hypothesis," *Midwest Journal of Political Science* 9 (November 1965). Also highly sensitive to this possibility is Leroy N. Rieselbach, *Roots of Isolationism* (Indianapolis, Ind.: Bobbs-Merrill, 1966); Ronald C. Moe and Steven C. Teel, "Congress as Policy-Maker: A Necessary Reappraisal," *Political Science Quarterly* 85 (September 1970), pp. 443–470.

4. Warren E. Miller and Donald E. Stokes, *Representation in Congress* (in preparation).

9

Patterns
of
Influence

One of the outstanding features of this study of congressional be-havior is the finding of a fairly simple pattern of policy positions among individual congressmen. The pattern's simplicity is comple-mented by a high degree of stability and reinforced by its dual ex-pression in the House and Senate.

Linked to the simple structure of policy positions are patterns of influence that can be comprehended without severe stresses on one's cognitive apparatus. It is these influences with which this concluding chapter is mainly concerned. This involves a description of the pat-tern of influence on each of the five dimensions, with the focus upon three general sources of influence: party, constituency, and the president.

Throughout this discussion, it is important to keep in mind that the object of influence is the *policy positions taken by individual congressmen in relation to the general policy concepts* that are the foci of the five policy dimensions. We are not talking about the deci-sions of individual congressmen on individual proposals, nor about congressional disposition of legislative motions.

As a preview of what is to follow let me say that my judgments on the patterns of influence lead me to the specification of four patterns. A pattern of party influence is seen on one of our policy dimensions; a party-constituency pattern is reflected on two dimensions; a con-stituency dominated pattern appears on a fourth dimension; and the fourth pattern, an unexpected combination of constituency and presi-dential influence, is found on the fifth policy dimension.

A *Party Influence:*
Government Management

It should be evident by now that I have a strong conviction that the government management dimension, which subsumes policies involving the regulation of the economy, relations between business and government, the care and use of natural resources, and tax and fiscal policy, is a partisan dimension. There is something akin to an ideological division between Republicans and Democrats regarding the involvement of the national government in economic affairs. In classical political-economic terms, this difference consists of opposing positions on the merits of the doctrine of *laissez faire.*

In application, the doctrine of laissez faire has lost some of its virgin purity. Whereas in its pure form the doctrine called for the government to keep "hands off" the economy, in practice the doctrine accommodates some degree of government activity in behalf of the business (or productive) enterprise. As Calvin Coolidge sparingly put it, "The business of government is business."

In a takeoff on this remark, Franklin D. Roosevelt asserted, "The business of government is government." This denoted that government was not restricted solely to those activities that aided the cause of business but could actually intrude into the workings of the economy on behalf of one business in relation to another, on behalf of the consumer in relation to business, or on behalf of the worker in relation to business. This view of the government's role was highlighted during the New Deal of the 1930s. However, its origins must be traced back, in this country, to at least the last half of the nineteenth century when the farmers and workers engaged in sporadic revolts against the financial and industrial giants whose names have become household words: Rockefeller, Carnegie, DuPont, Morgan. This was the era of populism, of incipient labor unionism, of frustrated socialism, and of attempts to get the government to regulate the mighty combinations of wealth and political power. *Then, later,* and *now* it is the Democratic party that has opposed the doctrine of laissez faire as the ultimate solution; *then, later,* and *now* it is the Republican party that has embraced the doctrine of laissez faire, if not as an ultimate solution, certainly as a highly desirable one.

But I must be careful lest I leave you with a caricature of reality. Neither party has been as strong in its position nor as united as I may have made it appear. The polar positions that I present should rightly be viewed as tendencies in belief and action. But I do believe the tendencies *are* discriminating, that the fundamental attitude differences *do* exist between the parties, that these differences *are* of an ideological form. What keeps the division from sharpening is the enormous capacity of influential members of both parties to bend their principles in response to the pressures of practical political demands.

The partisan division that I see on this dimension is shared by other political systems in the realm of Western democracies. It is the central component of the European distinctions between Left and Right, and between socialist and bourgeois. It remains a source of difference between the Labour and Conservative parties in England.

Actually, the division in the United States is a fairly mild one, and always has been, in comparison with the European experience. What is of interest to me is that it exists at all in a political society supposedly so devoid of ideology. Yet there it is. But why?

I believe that this dimension is partisan and ideological in character, its policy attitudes transmitted from one generation of partisans to another rather than being the product of current conditions, because many of the problems at issue are too complex for most to understand, are beyond the capacity of anyone to solve, and require temporary solutions whose effects are difficult to determine. Faced with problems of sufficient complexity and intractability, faced with the unknown, what is there to do but rely upon superstition, rain dances, and ideology? There may be no way to arrive at the best policy; therefore, let us follow the policy that is "right" according to our system of beliefs.

When I say that the problems at issue are too complex for most to understand and beyond the capacity of anyone to solve, I have in mind the continuing debate over the best ways in which to maintain full employment, stable prices, and increasing productivity. Clearly, the economists disagree on this; equally clearly, different presidential administrations try different policies in the search for the correct policy. The latest manifestation of this phenomenon is the Republican Nixon administration imposing wage and price controls. On the surface this appears to be a rather strong rejection of laissez faire although it certainly is not advertised as such.

Consistent with their preference for laissez faire, but making it a benevolent principle, Republicans favor the stimulation of the economy by direct aids to business through tax relief, subsidies, and investment incentives. The premise on which these actions are predicated is that as business expands, the economy moves forward, jobs are created, and more goods are produced. So the thing to do is to stimulate business to invest and expand, to provide direct aid to those who produce the jobs and the goods.

Democrats are, of course, also interested in stimulating business, but their economic experts favor entering into the economic cycle at a different point. The thing to do first is to create a demand for goods; as demands rise, production will increase to meet the demand, new jobs will be created, and the economy will soon be humming again. Perhaps some tax investment incentives to business will be of some use, but what is more beneficial is tax relief to the poor people who will spend every dollar they can lay their hands on because their demands are far from being satiated. This demand for more goods will stimulate production and create more jobs. If necessary, Democrats are willing to put people to work on government projects in order to provide the unemployed with a spendable income.

But something is wrong; neither system works well very long. Nevertheless, Republicans continue to believe that stimulating business directly is the way; Democrats counter with the belief that demand must be stimulated first. Both beliefs are politically advantageous to the respective parties. The Republicans' policy puts money in the pockets of their supporters while the Democrats' policy provides financial benefits to their supporters. Thus, the belief system jibes with the immediately economic advantage of the core supporters of each party.

In sum, government management is a partisan dimension, not a constituency dimension, because of the unpredictability and complexity of the policy alternatives. The voter is in no position to even have an opinion. His role is restricted to complaining when economic conditions worsen, not to choosing among policies. Therefore, to talk about constituency opinion in terms of concrete realizations of self-interest, which serve as constraints on the behavior of the congressman, is relatively meaningless. At most, the more involved partisans may share in their party's beliefs about economic policy. Although constituents on a fairly mass level may have ideas about welfare programs, aid to education, and racial integration, and may even have preferences on foreign aid, the United Nations, and farm subsidies, how to create jobs is beyond the pale.

Other issues included on the government management dimension are equally good examples of matters beyond the cognitive grasp and gut interest of the vast preponderance of American citizens. There is continuing debate in elite circles over the respective rights of business and government in the operation of electrical power utilities and transmission lines, over the control of patent rights when technological innovations result from government contracts, and over other questions concerning government-business relations in economic activities with a profit potential. It is a certainty that the same general question will continue to divide congressmen as, for example, new commercial uses of the space program come up for grabs and new sources of energy are developed.

Currently, there is developing an "ecological network" of issues concerned with pollution, the use of public lands, and the development of energy resources, which are likely to find a home on the government management dimension. The problems are complex and the solutions uncertain; in the effort to cope with this complexity there is a tendency to cast the issue in simple terms, like the gross national product versus a breath of fresh air. We can look forward to the Republican party favoring the gross national product, while the Democrats attempt to make hay out of the public interest. This does not mean either party will have a monopoly on clean air, fresh water, and open skies; it does mean that the two parties will differ on the methods of reconciling the need for production with the desire for a pleasant environment. The Republicans will, relative to the Democrats, make greater efforts to lessen the burden on business and be more likely to question the "realism" of the advocates of the sanctity of the environment.

Party-Constituency Influence:
Social Welfare
and Agricultural Assistance

Congressional policy alignments on the agricultural assistance and social welfare dimensions display a mixture of party and constituency influence. Although it appeared earlier that agricultural assistance might emerge as a party dimension closely linked to the government management dimension, with the partisanship just a bit muted by the effects of constituency interests, I am now persuaded that this is not the case. My final judgment is that social welfare and agricultural assistance share approximately equal status as party-constituency

dimensions. The reasons lying behind this judgment can be summarized quite briefly.

My initial inclination to view the agricultural assistance dimension
as a close blood relative of the government management dimension
was based on two things: the strength of the partisan division on
this dimension and the compatability of the substance of the two
dimensions. Remember that party accounts for almost 70 percent of
the variation on the agricultural assistance dimension, statistically
speaking, noticeably less than the 80 to 90 percent on the government
management dimension, but a much larger percentage than the 30
percent on the social welfare dimension. Substantively, the commonality of the government management and agricultural assistance
dimensions lies in the fact that both involve an intrusion of the
government into the economy. In the case of agricultural assistance
the farm industry must accept a measure of government control over
the program of production in exchange for a governmental program
of subsidies.

However, there is an important difference in the substance of the
two dimensions. In contrast to the government management policies,
there is little doubt regarding the beneficiaries of the subsidy programs: They are the recipients of the subsidy payments and the
growers of the crops whose prices are shored up by the subsidy program. It is also relatively clear who foots the bill. This is the point
at which constituency interests enter in. As a consequence, the
partisan lines are blurred somewhat. Some Republicans, normally
disposed against government intervention, support the subsidy program because it favors their constituents; and some Democrats, normally favorable to government aids, oppose the subsidies because
their constituents must bear the cost.

A second item entered into my reevaluation of the character of
the agricultural assistance dimension. Remember the observation that
party lines appear to be rather tightly drawn on the agricultural
assistance dimension. The information that qualifies a "partisan" interpretation of this observation is the evidence drawn from the study
of the effects of partisan turnovers of constituency seats, that is to
say, the change in policy representation that occurs when an incumbent congressman is replaced by a member from the other party.
According to this evidence, party is more important on the social
welfare than on the agricultural assistance dimension. Yet party seems
weaker on social welfare than on agricultural assistance when we

look simply at the voting alignments at fixed points in time. This apparent contradiction in findings can be resolved, and the key lies with the southern Democrats.

If we begin with the assumption that the Democratic party attitude is to favor federal social welfare legislation and support for the farmers, then we can see that southern Democrats, *voting their constituency interests* on both dimensions, contribute to a strong partisan division on agricultural assistance and to a weak one on social welfare, since southern Democrats tend to favor the former and oppose the latter. My expectation would be that southern Republicans taking the place of the southern Democrats would stand in stronger opposition to social welfare but provide some support for farm subsidies. Hence, if there were partisan turnovers in the South in large numbers, which clearly was not the case, then as more southern Republicans were elected, the party cleavage on social welfare would be increased and the division on agricultural assistance muted.

In sum, constituency is a powerful influence on both dimensions, but the existing arrangement of constituency interests and partisan alignments makes it only *appear* that party is a much stronger factor on agricultural assistance than on social welfare—when we look only at the voting division. This yields two judgments. First, constituency is a major force on both the agricultural assistance and social welfare dimensions, and probably equally important on both. And, second, it is very unwise to depend solely upon the properties of a policy alignment in Congress, at fixed points in time, for information on sources of influence.

In closing this review of the patterns of influence on the social welfare and agricultural assistance dimensions, let me affirm the presence of party differences on both dimensions, independent of constituency pressures. Party attitudes provide the best explanation for the urban Democrat's support of farm subsidies. Party attitudes also appear to exert a pull to the Left on the southern Democrats on social welfare, causing many southern Democrats to take a middle policy position. But in its contest with constituency, party comes off looking less impressive, by a good measure, than it does on the government management dimension.

Since this completes our review of the three dimensions on which the party influence is a demonstrably important factor, let me digress a bit to look at a difference in party strategies suggested by David

Mayhew after conducting a study of House voting for the period, 1947–1962. Mayhew suggests that the Democratic party operates on the principle of the "inclusive compromise" in which different groups, particularly in legislative bodies, who are seeking advantages from the government achieve their individual goals by each supporting the demands of the other.[1] The concept of the "inclusive compromise" is borrowed from Dankwart Rustow who also suggests an "exclusive compromise," in which some groups win and others lose.[2] According to Mayhew, the Republicans favor the exclusive compromise.[3] As it works out, this finds the majority of Republicans holding the line against government spending even when some of their brethren represent constituencies that demand the government programs.

For example, in the Democratic party the urban Democrats vote for farm subsidies in greater numbers than the farmers have any right to expect; but then rural Democrats, mostly from the South, support urban programs to a greater degree than may be appreciated by northern liberal Democrats. In contrast, the minority of Republican congressmen with "farm subsidy" constituents have to go it alone with the Democrats, as Republicans with urban industrial constituents have to do on urban programs on the social welfare dimension. Mayhew finds this pattern on four types of issues: city, farm, labor, and West.

The pervasiveness of the pattern of inclusive compromise in the Democratic party, in which party members support congressmen from constituencies that have an interest in a program, induces Mayhew to speculate that this strategy of legislative activity may be the hallmark of a successful (dominant) party.[4] A pejorative view of this phenomenon is expressed by the common criticism of the Democratic party: Everybody gets a free ride on the public express, with payment deferred to future generations.

Mayhew's interpretation is persuasive because of its fit with generally accepted views of the two parties. Republicans are expected to look hard and long at increases in federal expenditures and expansions of federal programs. Democrats are generally recognized as generous managers of the public treasury, reluctant to reject a half-way reasonable request for assistance.

One problem with the evidence from which the inference of the two parties' strategies is drawn is that it is collected by studying legislation only in those areas in which the Democrats have built up their reputation for "passing the gravy." What is more, it is also the case that in all four areas of legislation the proportion of Republicans representing "interested" constituencies (for example, metropolitan districts on city issues) is very small. In contrast, the proportion of Democrats in interested constituencies, in three out of the four areas, the West excluded, make up a much larger proportion of all Democrats. For instance, in 1954, one of the middle years of Mayhew's study, and fairly typical, the interested farm congressmen in the Republican party are outnumbered 4.5 to 1; in the Democratic party the farm congressmen are outnumbered by slightly less than 2 to 1.[5] (Since the definition of "interested" constituencies is arbitrary, it is the difference in the ratios of uninterested to interested congressmen in the two parties that is important, rather than the absolute number in each.)

The problem with Mayhew's evidence of party strategies, then, is that the members of the Democratic party are under much more pressure to support the constituency interests of their colleagues than are Republican party members. Indeed, one might very well imagine a loosening of the requirements that a constituency must meet to be classified as interested in the policy at hand, such that a majority of Democrats would be so classified while the majority of the Republicans would still be representing uninterested constituencies. In this light the behavior of the Democrats looks a bit more like representation at work and less like demagogic embezzlement of public funds.

Constituency Influence: Civil Liberties

The source of influence on the civil liberties dimension during the period under study is as exclusively *constituency* as the source of influence on the government management dimension is *party*. This is due in part to the fact that the black civil rights component so dominates the dimension that the North-South division is paramount in the voting patterns. However, voting on other civil liberties questions is consistent with the basic North-South alignment; otherwise such items would not be included on the same dimension. So, one is led to conclude that southern Democrats are unenthusiastic in their support of civil liberties, northern Democrats are most supportive, and northern Republicans fall in between, but clearly toward the high support pole.

The ordering of positions just presented should not be regarded as more than the description of the alignment at fixed points in time; that is to say, it should not be taken to imply that when a northern Democrat replaces a northern Republican, there will be a shift in the policy representation of the constituency because Democrats are more supportive of civil liberties. For the evidence of this study has been that a partisan turnover does not produce such a change. In both the House and Senate, the effect of a partisan turnover is virtually identical with that of a person turnover; in both cases, the new congressmen quite consistently take more supportive positions than their predecessors. (Earlier I attributed this phenomenon to a greater sensitivity of the new members to the national shift in support for black civil rights.) Consequently, the differences between the party regional groupings are more properly allocated to the differences in the constituencies represented by the congressmen from the various groupings, rather than to a divergence in partisan views.

One piece of evidence stands in the way of the flat conclusion that civil liberties is a policy dimension on which positions are taken in sole accordance with constituency views. This is the finding of a level of Republican party cohesion on this dimension that is barely exceeded by the cohesiveness of the party on the government management dimension. Normally, this level of cohesion would represent a partisan point of view shared by most members of a party. In the present case, however, it seems more reasonable to attribute this cohesion to the fact that nearly all Republicans were from the North in this period, and that northern constituencies were only slightly differentiated on civil liberties policies. In sum, I rest with the conclusion that constituency is king on this dimension.

Constituency and
Presidential Influence:
International Involvement

Of all the five policy dimensions, international involvement shows the most interesting pattern of influence. Part of the interest lies in apparent contradictions; the other part derives from a dynamism in the pattern that is absent on the other dimensions.

The international involvement dimension is distinctive in that it is the only nondomestic policy dimension. This takes us out of the realm of policies where party and constituency reign supreme into the domain of foreign policy, where the president casts a long shadow. The persistence of the presidential presence has been established first by Kesselman and later by my own work, for a period extending from the Truman presidency (1945–1952) through the first two years of the Nixon presidency (1969–1970), a time span of over twenty years. Actually, as will be pointed out later, the span of reasonably well demonstrated presidential influence on the policy positions of members of Congress reaches back to World War I (1918), about half a century.

In my judgment, the second major component in the policy positions of individual congressmen on this dimension is constituency. By this judgment, party influence is denied. Yet there is a role for party to play indirectly, through the loyalty of a congressman to a president of his own party. I have already discussed this role at some length in the chapter on presidential influence and will return later to implications to be drawn from it. For now, however, I want to turn to the enigma of constituency influence on the international involvement dimension.

The first and most obvious aspect of this enigma is that matters of foreign policy are usually considered to be beyond the interest and capacity of the vast majority of citizens. Granted, a fair degree of interest can be stimulated by posing war and peace as policy alternatives and by the conduct of current wars, but these are not the kinds of questions that congressmen of this study considered when voting in terms of the international involvement dimension. The principal issue was foreign aid and its many ramifications, although, in addition, congressmen were asked to support international conferences, organizations, and financial institutions.

The mythical average citizen may come up with an attitude on foreign aid as a general policy to be supported, tolerated, or condemned. Or, as I have argued previously, general attitudes toward international involvements may abound in the land. But that would be about the extent of it.

Another view of mass attitudes on foreign policy matters is based on policy attitude data collected by others during the period of the current study. In one such study, the meaningfulness of policy attitudes expressed in survey interviews was inferred from the stability of such attitudes over time. Among the eight policy questions analyzed for stability, foreign policy questions ranked fourth, sixth, and seventh. This finding is suggestive of friendly, but often random and meaningless, responses to the interviewers' questions.[6] In short, *the first requirement for constituency influence would appear to be lacking: the existence of a set of reasonably firmly held policy positions to be represented.*

Support for the proposition that constituency influence is absent from the international involvement dimension is augmented by the finding that constituency attitudes and the policy positions of their representatives show no degree of similarity. This finding is drawn from the Miller-Stokes study of representation referred to earlier and is based upon the following operations: [7] Interviews were taken with a sample of constituents from each of over a hundred House districts throughout the country. A mean score was computed for each House district, representing a mean attitude for the constituency, and this was compared with the congressman's score on a scale very similar to the international involvement measure used in the current study. Then an attempt was made to predict congressional policy positions from constituency policy positions, and it failed as badly as it possibly could. Nor is this just a failure of the techniques of the study, because a respectable showing was made with respect to a social welfare dimension and quite a good prediction was achieved on a civil rights dimension.

Despite this kind of evidence, I continue to insist that constituency is a major influence on the congressman's policy position on the international involvement dimension. This opinion is supported by the fairly high degree of stability found in congressional policy positions on this dimension, including a change in positions associated with a person turnover that is slightly above par for the course and a change in policy positions when a partisan turnover occurs that is far below par. Furthermore, there are definite differences in the level of support for international involvement associated with various regions, and urbanization is strongly related to the level of support for international commitments. What is more, both the regional pattern and the urban-rural continuum of support for international involvement have held up for years prior to those included in this study, as attested to by other research.

In other words, when one looks at congressional behavior on this dimension in relation to properties of electoral constituencies, a strong linkage is evident. But when one looks, instead, for a relation between constituency attitudes and congressional policy positions, one finds absolutely none!

A glimmer of understanding comes with attention to another analysis of public opinion in relation to foreign affairs. V. O. Key, Jr. observed, during the period at hand, that "on the broad question of toleration of, if not zealous support for, American participation in world affairs regional contrasts seem to have disappeared." This observation is based upon a review of questions put to American voters from the end of World War II to 1956, a date toward the middle of this study.[8] Furthermore, on a six-point scale of *urbanization*, Key finds the same level of support for international commitments across five points; only the people living in towns with populations smaller than 2500, or in the open country, appeared distinctly, but not sharply, less supportive.[9]

The import of Key's findings is that *inter*constituency variations in policy attitudes are minimal and provide a poor basis for predicting the variation in policy positions *that is observed* among congressmen. Whereas I can show, and others have shown, that differences in positions on international involvement among congressmen are associated with regional locations of constituencies and urbanization of constituencies, these eminent scholars have difficulty in coming up with evidence on mass public attitudes that provides any explanation for the differences among congressmen. If we were to go no further than this, I would be forced to conclude that constituency influence on international involvement positions is subject to debate, at best. However, there is a solution to the apparent enigma.

The contradictions among the findings given above are not difficult to resolve, particularly if we are spared the task of supporting the resolution by the systematic collection of evidence. The resolution flows from the premise that foreign policy matters are the concerns of a fairly specialized public; to put it less democratically, these are policy questions that engage only the political elites. Consequently, any measurement of constituency attitudes based upon a cross section of the voting population is unlikely to have much relevance to the behavior of congressmen. The search for constituency influence must be focused upon the limited number of constituents who maintain a steady interest in foreign affairs and form a specialized public on foreign policy questions.[10]

I can suggest some of the possible members of this elite, to whom future studies of constituency influence on foreign policy might give attention. Somewhere at the top of the list are the influential daily newspapers that serve a congressman's constituencies; their editors are typically not loathe to express their views on foreign policy topics. Another set of elites consists of the leaders of labor, business, and farm organizations, professional associations, and political organizations. Even though the organizational views are expressed only at the national level, the influence at the constituency level may still be felt through the strength of the organizations within the constituencies. Here I am not implying the issuance of a constant barrage of policy positions by these leaders; I am suggesting, rather, that their positions are fairly stable and relatively well known.

Finally, there is the circle of friends, acquaintances, and colleagues in the congressman's home constituency to which he is constantly exposed. Where the direction of constituency opinion is lacking, the views of such associates are potentially very influential.

This definition of the foreign policy constituency is reminiscent of the earlier discussion of a realistic definition of a constituency. The realistic definition held that the constituency of a congressman consisted of the people who voted for him in the last election, primarily kindred partisans. These are the people he can be expected to represent. In the case of international involvement, the "real" constituency is simply much smaller.

There is also the possibility that in the foreign policy domain, but specifically with respect to the international involvement dimension, the effective constituency may cut across party lines. An alternative way of putting this is that by representing an elite subset of his own supporters the congressman also represents people who voted for his opposition. In either case, we have a situation in which there is a general constituency point of view that is undisturbed by party differences. This is consistent with the rather surprising finding that the congressman representing a constituency takes the same position on international involvement whether he is a Democrat or Republican. In this respect the international involvement dimension is highly similar to the civil liberties dimension.

Having gone this far, a step further probably will not appreciably increase the chances that the evidential limb that I am out some distance on will break under the weight of my interpretations. Therefore, let me suggest that the call for *bipartisanship* in foreign policy may be as successful as it is because of the essential *non-*

partisanship of attitudes toward international involvement. Underscoring this nonpartisanship is the strong indication that presidents of both parties favor legislation that will maximize their influence on international relations. As I argued in the previous chapter, the legislation at the core of the international involvement dimension is designed to promote the national interest in a competitive, and combative, international arena—as opposed to legislation moving us toward a world order of supranational government.

In addition to the constituency influence on congressional positions on the international involvement dimension, I have proposed that presidential influence also is strong; furthermore, the conclusion that constituency influence is strong is interlocked with the conclusion that *party influence is weak.* I want to consider, for a bit, the juxtaposition of the conclusion that presidential influence is strong with the contention that partisan influence is either weak or nonexistent.

When the current discussion of the international involvement dimension was introduced, I said that although party was not a source of policy positions, it would be considered as having a role to play, in that *party* loyalty to the president has an effect on the behavior of some congressmen. This point will be pursued in relation to the finding that the partisan division on the international involvement dimension sometimes gives the impression of partisan differences.

If I had based my understanding of party influence on the international involvement dimension on the six Congresses of the core study, I would quite possibly have concluded that party influence was on the rise, based on the strength of the partisan division. Using a measure of the strength of the party division that goes from 0 to 1 (Pearson r), and looking at the House only, let us look at the way the party division varies. In the first Congress of the study, the Eighty-third, the measure of partisanship stands at 0.16, flutters up to 0.23 in the Eighty-fourth, plummets down to 0.01 in the Eighty-fifth, eases back up to 0.05 in the Eighty-sixth, and then comes the tide. In the Eighty-seventh Congress the measure of partisanship shoots up to 0.48, and in the last Congress of the core study it goes even higher, to 0.78.

What has happened in the Eighty-seventh and Eighty-eighth Congresses, in comparison with the Eighty-third through the Eighty-sixth, is that a Democratic president has taken over from a Republican president. When this partisan turnover in the White House occurs, there is a shifting of positions among congressmen (although some maintain a pattern of stability) that results in a strong party alignment under a Democratic president and a weak or nonexistent partisan division under a Republican president. Further confirmation of this pattern of partisan ebb and flow is provided by the Ninety-first Congress, under Nixon, in which the measure of partisanship drops to 0.13, the same level as observed during the Republican Eisenhower administration. Going back into time, and using the results of a study by Leroy Rieselbach, the level of partisanship in three Congresses of the Roosevelt administration (the Democratic Roosevelt) varies from about 0.60 to about 0.90.[11] The latter are very rough calculations, using the data as presented and looking only at foreign aid votes, but they are accurate enough to support the message that a Democratic administration results in "apparent" partisanship on international involvement.

My explanation for the decline of partisanship that accompanies a turnover from a Democratic presidency to a Republican one and the subsequent rise in partisanship that comes with a return of the presidency to the Democrats, is based on the period 1953 through 1970. It is conceivable that another explanation is needed for the earlier period, but I rather doubt it.

What happens is this: Each president has the primary responsibility for the information and execution of the nation's foreign policy. Much of this policy costs money, and congressmen generally see their voters as either passively accepting of the need to spend this money or as opposed to it. The president, on the other hand, wants all the tools he can put his hands on to exert his executive function in this area. In response to this presidential need, some members of both parties will alter their "normal" positions on international involvement in order to support the president of their *own* party. Some members of both parties support international involvement regardless of who is president. Some members of both parties resist presidential requests. The ebb and flow in the party division on this dimension is a function of the distribution of these three types of congressmen. To simplify the following description let me divide Democrats into their northern and southern wings and the Republicans into interior and coastal types. You will recall that these regional divisions mark the major points of regional differentiation, within the two parties, between low and high supporters of international involvement.

Under a Republican president, coastal Republicans tend to support international involvement while interior Republicans do not; the Democrats are also divided, with northern Democrats supporting the Republican president while southern Democrats lean in the other direction. In short, under a Republican president both parties are divided in their positions on international involvement, so partisan differences, per se, appear slight.

Under a Democratic president, southern Democrats join northern Democrats in supporting international commitments to produce a fairly unified party front; and coastal Republicans shift toward the low support position of the interior Republicans, who never moved from it, thereby increasing the difference between the parties and producing an apparent partisan split under a Democratic president.

It should be noted that the view on partisanship in foreign policy is different from the Senate galleries than from the galleries of the House. The appearance of partisanship is never as strong in the Senate as in the House because the coastal Republicans senators are consistent in their support of an activist foreign policy. They resemble the northern House Democrats in that respect.

In wrapping up the discussion of the pattern of influence on the international involvement dimension, let me make three points. (1) Presidential influence on congressional policy positions has the effect of causing large numbers of congressmen to shift their policy positions in the direction of higher support for international involvement when the president is of the congressman's own party. (2) Constituency influence emerges as an important component of the congressman's policy position; most notably, it causes some congressmen to oppose international involvement regardless of who is president and others to support international involvement under all presidents. (3) The distribution of constituency support and opposition to international involvement, in combination with the effect of presidential influence, produces what appears to be a partisan division on the international involvement dimension under a Democratic president; this apparent partisan division is virtually erased when a Republican moves into the executive mansion.

Just one last reminder. During the Ninety-first Congress, 1969–1970, we witnessed the emergence of a policy dimension, concerned with the Vietnam War and the defense establishment, that was independent of the international involvement dimension. This may be the birth of a new dimension of international military policy, or it may be the short-lived issue of a very long war in a faraway place.

Patterns of Influence—A Final Note

This discussion of patterns of influence has been carried on at a very general level—party, constituency, and the presidency—without going further into the properties of each that come to bear upon the congressman's policy positions. Such details may be found in the preceding text.

Although I have no intention of summarizing the more specific findings with respect to patterns of influence, there are two points from the detailed analysis that are worthy of recalling. The first point is the extraordinary degree to which congressional policy positions can be comprehended in terms of five variables: national party, urbanization of constituency, percentage of work force in constituency that is blue-collar, region party, and state party. Only on the international involvement dimension do these five variables fail us, and on this dimension the sixth variable of presidential influence comes to bear.

The second point, which is related to the first one, is that regional and state differences within each party make a very substantial contribution to an explanation of the variation in policy positions taken by senators and representatives. What is important about this point, in the annals of congressional research, is that studies that either leave out state and region or, as in many cases, take out the effect of region before continuing with an analysis that leaves out state party, will quite likely have a difficult time in getting their remaining variables to explain much of the variation. As I noted, simulation studies that *do* include region and state have been outstandingly successful in comparison with other studies of congressional policy positions.

The thrust of this second point is that there are highly relevant political characteristics of states and regions that must be taken cognizance of when seeking to explain the shaping of congressional policy positions. It would be preferable if this were done by developing indicators of the characteristics of states and regions that would more precisely indicate the crucial factors in the congressman's decision process. However it is done, region and state must be given consideration. The finding of this investigation was that state party explained a very high proportion of the variation in policy positions on the four domestic policy dimensions. In other words, the *differences in the policy positions of congressmen elected from the same state and party are minimal on the four domestic policy dimensions,* while remaining substantial on the international involvement dimension.

The Potential for Change

At this time I want to add a corrective term to the dominant equation written in this book: continuity + stability = Congress. The corrective term is change. Although change is unlikely ever to be a dominant characteristic of Congress, I would be engaging in extreme and highly misleading neglect if I did not point out very clearly and emphatically the opportunities for change that do exist.

I refer to change in the policy posture of the Congress as a whole; arithmetically, this may be thought of as the mean position of the total membership of Congress. Shifts in this policy posture, or mean position, are popular objects of journalistic prediction following an election: "The ——st Congress is expected to be more liberal than the last Congress"; or "the chances for ——— were set back by the results of the last election"; or "the election marked a defeat for the forces of conservatism in the new Congress."

Implicit in these kinds of predictions is the assumption that the character of the influx of new members will set the tone of the next Congress, whether this tone is a departure from that of a previous Congress or the same. In addition to the differences between the presumed policy positions of the new members and the known positions of their predecessors, which alters the political balance on policy questions, one also picks up the notion that holdover congressmen will be induced to bring their policy positions into line with the dominant direction represented by freshmen members. Of course, if there is no dominant direction in the election results, one expects no change on either count.

My research is certainly in accord with the view that the main impetus for change in the overall policy posture comes in the new

membership. I am less sanguine about the receptiveness of the continuing members to making changes in their individual policy stances
in accord with the election results.

The opportunities for change in the policy posture of Congress
are usually discussed with a view toward the policy output of the
Congress, the reasonable calculation being that the policy output
is determined by the policy input, so to speak, in the form of new
members with new ideas. However, even faintly knowledgeable
observers of Congress show an awareness that an unweighted
arithmetic mean of the policy positions of the membership of Congress may be a poor predictor of the policy output. It is clear that
some congressmen are more equal than others and that their policy
positions must be given more weight than those of others. This
unequal weighting of individual policy positions is a product of the
policymaking *process*. As proponents of direct democracy are well
aware, when a process intervenes between the participant's position
and the final policy decision, some people are going to be more
effective in pushing their individual positions into the final policy
product.

Where Congress is concerned, its collective response to the demands placed upon it is in part a function of the policy positions of
those members who move into the more influential positions as a new
congressional term begins. It is conceivable that the simple mean of
the policy positions of all the members can remain unchanged between Congresses but that the policy output will be altered because
the weighted mean of policy positions has changed with a turnover
in leadership positions. By the same token, there may be a strong
dominance of one policy view over another in the new membership,
but its effect may be stalemated by a counter policy shift in the
turnover of leadership positions. In other words, the policy impact
of electoral outcomes can be both immediate and delayed, with the
turnover of a congressional seat having as much or more of an effect
ten and twenty years later as it does in the immediate Congress.

The limitations of this study are such that further comments here
must be confined to the potential for change that is a function only
of the recruitment of new members and their effect upon the unweighted mean of policy preferences in the Congress. Let me
suggest the possibilities for change on each of the five policy dimensions.

Government Management

On the government management dimension, there is a strong possibility for change in the policy posture of Congress because a partisan turnover of seats results in a very sharp change in policy positions. As noted previously, when such a turnover occurs there is a virtual reversal of positions. Thus, when a Democrat replaces a Republican, the low support for government management is replaced by high support. There is simply no question about the fact that on this dimension the electoral choice is a significant one.

Social Welfare

The possibilities for change in the policy tone of Congress on the social welfare dimension also are substantial with a partisan turnover. However, there is less party impact because of the influence of constituency. Yet the choice is far from being one of little significance; a Republican congressman instead of a Democrat will probably mean a lower level of support for federal government involvement in, and support of, the many facets of the citizen's welfare. Of course, there will be individual cases where both candidates are equally sensitive to constituency demands, commonly perceived, and the choice between parties is irrelevant—as far as this dimension is concerned.

Because of the limited time period covered in this study and the analytic design used in the longitudinal analysis of stability and change in policy positions, the impression has undoubtedly been fostered that constituency influence is necessarily an impediment to change. But it is not at all a necessity, since changes in the constituency can produce changes in the policy attitudes of representatives. I do suspect, however, that the change in constituency attitudes is more likely to be registered by a new member of Congress than by an old hand.

Agricultural Assistance

The potential for change in the policy stance of Congress on the agricultural assistance dimension is, I think, quite possibly more variable by constituency than on some of the other dimensions. Thus, in a constituency where the subsidized farm commodities are a major economic element, the likelihood that a partisan turnover will lead to a major shift in policy positions is relatively small. In contrast, the absence of a strong farmer-based interest in subsidies leaves the door open to major shifts in policy positions when Republicans and Democrats exchange seats. In general, the proponents of farm subsidies, the main concern of the agricultural assistance dimension, can look for better times as the Democratic party majority increases. Or so one would conclude from the study findings from the period of 1953–1964.

Since 1964, however, the atmosphere in the farm policy domain has possibly undergone a change. The one look that we have taken at a later period, 1969–1970 (the Ninety-first Congress), provided a bit of a shock. In this Congress, the agricultural assistance dimension was nowhere in sight, at least not the old familiar dimension. Instead, there was a policy dimension primarily concerned *with limiting the size of subsidy payments to individual producers.* The traditional two party division on the dimension had disappeared; instead there appeared in both parties a division between the southern and interior states on one hand and the coastal and East North Central states on the other hand.

I am not interested in going into the details of the policy alignment on this "new" dimension beyond those needed to illustrate that Congress is not totally immune to change—new concerns may put a different light on old matters. Whether or not that was the case here, it seems at least fairly likely that the voting alignment on farm subsidies will never be the same again. But it is never wise to sell Congress short on its ability to come back to old habits.

Civil Liberties

The civil liberties dimension is a good example of one in which constituency is a force for change. On this dimension constituency influence is dominant *and* the collective policy view of the Congress changes. This is how I read the finding that new members of Congress are generally more supportive of civil liberties than prior occupants of congressional seats, during the period under study. Nor does the case for constituency influence as a dynamic element in the decision process rest upon the slender reed of a single study. I think the history of the period, in regard to civil rights for blacks, tells the same story. In sum, when there *is* a change in the national temper,

Congress reflects it through the mechanism of constituency rather than party or presidential influence.

Two points of clarification are needed regarding constituency influence as a force for congressional policy change, points that arise out of the particular example at hand. The first point is that the observation on constituency influence on the civil liberties dimension was made with respect to the new members of Congress only. They were more supportive than their predecessors, but there was no evidence that continuing members changed in their policy positions. This is illustrative of the proposition that changes in the constituency are more likely to be reflected in the new members than in the old members. However, we should be chary of coming to the conclusion that civil rights legislation was passed in the 1950s and 1960s *despite* the lack of increased support by the continuing members. All I can say is that I have no evidence of a change in the policy positions of continuing members. But I do want to insist that the policy positions of new members may have been the key to the congressional response to civil rights demands.

The second point to be made is that only infrequently is constituency influence expected to be a source of changes in the policy positions of the Congress, on *general* policy concepts. Constituency may much more frequently be the source of change with regard to *specific* questions such as school busing, revenue sharing, particular pieces of labor legislation, and specific instances of environmental pollution. Thus, I would consider the civil liberties dimension to be a rather unusual case. *Compared* with the emotional, physical, and intellectual energy expended on civil liberties during the study period, deliberations on the policies associated with the other four dimensions shared in the dullness associated with routine matters.

International Involvement

Change in the policy positions of senators and representatives on the international involvement dimension that is associated with changes in presidents has not only been observed but has been celebrated in this study. I shall forego another round of toasts.

It is not inconceivable, at least not at the time of this writing, that new dimensions and new alignments may emerge in the area of foreign and defense policy. It seems at least highly probable that the manner in which the United States secures its interests in the economics and politics of the world order will take on new form in the years ahead. Two world wars in this century laid the premise for the argument that the costs of active involvement in international affairs are a pittance compared with those to be sustained as a result of disengagement. The Korean and Vietnam Wars have perhaps laid the premise for another foreign policy argument, whose shape is dimly seen, if seen at all. There appears to be general agreement that American ground troops will hereafter be used very, very sparingly as the world's policemen; we may provide cannon to our allies but not cannoneers. The role of foreign aid has been diminishing, but I would be greatly surprised if this means of rewarding our friends were to be completely abandoned. It would be surprising if the current *rapprochement* with the Communist superpowers did not lead to further complications and possibly even turn out to be more trouble than it's worth. As I say, the future is seen dimly at best; it does seem, however, that we are approaching a turn in the road in foreign affairs.

In this review of the potentials for change in the congressional response to policy proposals on the five policy dimensions, I have attempted to add a little balance to the general picture of Congress that comes out of this book: a picture of continuity and stability. Change in the policy output of Congress can come with changes in party fortunes, changes in personnel, personnel movements within the Congress up the ladder of leadership, and possibly an occasional change of heart on the part of congressmen in service.

I am sympathetic to the cry of the critic that the appearance of continuity and stability that is projected from this study is, in fact, predicated on the analytic framework of the study. By focusing upon general policy concepts and policy dimensions, I have ignored the true quality of the frantic topsy-turvy everyday world of the congressman, in which he is confronted with the politics of specific issues. This criticism is valid. There is no doubt that a scene that is painted with broad brush strokes is deficient in detail, of both a mundane and an exciting kind.

The ordering of congressmen on a policy dimension may be compared to the ordering of buildings on a long street traversing a large metropolitan area. This street cuts through wealthy and poor residential areas, suburban shopping centers, parks, downtown, industrial areas. Paint this street with a sweeping stroke at two times, ten years apart, and the two pictures will show only modest changes. However, if the pictures were painted on very, very large canvases, showing the detail of each building on the street, a comparison of the two would find numerous differences: buildings that had been replaced, residential areas that had expanded, others that had contracted, drawing back from the wheels of commerce and industry. Yet the same *ordering* of areas, residential, business, park, would probably still obtain. This relatively unchanging *order* would have been captured in the boldly painted canvas, and the appearance of stability would have emerged. So it is, for the most part, in the current study.

However, this analysis of House and Senate voting and decision-making is actually more detailed in its description of congressional behavior than many other accounts. Although the five policy dimensions used to describe congressional voting in this study leave us with a pretty general level of description, consider some of the well-used alternatives. In the most extreme instance, we have the common labels, liberal and conservative, with moderate, reactionary, radical-liberal, middle-of-the-roader thrown in to define other positions on the *liberal-conservative dimension*. In place of one dimension, I have five. It is also common practice in research on congressional behavior to use, as single measures of voting behavior, such mixed-content measures of policy positions as "voting with the conservative coalition," presidential support scores, and support for the federal role.

But what is more important, and the only point that is really relevant, is that the five policy dimensions make sense and provide a sound basis for ordering the policy positions of congressmen. I have commented previously on the commonsense character of the five policy dimensions when viewed in the context of American politics and common descriptions of it, but let me affirm the faith once more.

The Five Policy Dimensions

It is unnecessary to document the fact that foreign policy, civil rights and liberties, farm policy, social welfare policy, and economic policy are commonly applied categories of policy. I have gone one step beyond these classifications of policy to the measurement of policy dimensions in relation to more precisely specified policy concepts, using the congressman's behavior as my guide rather than imposing my understanding of his behavior.

Three of the policy dimensions, social welfare, international involvement, and civil liberties, have commonly emerged from analyses of public opinion. I know of no measurement of the government management dimension in public opinion research, and I find no difficulty in accepting the possibility that this is not a dimension of public opinion, except as one accepts evidence of a dimension in the form of comments that the Democratic party is for the poor people and the Republicans for the rich, or that the Democrats spend more than the Republicans, or that the Republican party favors business while the Democratic party is for labor and the common man. Finally, with respect to the agricultural assistance dimension, I can only comment that the interest of social scientists in attitudes toward farm subsidies has been somewhat less than absorbing.

One of the most interesting research developments of very recent vintage is a study that provides strong indications that the five policy dimensions of this study are operative outside the Congress, within another branch of the national government. In an analysis of presidential State-of-the-Union messages, John Kessel finds evidence of six dimensions of policy concern: international involvement, allocation of social benefits, economic management, civil rights, agriculture, and natural resources.[12] The point of discrepancy between these six dimensions of presidential programming, and the five dimensions of congressional policy positions, is the separation of a relatively minor natural resources dimension from the economic management dimension (government management). Otherwise, the substantive parallels between these two sets of dimensions are extremely strong.

So perhaps the continuity of the five policy dimensions in Congress is indeed a reflection of a cognitive mapping or categorization of particular policy questions that is widely shared in the political culture, and particularly widely shared by the most active participants in American political life. Such has been my argument throughout.

References

1. David R. Mayhew, *Party Loyalty Among Congressmen* (Cambridge, Mass.: Harvard University Press, 1966), p. 150.
2. Dankwart A. Rustow, *The Politics of Compromise: A Study of Parties and Cabinet Government in Sweden* (Princeton, N.J.: Princeton University Press, 1955), pp. 230–232.
3. Mayhew, *op. cit.*, p. 155.
4. *Ibid.*, p. 159.
5. *Ibid.*, p. 30.

6. Philip E. Converse, "The Nature of Belief Systems in Mass Publics," in David E. Apter, ed., *Ideology and Discontent* (New York: Free Press, 1964), pp. 206–231.

7. Warren E. Miller and Donald E. Stokes, "Constituency Influence in Congress," *American Political Science Review* 57 (March 1963), pp. 45–56.

8. V. O. Key, Jr., *Public Opinion and American Democracy* (New York: Knopf, 1965), p. 106.

9. *Ibid.*, p. 114.

10. For an extensive discussion of the relation between public opinion and foreign policy see James N. Rosenau, *Public Opinion and Foreign Policy* (New York: Random House, 1968).

11. Leroy N. Rieselbach, "The Demography of the Congressional Vote on Foreign Aid," *American Political Science Review* 58 (September 1964), p. 578.

12. John H. Kessel, "The Parameters of Presidential Politics," a paper delivered at the 1972 Annual Meeting of the American Political Science Association, Washington, D.C., September 5–9.

Index